WHO'S WHO IN MOZART'S OPERAS

Joachim Kaiser

WHO'S WHO IN MOZART'S OPERAS

From Alfonso to Zerlina

Translated by Charles Kessler

SCHIRMER BOOKS
A Division of Macmillan, Inc.
NEW YORK

Copyright © R. Piper GmbH & Co. KG, Munich 1984
Translation copyright © 1986 by Charles Kessler

First American Edition published in 1987 by Schirmer Books
A Division of Macmillan, Inc.

Schirmer Books
A Division of Macmillan, Inc.
866 Third Avenue, New York, N.Y. 10022

Library of Congress Catalog Card Number: 86-10997

Printed in the United States of America

printing number
1 2 3 4 5 6 7 8 9 10

Library of Congress Cataloging-in-Publication Data

Kaiser, Joachim, 1928–
  Who's who in Mozart's operas.

  Translation of: Mein Name ist Sarastro.
  Includes index.
  1. Mozart, Wolfgang Amadeus, 1756-1791. Operas.
I. Title. II. Kessler, Charles.
ML410.M9K1413   1986   782.1'092'4   86-10997
ISBN 0-02-873380-0

To Jean-Pierre Ponnelle
in gratitude for many Mozart conversations

CONTENTS

Contents

WHO'S WHO
OPERA BY OPERA

TRANSLATOR'S NOTE

This book will, it is hoped, appeal to musical experts and laymen alike. The author certainly had the former, although not exclusively, in mind. My preoccupation has been with the latter: to them the following remarks are, with one exception, addressed.

To make reading pleasanter, opera titles have nearly all been anglicized. The same applies, unless the sense is obvious, to most of the libretti quotations – that is, the German or Italian comes first, the English rendering follows in brackets. It does not claim to be more than an approximation, but it has been done with the score at hand and it hopes to convey not merely the spirit but also something of the correct rhythm.

The numbered references are all to German texts: not, though, in the quotations from Mozart letters. Those are taken from Emily Anderson's *The Letters of Mozart and his Family*, of which twenty years after its publication Eric Blom in his preface to the excerpted Penguin edition wrote, 'An English translation of the Mozart letters need never be attempted again. Emily Anderson's is a classic.' And ineffably enjoyable.

Now for the exception. The list of figures includes Blonde, the *Abduction* girl. Mozart, his librettist and the present author make quite a point of Blonde being English. There is also the fact that she is generally called by the German diminutive of her name – Blondchen. The author is definite that this is a 'a diminutive that trivializes her', and the last sentence of his character-sketch is again emphatic about the matter. I have therefore taken the liberty of translating this diminutive into Blondie. It trips neatly off the tongue, meets the nationality point – and is at least as consistent as Mozart was when he accepted the Germanic 'Constanze' without insisting on Spanish transliteration.

C.K.

PREFACE

Then R. played to us from Mozart's *Abduction* and *Figaro* – he likes the old Simrock editions; Pr. N. observes that Mozart is said to have invented the music of intrigue and R. contradicts him, saying that, on the contrary, he dissolved the intrigues into music. It is only necessary to compare Beaumarchais's piece with Mozart's operas. The play presents shrewd, witty, calculating individuals cleverly dealing with and talking to one another. Mozart makes them into transfigured, suffering, eloquent creatures.

Entry for 12 February 1870 in the diaries of Cosima Wagner[1]

Mozart 'is musical drama's greatest realist', says Hermann Abert in his completely revised edition of Otto Jahn's standard biography. 'His figures are firmly rooted in reality, and nothing else concerns them.'[2] Can one really make such an unqualified assertion? But then, did not Wagner err in the opposite direction when, as Cosima Wagner's diary entry so vividly records, he contradicted 'Professor Nietzsche' with the superiority of the mature musician as against the young intellectual, contradicted him sentimentally, and transfigured personalities like Countess Almaviva, Susanna, and Figaro into *suffering, eloquent creatures*?

Mozart's major operas, composed between 1781 and 1791, are more than the sum totals of their characters. They continue a formal tradition which was at its height in his youth, but by the end of his life must have been somewhat dated and remote – that of Italian *opera seria* (*Idomeneo, La clemenza*). They broaden *opera buffa* into world theatre of a Shakespearian calibre (*The Marriage of Figaro, Don Giovanni, Così fan tutte*). They are, properly speaking, the true inaugurators of *Singspiel* and raise it to a serene, noble and humane level (*The Abduction, The Magic Flute*).

At this point, however, many life-long lovers of these works may want to add that each great Mozart opera has its own all-inclusive 'tone', no matter how diverse the characters appearing in it may be.

I

'Tone' in this context is meant not merely to signify that each of these operas is composed in one main key from its overture to its closing finale (unlike, say, the music dramas of Wagner). Even if the fact is incapable of precise proof, no one surely will deny that the finales in *Così* are in an idiom or 'tone' different from the two great finales in *Figaro*, let alone *Don Giovanni*. Each opera, in spite of occasional similarities and hybrid tendencies, is a world of its own. The characters, who are part of this world, create it by being as they are and singing as they do. Not that they alone create it, for from the very first moment of its overture it exists as an all-inclusive whole, to which every detail contributes. Let me venture a slightly strained metaphor for what seems to resist sober verbal definition. In Mozart's operatic masterpieces the tonal idiom deriving from the instruments and voices employed represents, so to speak, the waters of life, in which the characters, an integral part thereof, swim and disport themselves. Their essential being reaches down into these waters, while they rise above them as independent characters; and the varying relation between these two aspects is what constitutes the dialectic of Mozartian music drama.

The reader's intuition will tell him or her how, once we start speculating about the status of the individual in Mozart's melodic world, risky and vague formulations seem inevitable. For my part, I admit – and the older I become, it is increasingly the case – that I feel every attempt to provide an authoritative definition and discussion of the 'demonic' spirit in *Idomeneo*, the place of Eros in *Don Giovanni*, the initiation ceremony in *The Magic Flute*, or the revolutionary impulse in *Figaro* to be presumptuous as well as reductive. Since this book is intended as a work of reference in which, it is hoped, the user will be tempted to read further, I am not going to hazard any approaches to the profoundly difficult problem of the operas' overall meaning. I shall deal 'only' with the personages. The energies confined in each individual, taken collectively, amount to an almost inconceivable power.

In any case, the secondary literature on the operas is a stroke of academic luck. It goes back well before the awesomely learned and still definitive study by Jahn and Abert, and it has not ended with Anna Amalie Abert's agreeably concise, knowledgeable and informative volume.[3] We must be grateful to the many specialized studies, the Mozart year-books and complete editions; to scholars like Edward J. Dent, Ernst Lert, Alfred Einstein, Aloys Greither, and Bernhard Paumgartner, who has been so violently and unjustly attacked by

Preface

Wolfgang Hildesheimer; to this brilliant writer Hildesheimer himself, to the series of impassioned operatic studies published by the Rowohlt Verlag, and to an infinite throng of intensely devoted musicologists, sociologists, essayists and philosophers. All these achievements do honour to the academic profession. Mozart's genius has not only inspired great erudition; it has been actively requited.

My urge to count the gems in the rich coffer of Mozart character-ization has a twofold origin. First there was my ever clearer appreci-ation – through talks with producers, especially my friend Jean-Pierre Ponnelle, and from sitting through hundreds of performances – of the sovereign freedom with which the mature Mozart handled the antithetical forms of *opera buffa* and *opera seria*, not to mention *Singspiel*. Combined with this was my growing feeling that somehow everything said and sung by Mozart's figures in arias, ensembles and recitatives is part of each individual and seems suited to her or to him alone. (Even when practically identical formulae are uttered by several individuals in succession – it is worth noting that they are seldom completely identical – Mozart's skilful guidance of our sympathies or antipathies can persuade us that they are the necessary and inevitable expression, first of Donna Anna's hysteria, and then of Donna Elvira's vacillation.) Mozart tempts us to assume that his are living characters, each different, who can therefore be described as if they were real, though not solely in terms of realistic psychology. Obviously he did more than just load individuals with specific qualities. But, since he was always a musical dramatist, he used words and music to create unmistakable personalities.

This dictionary of Mozartian figures asks, single-mindedly and insistently, what do text, plot development, stage directions, and the dramatic context reveal about the individuals who sing (or speak) in the seven major operas? I stick as closely as possible to the musical facts of each case, and refuse to speculate on whether Figaro later filed a suit for divorce or whether the males in *Così*, disappointed by its unsatisfactory ending, became homosexual or even impotent. (Is there anything that producers, writers, and Mozart specialists have *not* brooded over?) I have only heeded how each utterance, action and attitude, whether expressed through words, gestures or singing, whether placed at the beginning or the end, helps to create character and describe an individual. The personal unity of Mozart's figures often results from a tension among barely compatible qualities.

My aim has been to compile a kind of Who's Who including more

3

than merely the 'important' individuals in the seven major operas. Of course the parts were not intended to be exhibited in isolation, as though in a portrait gallery. But they can take it! It is fun and it affords a lesson in astonishment to invest Mozart with god-like creative powers and then – laying the results, as it were, on the music-psychiatrist's couch – to see whether these dozens of souls really do differ in the womb of this operatic world.

The alphabet is a tricky instrument. It imposes completeness. The would-be lexicographer must not comment only on what catches his eye or his interest; he must also treat seriously those figures who are not altogether to his taste and whom he would have preferred to avoid. In my case, these included Despina, Arbace and Titus. It would, moreover, be wrong to assume that *The Magic Flute*'s harmless fairy-tale figures would prove fairly troublesome to describe, while those in such a differentiated piece as *Figaro* would turn out all the easier. The opposite is the case. The Queen of the Night and Pamina, Sarastro and Tamino furnish far greater contrasts than do Susanna and the Countess.

All in all, and leaving aside some of the less important *Idomeneo* figures, Mozart's characters do much more than just obey the rules, expectations and schemata of the various genres. This is especially true of the female roles. In *Idomeneo, La clemenza, Don Giovanni,* and *Così* the women are even more interesting than the men. I take issue here with Wolfgang Osthoff. In an outstanding essay on *opera buffa* he says, referring to *Così* and *Figaro,* 'usually it is the men who are superior and more intelligent'.[4] This remark certainly does not apply to the four above-mentioned works, and could even be challenged in respect of *Figaro, The Abduction,* and *The Magic Flute,* though about these last we should perhaps agree to differ. In most of Mozart, as with Richard Strauss and Wagner, it is the women who behave more spiritedly, more excitingly, and more in character. To cite a sociological argument, perhaps the dramatic soprano roles in musical drama should be seen as anticipating feminism.

All this is not to deny in the slightest that Mozart, an experienced craftsman from childhood onward, was of course thoroughly familiar with the specific requirements of the operatic genres. He drew up precise inventories of his personages. On 7 May 1783 he wrote to his father from Vienna:

. . . indeed I should dearly love to show what I can do in an Italian opera! So I have been thinking that unless Varesco is still very much annoyed with us about the Munich opera, he might write me a new libretto for seven characters. *Basta!* You will know best whether this can be arranged. In the meantime he could jot down a few ideas, and when I come to Salzburg we could work them out together. The most essential thing is that on the whole the story should be really *comic*, and, if possible, he ought to introduce *two equally good female parts*, one of these to be seria, the other mezzo carattere, but both parts equal *in importance and excellence*. The third female *character*, however, may be entirely buffa, and so may all the male ones, if necessary.[5]

Such demands reveal the professional seriousness with which he treated the schematic rules (here too he is thinking more about the women than the men). When it comes to composing, though, the figures break the bars of their typological cage. Donna Elvira is not simply a diverting *buffa* character; Monostatos is not merely lewd and funny, Osmin is more than just coarsely droll and vengeful.

Even before 1781 – and this explains why he was already a professional at the age of twenty-five – Mozart had composed a good dozen dramatic works. They included several *opere serie* with which between 1770 and 1772 (i.e. between his fourteenth and seventeenth birthdays) he enjoyed at Milan a string of successes such as never again befell him in the whole of his later life. *Die Schuldigkeit des ersten Gebots* (K. 35), the oratorio written at Salzburg when he was eleven, does not only contain music which is gifted, beautiful and unmistakably Mozartian from the very first bar: its 'justice' aria is so melodiously finished a piece of work that every composer, however grown-up, would be glad of such inspiration. The Judith portion of the *azione sacra* in two parts by Pietro Metastasio, dating from summer 1771 and entitled *La Betulia liberata*, contains the great C minor section for chorus and solo tenor whose ideas Mozart was to readopt and develop in his D minor piano concerto (K. 466). And who can fail to find overwhelmingly delightful passages in *Bastien und Bastienne, Lucio Silla*, and *La finta giardiniera*?

I admit that I am not (any longer) quite so sure of the case which I am about to put forward. Important performances or recordings of *Lucio Silla* and *Il rè pastore* have caused me to waver somewhat. Nevertheless it is still my conviction that the figures created in Mozart's 'operatic' works between his eleventh and nineteenth birthdays cannot be understood or interpreted as dramatic characters. That they sing lovely music, with the odd hint of character, is beyond question. But are they independent individuals, who can be described and can present themselves as living dramatic entities, to the same degree as Electra. Ilia, and Idamante in *Idomeneo* and thereafter all the others from *The Abduction* to *The Magic Flute?* I remain unconvinced. That is why this book deals only with the people in the seven consummate masterpieces.

Only brief reflection is required to show how far Mozart remains tied to the formal pattern underlying each of these works, while also rising above it. He creates ideal operas, but not 'ideal types'.

An ideal type (in the sense of Max Weber's use of the word) where *opera seria* is concerned is the completely intelligible presentation of straight theatre with music. Important textual passages are to be rendered comprehensible in recitatives. Special (and highly regarded) singers were employed for the arias, which were not intended to advance the action, but to convey emotions. Simultaneous speech by several characters, in other words ensembles, would have violated the principle of lucidity and the isolated utterance of pure emotion. Recitatives are followed by arias. 'Dialogue' signifies speech 'in succession', not 'together'. Ensembles, choruses and dances are in *opera seria* extraneous exceptions. These were rules which Mozart abandoned as early as *Idomeneo*, where he added a medley of French elements (the divertissements derived from the dance interludes in the *tragédie lyrique* which he had seen as a boy in Paris), ensembles and choruses. The major chorus finale in Act I of *La clemenza* is likewise not 'pure' *opera seria*; it is much more like a dramatic scene.

But Mozart's most effective mixing of genres occurred when he adopted and enriched the *Singspiel*. Emperor Joseph II was not far wrong in becoming indignant about *The Abduction*'s 'too many notes'. Ambition drove Mozart past the supposed confines of the genre when he wrote for Constanze, Belmonte and Osmin parts which have a considerable emotional range and even today continue to be thought exceedingly difficult, delicate, and only for the highly skilled. *The Magic Flute* became a virtually philosophical opera, the presentation of an idea (not an ideology). As for the Queen of the Night's coloraturas, Mozart was completely callous about the likely abilities of the *Singspiel*'s singer-actress, and what he composed had little to do with accepted *Singspiel* character. *The Magic Flute* surpasses it.

As for the *opere buffe*, in Mozart's hands they become more than the later and faster moving antithesis to *opera seria*, with the main aim of entertaining the citizenry. No cloudlessly blue stage sky stretches over his world of comedy. We 'moderns' sometimes, possibly with good reason, regard certain parts as too sentimental where Mozart meant abrasive comedy.

In *opera buffa* a happy ending occurred as a matter of course: that is why the sextet at the close of *Don Giovanni*, addressed to the audience and seeking to restore harmony, must not be cut. The old types are easily recognizable in the work's *buffa* figures. Its music, however, has other moods besides merriment. Thanks to Mozart's capacity for pity, combined with his all-pervasive propensity for laughter and for mockery, the old types are transformed into infinitely varied, differentiated individuals who can never be reduced simply to 'psychological' patterns. That holds good whether we recall Susanna's hope for happiness amid her present distress (something other than a Columbine's rage), Cherubino's adolescence, or Count Almaviva's more than purely rakish, possessive passion. The contradiction can be stated more plainly. The plots, with their exchanges of roles, disguise jokes, accelerations of pace and abrupt stops, have little bearing on what is glibly termed realism, the hard facts of life, verisimilitude. In any case, such terms seldom amount to more than a pretext for dismissing libretti, which have the assurance to do without these elements, as 'stupid' or fairy-tale ('operatic'). But although such theatrical situations are in no way beholden to reality, the ways in which the characters respond to them can none the less be psychologically revealing and capable of realistic reconstruction. Between operatic absurdity and truth of character Mozart struck a balance which in the history of music has never again been so naturally achieved. About the oracle in *Idomeneo* he wrote – and this modified illusionism was likewise his aims in the subsequent works – 'The voice must chill, it must penetrate to the marrow; it must be believed that things are really so'. The music of *La clemenza*, composed ten years later, may not seem very interesting, very dissonant, though it is demonstratively diatonic; but if one has the humility to immerse oneself in it, one may apprehend that Mozart not only practised dramatic, direct and pointedly distinctive characterization, but *also* an aesthetically indirect one which remains, in Goethe's words, a secret to most.

Mozart's voracious anthropological appetite impelled him to create figures who were quite different from the typical puppets in a well-calculated comic mechanism. From 1781 onward, at the time when he attained mastery in the field of opera, his characters, though based on traditional stereotypes, enlarge them into new hybrid forms. 'Suffering, eloquent creatures', they are also active, and hence resist becoming subservient to the functions they fulfil in each particular opera. By protesting as individual characters, they turn the particular opera's form into the function of their existence, their longings and their wishes. Mozart's singing creations are more than simply components of an operatic entity. They are also themselves. That is the proposition which this alphabetical sequence of portraits is intended to support. I hope that it will amuse as well as inform.

Munich, February 1984   J.K.

DON ALFONSO

Bass. A sceptic, firmly convinced that all young women are unfaithful. Alternates between irony, obstinate cynicism, and good nature. A sportsman rather than a spoilsport. Old and a trifle desiccated.

in Così fan tutte

The list of characters announces that he belongs to a generation senior to the other five *Così* figures: 'an old philosopher'. Once, quite briefly, the music makes the point. Suddenly, at the end of a longer *secco* recitative passage just before Act II, Scene 10, with the wager tilting in his favour and victory in sight, Don Alfonso breaks into a distinctly old-fashioned, baroque Siciliano melody, suggesting a proverb: 'a real fool is he who buys the bird which still sits on the bough'. It has a cosy, antiquated, confident ring, echoing an earlier style, and it intimates that he is of another provenance than the young officers and ladies whom he handles with such superior skill. (Analogously Dr Bartolo in Rossini's *Barber of Seville* delights in an 'outmoded' six-eight time arietta which allows the audience to hear the kind of music that was fashionable in the old gentleman's younger days. Beckmesser's lute serenade in *The Mastersingers* is another example of stylistic wit pointing to the difference between generations.)

Mozart, however, is not content simply to depict Don Alfonso, with these six unobtrusive bars, as 'bystander', 'odd man out', elderly friend but not intimate of the young people. That Don Alfonso inclines, like many comic elderly people in opera, to the plaintive repetition of a single note and often utters only tones in a narrow compass does not round off the composer's picture of this sceptical sophisticate. No, Mozart proceeds on sterner lines.

Neither text nor music show much interest in why Don Alfonso has become how he is. He is just terribly well informed about what women are like. Their infidelity is a fact of life, an innate quality, and they have to be taken as they are. And when you no longer have any illusions about female trustworthiness and female love, then you manage fairly well with the weaker, but amiable and attractive sex. Your good health, gentlemen. . . . Rather a repulsive attitude. Is it the result of hatred, of a blasé outlook, or of disappointment in a love affair for which our friend could himself have been to blame? The answer is never disclosed, however ugly the suspicions that obtrude.

At the outset Don Alfonso slightly hesitates risking the experiment. He claims to be reluctant to disturb people's peace of mind. The bet once laid – his barren mental superiority is perhaps a bore to the fiendishly sceptical old fellow, maybe he needs a little sultry turmoil around him as a brief change from his frosty rationality – he avails himself of a smoothly running intellect. He elegantly spans the breaks in the dialogue when the young officers, gradually realizing what they have let themselves in for, are shocked into speechlessness. He conducts the procurement operation with great intelligence, commenting with cheerful irony on how convincingly he has played his part of mourner in the farewell terzetto ('I'm no bad comedian'). Occasionally, as when he declares a scorching contempt for the fair sex, he breathes sombre fire. In the end, though, he again becomes pleasant and conciliatory because, after all, one has to come to terms with the world. (Besides, he does not want to be left entirely on his own.) Temperament, as far as he is concerned, is weakness, a sign that the brain is not in complete control.

Why, in his view, do all young ladies betray men when they get the chance? Because 'like all the rest of us, they are made of flesh and blood'. They are not angels, but women. For this aphorism the opera wreaks vengeance on Don Alfonso. The score depicts how terribly lacking he is in living flesh and warm blood. This takes the form of denying him what all the rest are allowed, even Despina, who God knows is earthy enough – the hues of the wind instruments. The sensuousness of the clarinet, the bassoon's contentedness, the tenderness of the flute, the mellifluence of the oboe, the horn's sensibility – Don Alfonso is denied all these, in a way that is nothing short of systematic. Alone, he barely opens his mouth before the orchestral coloration ceases. His accompaniment is always 'only' the strings. In an operatic world where wind instruments participate to such a distinctive extent as in *Così*, this signifies an impoverishment, a deprivation of vitality, a taint. The others, embraced by the wind, are women of flesh and blood (seducible, granted) and officers (impulsive sparks given to levity). Don Alfonso alone is bereft of the vivid complexions that the woodwind section lends. He manages tiresomely to be always right; he is witty, sensible, well-off, and in the end he is willing to come to terms. Worse characters may inhabit Mozart's world, but none more withered, none more numb. Can it be mere chance that Don Alfonso is deprived of the woodwind? In the opening terzetto, when he tries mollification, 'No more argument, I have had my say' (bar 33), the oboes and the bassoons keep silent in this very bar, and begin again with Ferrando's and Guglielmo's answer. When Don Alfonso jokingly compares female fidelity with the legendary phoenix in Arabia, it is again the wind's turn to stay silent during his first six bars. The wind does join in briefly afterwards, but vanishes as soon as Don Alfonso ironically declares that there is no such thing as a phoenix – far less two of them at once in the shape of a pair of noble sisters. When he rattles off his F minor aria, which launches the imposture, once again not a single wind instrument note is to be heard, only an arid string accompaniment.

In all this a deliberate method of characterization is apparent. Therefore, in the rare cases where Don Alfonso and the wind section do coincide, one should not dismiss the matter as evidence that Mozart is no stickler for principles and his rules allow exceptions; instead, one must ask what the wind instruments signify. Are they implying that this dry stick is no longer an isolated figure, but part of an ensemble which they accompany? That even he, well supplied with money but poor in emotion, feels a little pale fire coursing through his veins?

One set 'loves' from the heart, another at least for the fun of it; but Don Alfonso's shrewd, know-all gratification consists solely in being able to prove triumphantly that a young woman capable of love and fidelity is only an idealistic mirage.

COUNT ALMAVIVA

Baritone. Accustomed to having everything in his castle follow his wishes. His relationship with his Countess is in difficulties, and it is her personal maid Susanna whom he is now after. After assuring his wife of his continuing love he adds (in Beaumarchais's original text) the not unduly gallant observation, 'Three years together lend a marriage great dignity'. He covets Susanna passionately. Neither his earlier promise to abandon the antiquated 'droit de seigneur' nor the Countess's distress, let alone Figaro's wish to marry, can inhibit this aristocrat's addiction to erotic play and pursuit. However, matters are no longer quite as easy as they used to be for the members of his caste.

in *The Marriage of Figaro*

'His lordship the Count,' Susanna informs Figaro, 'tired of chasing outside beauties, wants to try his luck again inside the castle, although it is not his wife, and listen carefully here, who has whetted his appetite.' 'Who then?' 'Your little Susanna.' The music teacher Basilio has performed his pandering. All is perfectly clear. Over and above this the Countess complains of neglect and Barbarina babbles about how sweetly the Count has fondled and kissed her, not to mention all that he has promised during the process.

Our sympathies could hardly be more clearly channelled. The Count, a miscreant, completely bored with his wife, dallies more or less passionately with the womenfolk in his castle. That is what they tell us; that is what we see happening. What could possibly speak against it? The music, for a start. Remember those grand, chorale-like moments in Acts II and IV when the Count's lingering love for his Countess, his repentance, his genuine goodwill seem to be preserved in sensitive, soulful and enraptured tones. These gentle ensemble climaxes admit of no doubt. They lack the slightest touch of irony, of superficiality, of reservation. But what about the Count's palpable philandering? More souls than one, shall we say, appear to inhabit his breast – perhaps four.

To view him solely from Susanna's or Figaro's perspective is probably to underrate him.

He is a young and impetuous nobleman. When he was played by Dietrich Fischer-Dieskau, everyone thought he must have been born with a hunting-crop in his fist. Resistance to his wishes or whims seems utterly out of the question. And now a servant of his is to enjoy a pleasure that he has unavailingly aspired to? Almaviva has yet to learn his lesson in social history.

His marriage to the beautiful Rosina no longer holds him, or at least not very exclusively. There is not the slightest doubt about that. This aristocrat is full of erotic dynamism; his instinctive passion is more ardent (and deserves, in a way, more respect) than dalliance out of sheer boredom or from a sort of sporting ambition. The man really does want Susanna, and that to the point of despair. He does not wish simply to 'buy' her like a whore. He wants to have and, so he at least imagines, to love her. Money need do no damage. Early in Act III, after she has pretended that she will meet him, he gives a display of anticipatory pleasure – the feeling of happiness that comes from talking about a forthcoming rendezvous. No less than a dozen times he repeats obsessively, 'So you will come into the garden?', 'You will keep your promise?', 'You will come?'. The sequel in the A major duet (no. 17), 'Mi sento dal contento, pieno di gioia il cor' ('oh, how I feel contentment, so full of joy my heart'), discloses a blissful mutual harmony, although it exists in his mind alone. (Susanna, at this point playing the coquette, has quite other things on her mind.) Almaviva is head over heels in love. This, then, is one of his numerous souls; and it makes him quite likeable.

Another aspect of him fascinates us, without necessarily engaging our sympathy – namely, the masterful bearing of the powerful aristocrat. If Figaro is often noticeably restrained, soft in his enunciation, his lordship invariably sets the tone. He does so, for example, when in the Act II trio he sings C major and then with sovereign authority proceeds to A flat major, or when in his Act III vengeance aria 'Vedrò, mentr'io sospiro' ('pleasure am I to forgo'), he declares in an aggressive forte that if he has to relinquish Susanna he will suffer the torments of hell. He even avails himself (bars 77–81) of a rhythmic and melodic belligerent gesture which at a later date made Carl Maria von Weber's *Schwertlied* so popular. (Weber, incidentally, is more likely to have adopted this characteristic intonation from late-eighteenth-century convention, on which Mozart also drew, than from Mozart himself.) The Count's egotistic pride also includes some malice. 'Poor devil' is his ironic comment when Cherubino has once again been caught. As he is firmly convinced that a lover is concealed in the closet and rightly regards as an evasion his wife's whispered assertion that it is Susanna who is there, he says ironically, when all doors are locked and he offers the Countess his arm to accompany him in the search for tools, 'Susanna shall stay there till we return'. When they do return, the dupe announces, guilelessly and quite wrongly, 'All as we left it'. The plot, however, repays his irony twice over in the same coin. Susanna, unfortunately for the Count, is at that stage really in the closet. Thus, even in da Ponte/Mozart's deliberately depoliticized drama the power of coincidence questions Almaviva's arrogance. His pride leads him cuttingly to interrupt his compromised wife, as she tries to proffer some excuse: 'Speak then!'. The orchestra's forte deprives the terrified Countess of breath. Without such a miracle and opportune accident, she would not have had a chance.

Just as Almaviva's arrogance is allied to obviously justifiable jealousy, so is his darkest, most dangerous soul a compound of elements – delusion combined with rage make him grim and unapproachable. Half a dozen times in succession he croaks, 'Death, death to him!'. If Cherubino were actually obliged to emerge from the closet, he would receive short shrift. The matrimonial row assumes titanic dimensions. The music asks what fate innocence can expect in this world.

In this Othello mood, where nothing other than 'Death, death to him, no longer shall the wretch make me suffer' can penetrate his brain, the Count is hardly inclined to discuss the divine order of things. Believing, in the finale of Act IV, that he has caught his wife in shameless adultery, he can do nothing but repeat with increasing violence that he cannot forgive her. For bar after bar he thunders his 'No' in unison with the orchestra. Despite all this, it is conceivable that he may still be able to love his Rosina, just as somebody awaking from fantastic dreams suddenly appreciates the value of reality. This is the purest of his many souls, though also the one most deeply buried.

At the end of Act II, Scene 8 the Count, the Countess and Susanna have all learnt something. 'From this moment forward his heart will be wiser', sings the Countess, 'my heart will be wiser', sings the Count. They aver that their two hearts will now at last be wiser and wholly able to understand each other in a gentle, *sotto voce* whisper which rises to a crescendo exceptional not only in *Figaro*, but in the history of opera. The triad theme, at first apparently quite inconspicuous, rises after a thoroughly symphonic development into sublimity (bars 296–327). Such spiritual power can only derive from the most exquisitely pure instrumental music and the most consummate vocal art. It is a marvellous instant of logical development combined with harmonic richness, of gentle chorale-like lingering and of large-scale forte.

The music is now not merely far beyond any suggestion of irony, but, thanks to its emotional impact, attests that here the individuals are truly trying to find happiness. The Count means it, at the moment at any rate, in all sincerity. He even forgives Cherubino, so that peace reigns supreme.

The pattern is repeated at the close. Almaviva – paying enamoured compliments to his wife whom he believes to be Susanna, then realizing that he has wronged her and become the victim of her stratagem – again begs and receives forgiveness. This time a *tutti* chorale in G major is consecrated by an effusion of violin quavers. Everything ends in 'Love, contentment, gladness' and the hope of living happily ever after.

True, the sceptic may say that the course of the plot sufficiently proves how brief reconciliations are and how little difference they make. But does the opera conclude with a question mark? Or with no more than the suggestion of a happy ending? Surely not. The opposite assumption is no less warranted, and is confirmed by the music. Strained relations between the Count and the Countess will keep recurring, but they will eventually be surmounted, in love and harmony.

COUNTESS ALMAVIVA

Soprano. The unhappy, neglected, but affectionate wife of Count Almaviva. Undoubtedly finds a little distraction in Cherubino's pleasurable, rapturous devotion to her. Risks much, apprehensively and bravely, to shame her husband and to win him back to her side.

in The Marriage of Figaro

During the turbulent quarrels, concealments and discoveries in Act I the Countess is not on-stage. For the present she has no part in them. After a long, nobly lyrical orchestral prologue she introduces herself at the beginning of Act II with the larghetto cavatina in which she implores the god of love either to restore her husband's attachment to her or to let her die. She brings a new tone – that of complete seriousness – into the comedy, a tone wholly free from adolescent exaggeration, *opera buffa* playfulness or complacent superiority. It is the tone of heartfelt seriousness.

It is worth raising the difficult question whether in the world of *Figaro* this confessional tone is not intimated (leaving aside the large-scale ensembles, to which the observation cannot apply) in the solos, duets and trios by a negative indicator – the absence of the flutes. In the Countess's two slow arias – 'Porgi, amor' and 'Dove sono' in Act III – the flutes are missing: likewise in the Act II trio, probably the most agitated brief ensemble passage in the whole work. And the flutes are also absent in Act I, when Cherubino describes his despairing state of mind. On the other hand during the less direct, deliberately stylized canzone in Act II, accompanied by Susanna on a guitar, the flute is characteristically present. In each of her two solo arias Mozart gives Susanna's soprano the support of a flute. Yet, curiously enough, he withholds it from the Countess.

One can smile at the Countess's luxuriant tearfulness and poke fun at the misunderstood woman who indulges herself in elegiac lamentation and gives the impression of inclining in moments of exquisite loneliness to a constant megrim. (Not, unfortunately, to the rather more entertaining variety from which the *Feldmarschallin* in *Der Rosenkavalier* suffers: 'I had the megrims this morning'.) Such derision, however, would do the Countess a grave injustice. She is not striking a pose, for the issue really is love or, failing that, death. During the course of her E flat major aria the thought of death becomes ever more insistent. The line 'O mi lascia almen morir' ('or give me death as a release') recurs more often than its preceding antithesis, 'O mi rendi il mio tesoro' ('restore to me the love that once was mine'). The poor lady not only repeats her desire for death more frequently, but also more vehemently. The aria's top note is an A flat, fermata, on the repeated 'morir'. Such is her despair at believing herself no longer loved where her own love is engaged.

Not that this young woman – it is only some three years since the Count conquered the enchanting Rosina – lets the purity of her unhappiness and her despair drag her down into depression or apathy. True, she recalls her past felicity with an indescribable sincerity, dreaminess, and nobility of mind (Act III, C major aria) as though by such invocation she could bring it back again. She is not content, though, to leave matters at that: she hopes and she acts. A tempestuously lofty moment in the allegro of this same aria reveals the strength of her hope. When it comes to the plea 'Ah! se almen la mia constanza . . . mi portasse una speranza di cangiar l'ingrato cor' ('ah, could but one day my endurance . . . inspire a hope of change in his ingrate heart'), the music radiantly reflects the significance of 'change', the return to a state of harmony. First the score prescribes the Countess a pure C major triad, G to C at the start, then C to E, and finally not E to G, as would logically be expected, but E to A: something original and irregular, this sixth step, with its minor key undertones instead of a fifth. The high A not only comes as the climax and top note of the aria, held for an entire brilliant bar, but it shifts precisely at 'cangiar', at 'change', returning via A flat to G and ending in a regular C major cadence. Here we are direct witnesses of how lustrously the desired transformation from a painful feeling of exclusion into the 'homecoming' triadic harmony is effected.

The Countess knows but too well that her husband can be madly jealous; yet she too has a passionate temperament! The recitative preceding her C major aria has turns of phrase unmistakably reminiscent of the Count's recitative motifs (hers, no. 20, bars 4–9 corresponds to his, no. 18, bars 30–40).

Be that as it may, Rosina does not allow her troubles to reduce her to lachrymose inactivity. Her state of mind is fortunately no obstacle to her efforts to repair the marriage. During the preparations for the decidedly daring masquerades she wavers between courage and anxiety. The latter amounts to more than mere apprehension. When the Count returns unexpectedly, a half-dressed Cherubino is hidden in her closet, and catastrophe impends, anxiety flares up into terror. Her coloraturas reach as far as high C. The poor lady's self-control is on the point of breaking down. (In older, erroneous versions Susanna sang this passage, although here, heaven knows, she has less reason than her desperate mistress for such an expression of fear.) Even at this critical juncture the Countess proves herself a worthy match for her spouse. Driven into a corner, obviously in the wrong, she still has the presence of mind to answer the Count's not unreasonable question why she should tremble on Susanna's behalf with a breezy, 'This maid, my lord, perturbs you more than me'. And when Barbarina has frankly compromised the Count, she does not suppress the malicious whisper, 'Your turn now, I think, my lord'. She certainly does not lack repartee.

Cherubino's adoration is not only flattering, but undoubtedly of some consolation in her sufferings; what a pity that he should remain so restrained. To watch Susanna flirting with the boy can make her positively jealous. . . .

Her plaint and her longing for happiness stand out against the comic confusions arising from the exciting game of hide-and-seek being played in the castle. Her courage may sometimes waver, but never her feelings. Difficult though she finds it to forgive herself for doing so, and sceptical though she may be, she does forgive the Count. Thanks to the irresistible persuasiveness of the orchestra, the chorale-like tutti, the wonderfully composed exaltation (Act II) and the happy restoration of order confirmed by the exultant violins (Act IV) – she allows herself to be reconciled and accepts the love of her husband, who has just been rhapsodizing about the delicacy of her hand (in the belief that it was Susanna's). No more than a few sombre touches in the modulation leading to the allegro assai cast brief, evanescent shadows over the joy that Mozart, contrary to the 'verisimilitude' taught by dour experience, concedes the Count and Countess at the end.

DONNA ANNA

Soprano. Daughter of the Commendatore. Falls under the spell of
Don Giovanni, who tries to ravish her and kills her father. Under
immense emotional strain. Very emphatic and highly strung. Her
betrothed, Don Ottavio, cannot at present do much for her. Their
wedding is postponed. Will time prove a healer?

in *Don Giovanni*

About one thing there can be no doubt – Don Giovanni laid hands on
this young woman, in the most literal sense, while trying to ravish her.
In her distraught recitative, to the accompaniment of panicky and
agonized chords from the orchestra, Donna Anna tells Don Ottavio
what happened to her during the night. It is clear what she wants to
say, but by no means clear what she actually does say.

Donna Anna: 'Silently he approaches and tries to take me in his arms. I seek
to free myself. He clasps me closer. I scream. No one comes. With one hand he
tries to stifle my cries, with the other he holds me so tightly that I think myself
already overwhelmed.'

Don Ottavio: 'The ruffian! And then?'

Donna Anna: 'The pain and the horror at this infamous attack finally
increased my courage so that by twisting, wriggling, squirming I was able to
free myself.'

Don Ottavio: 'Thank heaven! I breathe again.'

'No one comes' or 'I think myself already overwhelmed': such
utterances intimate a ghastly lapse of time. They imply that something
may have been happening about which Donna Anna does not speak –
perhaps because she does not want to remember, in which case she
would be a liar; or perhaps she lost consciousness for a few seconds, like
Kleist's Marquise von O., so that she did not actually experience the
rape, but is now deeply upset by feeling its after-effects.

Either interpretation is admissible. Her description of her resistance
– 'twisting, wriggling, squirming' – may be thought to have a strangely
erotic flavour. (Granted, Don Giovanni as a type is no rapist. None the

less, the speed with which at the end of Act I Zerlina is hustled into a closet and a scream follows, not of pleasure but of fear – obviously because she has been assaulted – proves that this seducer's amorous 'foreplay' is not always deliberate and time-consuming.) Don Ottavio's 'I breathe again', coming just after what may be the most delicate and ambiguous moment in Donna Anna's tale, can only be described as extremely positive and optimistic. It may well make us smile.

In one manner or another, Don Giovanni has laid vicious and violent hands on Donna Anna's person. She cannot erase the memory of this contact, and it may have leapt into her mind just before her dramatic narration because of some unpremeditated gesture on his part. We may be sure that her noble and sincere fiancé was not in the habit of treating her as Don Giovanni did in his nocturnal assault. Still, we must not overlook the ambiguity of Donna Anna's words.

Leaving aside what well- or ill-intentioned interpreters may say about Mozart's 'eroticism' or about supposedly 'natural womanly reactions', we must respect the fact that da Ponte and Mozart have endowed Donna Anna with a secret. It consists partly in the ambiguity of the physical contact that has occurred, partly in the emotional impact which the death of her father in a duel for which she was indirectly responsible has had on this excitable young woman. To pass definite judgement on Donna Anna means imposing one's own conclusion on a matter which Mozart did not wholly disclose but preferred to leave mysterious.

Those who declare Donna Anna to be a 'straightforward' character are determined to find harmony among qualities which are at best strange, and not so much 'straightforward' as incompatible. Her mixture of expressivity and instability, her strained behaviour and her tendency to lose consciousness and control of herself do not worry them at all. Others interpret her oddities from one or another arbitrarily chosen angle. This means pressing a carefully composed enigma into the service of an ill-considered psychological theory. For Donna Anna wants to escape, not simply from the body of Don Giovanni and the urgings of Don Ottavio, but from the pens of her interpreters.

When Donna Anna recalls the events of that particular night – 'it was already late' – her recitative has progressed from B flat major to E flat minor, which is an incongruous key in *Don Giovanni*. True, B flat is soon adjusted to A sharp, enabling Mozart to introduce a modulation to B minor which is at least an approach to the D region. (Chopin, incidentally, incorporated into the slow movement of his F minor piano concerto, whose middle part constitutes a powerful recitative, a literal quotation from Donna Anna's E flat minor notes. An admirer of *Don Giovanni* with a thorough knowledge of it, his Opus 2 was a set of variations for piano and orchestra on the theme of 'Là ci darem la mano'.) Perhaps the word 'enigma' is too orotund and tends to obscure rather than explain the characterization of Donna Anna. Her various modes of behaviour are perfectly intelligible; it is just that they seem to lack complete consistency. It is certainly an essential part of her character that she has moments of melodic ardour surpassing those allotted to anyone else in this drama (in the Act II sextet, for instance, bars 45–61, her C minor cadences, 'Death, and death alone, can still my tears', are of indescribable beauty).

Whatever she may have suffered, at the end she no longer seems to be struggling, but appears calm and self-assured. The appeal by Don Ottavio that she shall at last agree to the nuptials – Don Giovanni, the scoundrel, has meanwhile gone to the Devil so that honour and parricide have been avenged – is met with a promise. She explains that she needs a year to recover her tranquillity, after which her faithful love will gladly yield to his heartfelt pleas ('al desio di chi m'adora ceder deve un fido amor'). In other words, she cannot face marriage as an immediate sequel to Don Giovanni's brutal and destructive intrusion into her life. In twelve months' time, she thinks, she will be ready.

What is there to suggest that Donna Anna, at this outstanding moment during the very last instants of the work, does not mean what she says? Nothing at all. The larghetto of this duet in G major sung by her and Don Ottavio contains not the slightest musical indication either of any feminine reservation or of any disagreement between the pair. What is made clear is, on the contrary, a perfect harmony in outlook as well as in musical phraseology and gestures. A purer expression of consonance between two personalities is not possible. The young woman accepts entirely naturally and in almost identical tones what her betrothed has just said. In the earlier scenes it has hardly ever been he who has given their exchanges a decisive turn. The cantilena of 'to him whose faithful love seeks this' sounds, as Donna Anna sings it, like an unruffled response matching the purport and expression of Don Ottavio's appeal. The two voices remain intimately and smoothly together (bar 727 in the final scene), and Mozart sees to it that with the repetition of 'al desio' – bars 724–5 are reproduced by bars 730–31 – Donna Anna adopts Don Ottavio's phrase while he echoes her answer. If musical characterization can serve any purpose and supply any proof, all the foregoing must mean 'these two are one and in accord'. Donna Anna loves her betrothed, promises him marriage when a year of mourning and quiet has gone by, and the music confirms this unity, this serene harmony.

Thus a subdued happy ending follows a frightful convulsion. Before Don Giovanni had justice meted out to him, Donna Anna did not seem capable of such an equable concurrence (which now appears real and unaffected).

From the outset she has been on remarkably close terms with death. Her very first sentence – she tries forcibly to detain the escaping ruffian – speaks of it, declaring that she is ready to sacrifice her life for the truth: 'Do not hope, unless you kill me, that I shall ever let you flee'. Then – consistency is not her strong suit – she hurries into the house, returning with her betrothed and with servants carrying torches to what has meanwhile become a duelling-ground. The flickering light falls on her dead father.

Similar illumination, almost ceremoniously created by another group of torch-bearing servants, again originates with Donna Anna and Don Ottavio when Mozart's trumpet modulation from B flat major to D major, symbolizing light, resounds in the sextet of Act II. (For the inspiration of this particular passage, bars 27–30, Richard Strauss would gladly, according to the conductor Karl Böhm, have sacrificed an entire opera of his own. 'And he thought very highly of his operas', Böhm added.) A light now shines in the vestibule. Don Ottavio implores his beloved to stop weeping. Overcome and with over-powering splendour – it is a rare moment – she continues his gravely beautiful D major cantilena to that glorious sequence 'Death, and death alone, can still my tears', already quoted.

In her last scene but one we encounter Donna Anna in a dark room where her father is lying. No, she cannot marry now, she tells Don Ottavio. 'What would my father say!' she argues. Then, of course, she promptly produces a different argument: 'What would the world say!'. She is under such strain that her self-control and her reason are in peril.

In the agony caused by the death of her father she fails to recognize her betrothed, and can manage only a confused apology. Later, when in the company of Donna Elvira and Don Ottavio she meets Zerlina, another victim of a seduction attempt, in Don Giovanni's country house, she again comes close to losing her self-control. This over-strained young woman is at the mercy of her own clashing emotional qualities. Extreme excitability, eccentricity, wildness and a courage which defies death coexist somehow with psychic instability, weakness and an unquestioning willingness to let her father and her betrothed act in her name. Here she behaves in accordance with the custom of her day; yet a moment earlier she has forced Don Ottavio, who wants to be both father and friend, to swear 'fealty' like an underling.

Thus her instability is in simmering conflict with her iron determination to obtain vengeance. Don Ottavio, gentle and sincere, has occasionally been mocked for his 'Hamlet-like' hesitation; but Donna Anna bears rather more resemblance to the Danish prince faced with a task beyond his strength. She may vigorously clamour for revenge and in ensembles she sets the tone, but we hardly ever see her taking decisive action. The strange thing is that in ensembles with the much more self-reliant and active Donna Elvira she is never subordinate or less eloquent, but always holds her own and is generally dominant. This is the case even when Donna Elvira, as happens immediately before the Act II sextet, has been the victim of Leporello in the guise of Don Giovanni and would have the better cause for lamentation. Yet even if Donna Elvira shows herself to be the more energetic, as in the prosecution of Don Giovanni and when she tries a last time to save the scoundrel, it remains the case that Donna Anna, although less steadfast, is generally the more expressive of the two.

Her enigmatic personality combines a marvellous resoluteness – the wonderful soaring sixths in her D major aria – with a hunted, gasping quality as when, precisely in this aria, barely able to breathe, she recalls her father's death struggle, 'Remember the wounds, the pains of my poor sire' (Act I, Scene 13, bars 116–18).

In her last major recitative and in the rondo the clarinet gently confirms Donna Anna's assurances to her betrothed about the love she bears him. Though formerly unruly, she now submits. Mozart's music at least is convinced that Donna Anna, in harmony with Don Ottavio, will gradually get over the death of her father and Don Giovanni's violence.

ANNIUS

Soprano. Friend of Sextus, loved by Servilia. A docile figure among more vigorous personages. Properly speaking, a castrato second lead, but for lack of castrati singers composed for a female voice.

in *La clemenza di Tito*

Annius sincerely loves Servilia and believes himself to be on terms of intimate friendship with Sextus. Two solo arias and his participation in numerous ensembles nevertheless fail to establish him as either an independent or even a strong character. He appears anxious always to subordinate his own wishes to those of the Emperor, Titus.

At the beginning he relies on the help of Sextus, a close friend of Titus, to obtain for him the imperial permission to marry Servilia. The simple, *Singspiel*-like duettino (no. 3) between him and Sextus shows the complete and delightful harmony between them reflected in their fraternal, friendly union of thirds and sixths. However, before learning that Annius wants to marry Servilia, Titus himself selects her to share his throne. Annius is prepared unhesitatingly to acquiesce in the imperial will: emperors are not to be contradicted. He goes so far as to interpret Sextus' brief hesitation in front of Titus as an effort to sustain his hopes by suggesting that Servilia would be an unsuitable bride for the august ruler. For his part, however, Annius gives way immediately: 'How could you have chosen a spouse worthier of your empire and yourself? Virtue and beauty – Servilia has both. I saw it in her that she was born to rule. What I always surmised is now true.' Astounded, Sextus comments in an aside, 'So speaks Annius? Do I dream or am I awake?'. Or is it that the charming, submissive Annius does not wish to stand selfishly in the way of his beloved's career as Empress?

The burden of his subsequent song rebuts, thank goodness, the doubts raised by his pussy-footing behaviour. In his duet with Servilia, whom he is despairingly resolved to abandon, he launches into an A major cantilena whose tones of pure and sincere love touchingly testify to the pair's mutual attachment. (It is followed by Servilia's revelation to Titus of her eternal love for Annius and his for her.) Private love on the one hand, concern for the public good on the other. In Annius' eyes this produces no conflict, but simply a feeling of distress which his beloved manages to soothe.

Shy of collision as Annius is, he has no idea of his friend's intentions. In the trio with Vitellia and Publius he completely misunderstands Vitellia's appalled desperation. After goading Sextus, for reasons of jealousy, into treasonable conspiracy, she has just learnt that the Emperor (after his rejection by Servilia) has decided on her as his bride. She fears that her murderous plans will be carried out, but Annius mistakes her terror for the confusion produced by happy love. Sincerity and adaptability are his strong suits rather than perspicacity and courage – not that these qualities should be misjudged as cowardice. He devoutly affirms a divine order of things, and thinks that Sextus should rely on the beneficence of its authority and remain on the spot instead of fleeing. Of this he tries to convince his friend in an allegretto aria which lacks intensity of feeling and proceeds more on a flowing, urgently imploring note. Exemplary remorse and devotion, he avers, will put everything right. Honest distress, without any opportunistic exaggeration, is to be heard in his plea to Titus on his friend's behalf. 'Gaze graciously down upon our sufferings', he sings. His diminished seventh is eloquent, while the cantilena's sweep is broad and ventures on expressive inflexions. So towards the end of the opera there are moments when Annius emerges from the shade into which the more fiery or strong or powerful figures normally put him.

ANTONIO

Bass. Although Susanna's uncle and Barbarina's father, this sot sides neither with the threatened lovers nor with the dependants in the *Figaro* world, but with his master, the Count.

in *The Marriage of Figaro*

In Beaumarchais's five-act drama *The Follies of a Day or The Marriage of Figaro*, the model for the *Figaro* libretto written by da Ponte for Mozart, the gardener Antonio occasionally displays a certain proletarian brashness. Impudently, but not illogically, he answers back the Countess's reprimand for being drunk without reason: 'Drinking without being thirsty and bedding down a woman any time, that's the only difference, ma'am, between us and the animal world.'

Such remarks were cut by da Ponte. In Mozart's version Antonio is not whimsically tipsy, merely maudlin, when he makes his entrance and nearly destroys the splendid web of lies in which Susanna and the Countess have just ensnared the Count. His alcoholism is musically reflected in a pretty monotonous whimper. He sings more than seventy (!) individual notes one after another before an interval bigger than a second occurs; for a long time he cannot even achieve a third. Almost throughout, steeped in alcohol, he progresses precariously, practically howling, from second to second. Would he be sick if he had to make the effort for larger tonal leaps?

Figaro and those of his party should not complain about the gardener's inebriation, however. Alcohol renders Antonio – whose suspicion and annoyance are in fact quite justified – irritable, but also credulous. For after listening to Figaro's story about having jumped out of the window and lost the correspondence in the process, he is so idiotically gullible that he hands him the compromising papers without any ado. In a state of greater sobriety he can be more dangerous. That is how he comes to blab ironically on Cherubino: 'Today, if you will forgive me, Seville is in my house. There they dressed him as a girl and that's where his own clothes have remained.' And his effort, immediately before Act III finishes, to land Figaro in difficulties is shrewdly undertaken. His whining monotony sounds more artless than his less tongue-tied, more sober recitative (in Act III, Scene 9), but under the influence of alcohol he is of course easier to manipulate.

All the same, the contempt that he, the tipsy old father and uncle, earns from the others is not too great. At the moment of greatest happiness, immediately after the blissful sextet in Act III, Susanna says 'Now let us go and tell all these happy events to my lady and our uncle'. This grumpy and zealous gardener is, after all, part of the family.

ARBACE

Tenor. Confidant of Idomeneo. With perfectly good intent, he makes a proposal that has fateful consequences.

in *Idomeneo, King of Crete*

'O beloved, faithful Arbace', says the King to his counsellor with grateful relief after Arbace – not on the spur of the moment, but after a brief pause for reflection – has tendered his advice on how to try and circumvent the situation. Arbace knows that Idomeneo, on the point of shipwreck, promised to sacrifice to Neptune the first person whom he should meet if he reached land safely. He also knows – he practically fainted when he learnt of it – that this first person was Idamante, the King's son. And Arbace senses the tone of command in Idomeneo's plea, 'Advise me, save my son'; that is why he recommends that Idamante shall 'seek refuge in another land. He must remain hidden from the people. Meanwhile a way will be found to placate Neptune. Some other god will see to matters', which is expedient for the time being, but very dangerous for the future.

The King, in other words, is to break the vow that he has made to a god. Barely has Idomeneo heard what he wanted to hear before he believes that, thanks to his counsellor, he can now enjoy peace of mind. Arbace, whose recitative sounded gloomy and sorrowful, in turn ponders in his first aria, a C major bravura piece lacking almost any darker tones, on the lofty but exposed position in which rulers (even given good advisors) are placed. Calamity and sorrow are unavoidable for crowned heads: 'Remain aloof from thrones or else do not lament'. He is far from being either cynical or spiteful; he simply has no doubts as to the right order of things (why should a loyal and devoted confidant do so?). *Opera seria* was, after all, also a 'mirror of princes'. The didactic conclusions to be drawn from its scenes and situations need not reflect the emotional state of a character whose function is to utter the sententious remarks required by convention.

In Act III it becomes clear that the sea god is not to be defied: Neptune has sent a sea monster to which thousands have fallen victim. Arbace recognizes that his calculation about some other god conciliating Neptune or diverting him from his purpose has not worked out. He not only admits his mistake, but bewails it in an emotional adagio recitative telling of death, devastation, and even violent anger against divine 'deafness'. This is the second time that Arbace's aria is given to analysis of the situation. His sensitive contemplation in A major reveals that his love for his lord, the King, and his son Idamante surpasses that for his country. If Crete has incurred guilt, let doom take its toll, but the gods should at least save the King and the Prince. He does not touch on the problem of guilt and innocence (after all, he knows the facts). He adds a rider: if his own blood can help to palliate the divine wrath and extort compassion for the realm, then it will be offered to the gods.

Arbace is a noble figure of the second order. He is deeply shocked by Idomeneo's unfortunate vow, and painfully affected by his compatriots' suffering, but when his aria reveals his inmost thoughts it is plain that he completely accepts the situation. Not for a moment does a doubt cross his mind. He knows straightaway what a king must do or suffer, or for what sacrifices anyone must be prepared who has the honour to be a royal confidant.

BARBARINA

Soprano. Antonio's daughter and Susanna's cousin. Passes in Almaviva's castle from hand to hand. Loves Cherubino, kisses the Count, and is a clumsy go-between.

in The Marriage of Figaro

Dramatists demonstrate often enough that people are not what they seem. Noble, magnanimous attitudes are critically analysed and revealed as either deception or self-deception. At the end of *Così fan tutte*, for example, Fiordiligi and Dorabella are probably no longer so serenely sure of themselves and their feelings as they were at the beginning.

The way that Mozart treats Barbarina is totally different. At first this childish but artful creature with her ready flow of prattle gives the impression of being a little hussy, yet at the close she seems almost transfigured. In front of the Countess she chatters about how much the Count likes to kiss and fondle her – however disconcerting at that particular moment it may be for the aristocratic husband. With Cherubino she plays the same sort of high jinks, and the Count catches her in these frolics. She announces innocently that she would like to marry Cherubino and to love the Count like her kitten. As a go-between for lovers she is below par, loses the identification token, and discloses to none other than the astonished bridegroom what her employer, his lordship, told her to keep secret.

So what we have here is a pert little girl who already dominates the circle of her female friends and glides from one pair of arms to another in a spirit of innocent hilarity. If she is still a child, she must be a pretty precocious one; if she is no longer a child, then she has retained many child-like qualities. Our interest in her, as she is occasionally mentioned during the course of three Acts and then heard uttering a few words of recitative text, is rather slight in any case. She lacks Despina's presence of mind, Zerlina's physical warmth; she strikes no note of her own, this Barbarina, with her medley of frankness, cheerful simplicity, and gentle waywardness.

At the start of Act IV, though, there occurs her cavatina, thirty-six bars in F minor, and it is hardly possible to hear this piece the first time without being deeply moved and feeling ashamed of the casual malice with which it is so easy to dismiss the little trollop. Barbarina is in trouble. She is looking for a lost pin. She is suffering from guilt and fear. Mozart wonderfully complements what has gone before. He adds to the picture of Barbarina, who so far had merely fluttered through the opera like a bright-hued butterfly, a deeper dimension: we divine something of a sensual sadness, of melancholy underlying her thoughtless instincts, of the purity of such unhappiness.

The cavatina is in an F minor confined to its own track and it rarely approaches a direct outburst: when that does happen, the violins at once strike up sixteenths; otherwise a steady flow of quaver accompaniments is maintained. Utterly simple, yet far from trite, it represents the essence and the alibi, with no need for psychological explanation, of a child who in a moment will again be a little pert, a little silly, and babbling away thoroughly unabashed.

DR BARTOLO

Bass. Intrigues against Figaro till it turns out that the latter is his long-lost son. Later he even takes sides against the Count's despotic ways. As long as he remains an evil figure, his music is richer and has more character. At the end, though, he has at any rate a son and a wife.

in *The Marriage of Figaro*

Dr Bartolo is an elderly doctor who behaves like a lawyer. Not so long ago young Count Almaviva had, with Figaro's cunning assistance, snatched from under his nose and married his ward Rosina whom he would have liked to wed himself: that is why he bears Figaro a grudge. What further ingredients are required for this tribunal of revenge that he proposes to hold? In his 'vengeance' aria he lists them. In the first place there is pompous self-confidence and utter lack of scruple. Drums and trumpets are at this stage heard for the first time in the orchestral accompaniment. Revenge is a tribunal, and Bartolo savours this fact with pride. Anyone who can 'forget' – the strings wriggle in a narrow, illustrative compass – shows a 'base-born' mind. Pride and ostentatious ruthlessness are not sufficient, however; one must set about the task of revenge with furious energy. Bartolo describes this like a man possessed, and his assertion that he will assuredly succeed sounds somewhat like an unquestioning, lip-smacking slogan.

At the end of his aria the triad fanfare motif of the beginning is resumed, but instead of 'Now for vengeance, oh, now for vengeance' the text runs 'All of Seville knows who I am – Bartolo'. Mozart characteristically continues the initial motif to the triumphant close which both the avenger and his client Marcellina seem to find equally convincing.

The voice of nature had failed to make itself heard in the offended Bartolo, and likewise in Figaro. No instinct told either the infuriated senior or the quick-witted junior that they were blood relatives – father and son. Subsequently Bartolo, a trifle exhausted by life, no longer vengeful but only moved, seems a little awkward in the role of father, but he is sufficiently happy finally to decide to marry Marcellina. His spirit is unbroken. When Basilio remarks that for counts to lead ladies' maids astray is the way of the world, the old doctor rebels against aristocratic despotism on behalf of his offended son: 'You think then that he should suffer it in silence?'. He is on Figaro's side now, but cannot sing any vengeance arias on his behalf. Benevolent, he has long ceased to be a central figure.

BASILIO

Tenor. Music master in the castle of Count Almaviva, where he is also busy as a pander.

in *The Marriage of Figarro*

As a youth, so Basilio assures Bartolo in his major Act IV aria, he too had been a hot-tempered fool; experience has meanwhile taught him how the powerless must behave among the powerful. Let a man phlegmatically renounce pride and dignity. Let him slip into an ass's skin and his foul smell will then save him from the wolfish threats of the dangerous world. True enough, the music master's conduct leaves little that is detestable to the imagination. His master's cravings are his command: hence he serves the Count as pander, snooper, and prudent advisor, representing an eighteenth-century hanger-on, lackey and informer in Almaviva's castle. He brings Susanna the Count's lucrative offers. He is also quick to discover that Cherubino, crazy with love and consequently reckless, proposes to dedicate his canzonetta to the Countess. It has not escaped him how the careless boy has spent hours prowling around Susanna's room.

Is Basilio a thrashed dog whose spirit has been broken by life? Someone who has craftily and cowardly allied himself to the wicked way of the world because he would otherwise not stand a chance? That is how he puts it, overlooking the peculiarities which make of him a mini-character, although a shabby one. Like many a musician, Basilio lacks neither wit nor spite. It is he who invents the nickname 'Cherubino d'amore'. He has a gift for elegant malice. During the Act I trio (no. 7), where after an unpleasant beginning everything turns out for the best for him, he renders his somewhat oily falsetto motif 'In mal punto son qui giunto' ('at this point I am out of joint'), first in alarm, then waiting for the outcome, and finally with ironic malevolence, without ever really introducing any change into the line.

Rather than being phlegmatic, he seems gleeful and cynical. The opportunities for mischief and venomous delight provided by other people's mistakes are evidently a fine reward for his vigilant detective work. He rejects reproaches with the argument that he is no liar, but simply bows to the actualities of power; he always passes on what he learns, and he resents being called a 'wretch' just because he has 'eyes in his head'.

It is ironic that in *The Marriage of Figaro*, a peak of ethereal achievement in western music, it is of all people the *musician* Basilio who is far and away the meanest, most unsympathetic figure.

BELMONTE

Tenor. Has organized a ship and a rescue operation to bring back to Spain his sweetheart, her maid, and his servant from the country estate of Pasha Selim where they are now held prisoner after being sold into slavery.

in *The Abduction*

Belmonte is an ecstatic lover. He raves so sincerely about his Constanze that the everyday reality with which he has to deal and the mortal danger of his undertaking hardly impinge on his mind. When he trembles, becomes afraid, doubts, he is not subject to the vulgar fear of brute force and death that other mortals feel, so much as to the delicious mixture of anxiety and bliss produced by a great love in mortal danger.

The anxieties and troubles of anyone capable of such love elevate the *Singspiel*'s character. This transformation is deliberate and systematic. For instance, the melody of Belmonte's entrance aria is already heard in C minor in the overture. His situation, that of a man on foreign soil who proposes to abduct his beloved, his agitation, his words 'Ich duldete der Leiden, O Liebe, allzuviel' ('of torments, O my love, I have borne all too many') – for these the expression C minor extending to the diminished seventh chord is indeed the appropriate key. When however the young lover does make his entrance, it is in a major key that he sings, and he evokes the torments he has endured without a trace of minor-key plaintiveness.

The love which throbs through Belmonte's arias is a tender, ecstatic, sincerely felt emotion lacking the slightest *stretto*-like vaunting quality. On his own, not roused by partners to vehemence, rage or other transports, he normally confines himself to a moderate andante (arias nos. 1 and 4). 'Wenn der Freude Tränen fliessen' ('when tears of joy run down our cheeks'), aria no. 15, is even labelled adagio; its allegretto section is distinctly restrained. Similarly his last solo, at the beginning of Act III, is an andante piece, though packed with coloraturas. At this point, just before the abduction venture, he does feel afraid, or so he says; but his singing, his idealistic self-expression, does not convey fear.

Love renders Belmonte's tones all the more mellifluously persuasive. Glorious turns of phrase emanate beguilingly from the flow of lovely melody and elevate the rather clumsy words 'Es wird mir so bange . . . Es glüht mir die Wange' ('in me alarm does grow . . . my cheek is all aglow') to the outpourings of an enraptured lover. He is often enveloped in a gleam, an aura, of gracious radiance.

The cunning deceit and the sly tactics required when dealing with difficult customers like Osmin are not for him. He is not worried by the risky situation, but merely by the momentary doubt whether Constanze has been faithful to him. As the organizer of an abduction his conduct is not very adroit. Asked to be a little more careful, his answer is 'Ah, Pedrillo, if you but knew love!'. Apart from being somewhat offensive to his servant, the remark reflects the blind assurance of the entranced lover, confident that he can get away with anything because to help a love like his is what guardian angels are for.

The finale demonstrates that he is proud, wealthy, and has never 'bent his knee to anyone'. We have his word for it. At the beginning, however, he displays the arrogance of a Spanish nobleman in his notably imprudent handling of Osmin. It ought after all to be in his interest to ingratiate himself (as the shrewd Pedrillo has unsuccessfully tried to do) with the overseer, but he is unaccustomed to practising caution. 'Hey, friend,' he asks, 'is this not Pasha Selim's country house?' Osmin does not allow himself to be disturbed in his singing. Belmonte at once becomes more aggressive. 'Hey, old fellow, hey! Are you deaf?' As Osmin imperturbably sings his song to its end, Belmonte indulges in a minor tantrum by taking over the start of the song and propelling it into a fast four-four time direction to the accompaniment of the uncivil text 'Verwünscht seist du samt deinem Liede, ich bin dein Singen nun schon müde' ('a curse upon you and upon your song, to which I've listened far too long').

Not for a moment does it cross the nobleman's mind that he might attempt to curry favour with Osmin, whose jealous dislike of Pedrillo is obvious. In their presto duet his behaviour is that of an opponent on equal terms who happens just at this juncture to be at a disadvantage. Osmin quickly guesses what the impertinent stranger's intentions are. He complements Belmonte's 'Ich möchte gerne' ('I would much like to') perfectly logically with 'So hübsch von ferne ums Haus rumschleichen, und Mädchen stehlen?' ('nicely from afar steal about the house, and its inmates too?'). Of course Osmin is quite right. But instead of changing his tactics and yielding, Belmonte replies testily, 'Ihr seid besessen, sprecht voller Galle mir so vermessen ins Angesicht' ('you are quite imbecile, to look me in the face and dare talk to me so full of bile!').

In a land where torment and torture are commonplace, Belmonte behaves like a cross between an impatient prince and a sleep-walker. His heart beats audibly (aria no. 4). The first larger-scale coloratura is launched by the word 'liebevoll' ('full of love'). Longing and the joy of love deeply move him ('Ach, lass mich zu mir selbst kommen' – 'ah, let me come to myself'). His brief suspicion of Constanze (although she has always bravely resisted Pasha Selim) is a weakness quickly and repentantly overcome. Whatever happens, the mellifluence of his singing – 'Ist der Liebe schönster, grösster Sold' ('is love's sweetest, greatest boon') – remains unaffected: even the pauses in which he draws breath seem to throb with bliss.

The *Singspiel*'s sympathy lies on the side of those able to surrender entirely to love. It is not good sense, which Osmin possesses too, but the heart, that receives its reward. When the worst befalls, the abduction fails, and death by torture is a settled prospect, Belmonte and Constanze have not a thought for their own troubles, as more sensible and practical people would in such a situation, but only for the other's affliction. And then it occurs to the heroic pair that death with the beloved for the sake of love is indeed a blessed and delightful fate; however, they are not obliged to put this hypothesis to the test. Their ability to entertain such fabulously lofty feelings itself deserves a fairy-tale reward. 'Du linderst mir den Todesschmerz, und ach, ich reisse dich ins Grab!' ('you ease for me the mortal pain, and oh, I bring you to your grave!') closes Belmonte's generous-minded recitative. Each is responsive only to the other's suffering. Their own is thereby mitigated, dissolved. Thanks to his exaltation, Belmonte evinces composure and a sense of justice. 'Extirpate the wrong my father did you,' he tells Pasha Selim, bravely adding, 'I will face anything and do not blame you.'

At least Belmonte realizes that the happy turn of events at the end is not a matter of course, but that a miracle has supervened. It is he who strikes up the vaudeville, that rhythmic paean to Pasha Selim for his benevolence, great-heartedness and magnanimity.

BLONDIE

Soprano. Maid to Constanze, steady girl-friend of Pedrillo, pursued by the love of the overseer Osmin. Manages the complications that result from this set of relationships in a gaily robust way. Not in the most hard-pressed situation does she allow herself to be intimidated, for she is a proud and free-born Englishwoman.

in *The Abduction*

Everything that Blondie says and does shows vitality, toughness, vivacity and forthrightness. Either she is incapable of fear, or she forbids herself to indulge in it, even fear of death. After the failure of the attempted abduction she and Pedrillo are brought to account. Appalled by the thought of the prospective torments, he turns to his girl-friend; 'Oh, Blondie, Blondie, what will they do to you?'. Her answer is fatalistic and stoic: 'It is all the same to me. Seeing that we have to die some time, I don't mind what they do.'

Her courage comes to the fore not only when all seems lost in any case and neither moaning nor wily dissimulation serve any further purpose. Earlier, when she could undoubtedly have improved her situation by hypocrisy or compliance, it never crosses her mind to try to deceive the terrifying Osmin, in full pursuit of her. She tells him straight out that she likes Pedrillo far better than his 'bellows face'. Osmin pulls out every stop, the deepest not excepted, to display his manliness. He sings shattering minims of blood-curdling seriousness, and will not yield a step, he tells her, 'bis du zu gehorchen mir schwörst' ('till to obey me you do swear'). She is not in the least impressed. Unabashed and jaunty, she too pulls out every stop and derisively imitates the old growler's deep tones and inflated dignity. She will not submit, 'und wenn du der Grossmogul wärst' ('and if you were the Grand Mogul'). She repulses him and the overseer retires 'timidly'.

What is the source of Blondie's courage? Is she so spoiled, so flippant or so feather-brained that she simply does not realize how dangerous the situation of a prisoner is? Or does her courage not count because, as is well known, the task of a *Singspiel* coloratura soubrette is to be constantly lively, amusing, cheerfully amorous, not a jot more, and in any case she can rely on a happy ending? Yes, Blondie clearly comes close to the soubrette category, that is the part of lady's maid, and in opera signifying the role of vivacious girl-friend. She fits the convention. Belmonte and Constanze represent the 'upstairs' pair and their feelings are high-minded. What else then can Pedrillo and Blondie, the 'downstairs' pair, do than be the cheerful, more naive, more superficial *opera buffa* team?

I have no wish to exaggerate: Blondie is certainly not a majestic figure, and her character is not opposed to the category to which she has been assigned by the operatic system, aided by producers and sopranos whose coloraturas stretch to the top E. Nor is she a passionate heroine. At the same time she is not merely a brainless nonentity. To regard all her words and actions as typical of a vivacious soubrette, just because one has prematurely formed a conventional image of her, is to blur an important difference. It reduces a brave girl to a conventional puppet. What first belittles her is that everyone calls her Blondie, a diminutive that trivializes her. Someone who loves her, like Pedrillo, may feel an urge to address her by way of such an endearment, but as an individual and a young lady her name is Blonde.

Good-natured and plucky, she does her best to encourage the wholly despondent Constanze ('Do but listen. Not once in a lifetime do I give up, however bad things may look. For whoever is always imagining the worst really does get the worst of things'). Is that a piece of unthinking optimism? Likewise, her stoic indifference to inescapable death is not the imperturbability of an operatic stereotype, but springs from her conviction that a girl born to freedom still retains her freedom of mind, 'even when of freedom deprived'. Her conviction is based on her origin, for she is an Englishwoman, and hence free from the innate submissiveness usual in petty German states or the Habsburg realm.

Let the rest sing or complain sentimentally and sadly; she has a stronger, more resilient nervous system. Her entrance aria, 'Durch Zärtlichkeit und Schmeicheln, Gefälligkeit und Scherzen erobert man die Herzen der guten Mädchen leicht' ('with tenderness and favours, blandishments and kindliness to conquer good maidens' hearts is no laborious task'), tells Osmin that with her he began on the wrong tack. Grumbling and squabbling only means that love flies out by the window. At 'flies out' ('entweicht') she sings an almost unrestrained demisemiquaver run, three times, and with a vigour that expands the coloratura longer and higher, each time rendering it the more convincing.

She does not lie. She is fearless towards Osmin and also Pedrillo, who earns a well-deserved box on the ears. Can it be that this lady's maid is a lofty-minded idealist? No: Blondie simply turns the situation decidedly to her own advantage. Her threat to Osmin, 'My mistress . . . is the Pasha's love, the apple of his eye, his all, and it will cost me but a word for you to have fifty strokes of the cane on the soles of your feet', demonstrates that her boldness rests on a realistic foundation. She knows just as realistically how to distinguish between her own situation and that of her mistress. For her part, she at least has Pedrillo on hand for consolation whereas Constanze has to resist the Pasha's advances without Belmonte's support. The realist Blondie is, however, no priggish stickler for principles either. She has so much courage that Osmin, quite rightly, fears that, given the chance, she would be capable of remodelling Turkish women's behaviour and inspiring them to revolt. All the same, she is far from puritanical. When she tells Osmin that his approach is wrong, an expert is heard speaking. Be as ugly as you are, act as badly as you do, and success is out of the question; 'blandishments and kindliness' achieve more. He sets about it in completely the wrong way. At a later stage she has no hesitation in calling him an unbearable beast.

Not for a moment does she attach supreme importance to entire faithfulness; 'Caliban' Osmin happens not to have presented any real temptation. Should so noble an individual as the Pasha take some pains, then it is far from clear that one should reject such a promising liaison just because one is already engaged. The high-spirited Blondie coolly opines that Constanze is too sentimental. 'But I would not be of such sensibility as she. Men truly do not merit that we should pine to death for them. Perhaps I would think along Mussulman lines' (i.e., not adhere to monogamy).

An English heart of oak and a robustly plebeian sense of reality combine to give her natural attraction a warm-hearted background. She reveals the strength of her soul when, at the end of the aria 'Welche Freude, welche Lust' ('what a pleasure, what a joy'), her momentum during this moment of overflowing happiness makes her utter her 'Freud und Jubel prophezeien' ('delight and cheer foretelling') with an almost Handel-like acclaim over and against a forte in the full orchestra. Here she displays a radiant greatness, concise, content, and free from affectation; after all, she is not a doll named Blondie, but a human being named Blonde.

FIRST, SECOND, AND THIRD BOY

⌣

Soprano, mezzo-soprano, and contralto. Always act, advise or
impede together and unanimously. They are not three more or less
individual people, but constitute something of a triumvirate or, to
be pedantic, a triumpuerate. A gaily attractive, musically rich
boys' trio.

in The Magic Flute

The Three Ladies in the Queen of the Night's service, who, as
individual women, consider themselves rivals for the handsome Prince
Tamino, instruct Tamino and Papageno in the Act I quintet (no. 5)
that three boys will help them in the task of freeing Pamina from
Sarastro's clutches. Their help will consist in hovering around them
and acting as guides: 'Follow their guidance quite alone'.

There is no doubt that the 'three boys, young, fair, sweet and wise'
seem at first to be actively on the Queen of the Night's side. But their
actual behaviour, summoning the Prince to manly conduct, having to
refuse him certain information, singing him encouraging exhortations,
suggests that they are on Sarastro's side. Act II brings no change.
There in Sarastro's name they return, from an 'aerial carriage covered
with roses', the instruments previously handed to Tamino and
Papageno by the Three Ladies to help them in an emergency – the
magic flute and the chimes. All the high-minded words and directions
uttered by the Three Boys clearly reflect the outlook prevailing in
'Sarastro's realm', with which in the A major trio they expressly
identify themselves. This inconsistency in the plot has led ingenious
interpreters to conclude that the text's author, Emanuel Schikaneder,
was less ingenious than they. Who is it who really gives the Three Boys
their orders?

Given that the Three Boys apparently serve two masters in
succession, is this inconsistency serious, even intolerable? In a fairy-

tale, why should we not imagine the existence of neutral beings, forces, magical figures whose services are available to all powerful people? The Three Boys might then to some extent be 'for hire', equally at the Queen of the Night's as at Sarastro's disposal, and able in given circumstances to confer their sympathies on the nobler of their patrons. This is one possible explanation. Or it may be that everything that is pure and innocent within Sarastro's orbit gravitates inevitably towards his lofty sovereignty. Once the Boys have come into contact with the sanctuary, they henceforth serve Sarastro exclusively and no longer the Queen of the Night.

It might be too much of a rationalization to argue that the triumpuerate proves how Sarastro has the upper hand from the start, even in the Queen of the Night's realm. This would suggest that the Boys, never seen acting firmly on the Queen's behalf, are throughout Sarastro's creatures without the Queen and her Three Ladies knowing it. At any rate, it is perfectly easy to render the trio's apparent 'reorientation' plausible. But is it equally possible to replace boys' voices with those of women?

Experienced opera-goers have often found that boys' voices are not resonant and strong enough to carry clearly and impressively in big houses: they are too thin. Herbert von Karajan has said that he has rarely heard really 'pure' and really clear boys' choirs and voices. If this trio of helpers does not consist of rounded, sensuous female voices, but of three adolescent singers who are past childhood but have not yet reached puberty, still less the world of adult sexuality, this is not a gratuitous addition, but relevant to the themes of the opera. This is not just because the Boys are still too young for erotic rivalry and form a homogeneous group, a trio, rather than three individual beings receptive to love. Their conduct must on no account be innocuously childish. It is they, after all, who initiate the two finales to the accompaniment of measured, serenely ceremonious music which underlines the significance of the ensuing proceedings: 'Zum Ziele führt dich diese Bahn, doch musst du, Jüngling, männlich siegen' ('to your goal this way will lead you, yet, fair youth, brave must be the victory' – Act I) and 'Bald prangt, den Morgen zu verkünden, die Sonn' auf gold'ner Bahn, bald soll der Aberglaube schwinden, bald siegt der weise Mann' ('soon the sun shall take its golden way, presaging another day, soon all superstition shall away, and the wise man have the say' – Act II).

The true and satisfying meaning of their pre-adolescent innocence only becomes clear when the Boys, not yet tormented by sexuality, encounter two victims of love's rapture. The Three Boys hold back Pamina and Papageno – the true 'victims' in *The Magic Flute* – from suicide. They realize that love is anything but amusing. 'Sie quält verschmähter Liebe Leiden. Lasst uns der Armen Trost bereiten! Fürwahr, ihr Schicksal geht uns nah'! O wäre nur ihr Jüngling da' ('rejected love's pains are her torments. Let us offer consolation! Truly we are deeply touched! Oh, were but her lover here'). The Boys regard love's pains as a kind of illness; they sympathize and sing chromatically in C minor. Pamina's madness, which brings her close to death, is reflected in the naive, tender solicitude of three friendly helpers to whom Eros' dark depths are as yet unknown, although they sense them to be indubitably sinister. That is why, agitated, they seek actively and decisively to be of help. When appeals to morality – 'Self-destruction God will punish!' – are of no use, they seize the dagger from her.

The Boys intervene too in Papageno's case. Since, however, his despair is less love's madness than a problem of deprivation and disappointment, they adopt a pragmatic approach: use the chimes and you will no longer be alone.

The trio's part-writing is sometimes homophonic, sometimes elaborately canonic and polyphonic. The group none the less always 'voices' only one view, a voice that is sometimes wise and sometimes sounds deliciously like precocious wisdom. It is also the voice of kindly pity of those whom the power of Eros does not affect for those who suffer under its power. Only boys are capable of enunciating such delightfully unsentimental and objective compassion; were this to be performed by three young women, were expressive female voices to hurry to a suicidal maiden's aid or that of a Papageno about to hang himself, the tones would be identical, but the scenic tension no longer the same.

CHERUBINO

Soprano. Count Almaviva's page. Gets in the way during his master's love affairs and is therefore ordered by the Count, who is also his military superior, to leave for Seville. He is easily persuaded to disregard the instruction and to remain, because there is hardly a woman in the *Figaro* world whom he does not love, as well as being painfully in love with love itself. The ladies spoil him accordingly. The music teacher Basilio spitefully labels him 'Cherubino d'amore'.

in *The Marriage of Figaro*

Cherubino is a very young man, still in the throes of adolescence. Being courageous but by no means adroit, he easily lands the ladies who like him in awkward situations. Not only artistically gifted – 'What a charming voice', says the Countess after his arietta, to which Susanna flatteringly adds, 'Oh, as far as that goes, everything he does is well done' – he is to all intents and purposes so lovable that Barbarina asks the Count to give him her for a husband, the Countess not only dries his eyes but is more than willing to tolerate his rapturous adoration, and Susanna, a bit jealous, finds pleasure in fiddling around with him while taking his measurements (as Figaro in Act I does those of the bridal bed) in order to disguise him.

If he blushingly casts the Countess yearning looks, he is by no means always so shy with women of lower station. (In the last piece of the Beaumarchais trilogy, incidentally, it appears that he proceeded beyond harmless idolization. This play, *A Mother's Guilt*, was, however, not known to Mozart. Set in the year 1790, it was first performed in 1792. There the Countess has had a child by Cherubino.) At present worshipping the Countess at a decent distance, he is all the saucier with other females. In Act IV he is downright impudent to Susanna: he knows only too well, he says, that with the Count she is anything but prudish (he has no idea that it is really the Countess to whom he is speaking). 'Why then may I not do what the Count may do at any time?' Impertinence indeed.

Since Cherubino chases women obsessively (endangering himself) and thoughtlessly (endangering others too), he has been called an adolescent version of Don Juan or compared to Count Almaviva, who leaves no woman, except his wife perhaps, in peace. Such comparisons do him an injustice. His amorous obsession results neither from boredom nor from manic pleasure-seeking, neither from pure enjoyment of pursuit and capture nor from male erotomania; it always takes into account the other person and the longing that she inspires. He is entranced by the opposite sex. They allure, confuse, make him both happy and unhappy. He is not calculating. His loving has nothing of swagger or ostentation. He obeys an instinct and feels himself to be its bewildered victim.

Although Cherubino can get on everyone's nerves, Mozart's music enhances his personality. 'Cherubino d'amore' touches the hearts of all women as well as of all men who have not wholly forgotten their own adolescence. For him the unequivocal fiery absoluteness of his urge to love is neither a pleasant frenzy, gay desire, lustful earthiness nor the morose opposite of all these, insane passion, infernal fire, a desire for an endless succession of conquests. He suffers the ambivalence of love – sweet distress, heat and cold, laughter and tears, boldness and shame, stylish self-confidence and complete loss of countenance. Eros speaks through him, but not as a cynical quest for enjoyment. The purest unity of character, subject to an urge whose essence is conflict – that is the miracle which is Cherubino.

'Such a longing' ('un desio') 'as I am not able to name' forces him, waking and dreaming, to talk of love: so the middle portion of his allegro vivace aria in Act I reveals. 'Un desio' recurs four times: first (we are in B flat) as a minor third in a pained minor chord, then as a major sixth in a kindling major chord (the voice is never taken higher than this G), back to the minor third, pointed up by syncopation, and finally once more as a major sixth. It is difficult to imagine how the ambivalent pain and happiness caused by adolescent yearning could be more clearly conveyed than by means of this carefully considered and acoustically irresistible alternation. A corresponding quality is demonstrated in this passion-laden *aria parlante* by the relationship between the lines 'I speak of love waking/ I speak of love dreaming'. Instead of illustrating the difference between waking and dreaming, the tones descriptive of 'Parlo d'amor vegliando, parlo d'amor sognando' make of waking and dreaming something analogous, even homogeneous.

Whether the effect is described as psychological programme music or as a helpful accident latent in the operatic genre is of small concern to the figure of Cherubino which emerges from such tones. They portray him realistically, but transfigure him as well. Likewise in the arietta 'Voi che sapete' ('you, lovely ladies'), sung by him to the Countess in Act II while Susanna plucks the guitar, the musical interpretation and elaboration of emotion goes so far that, despite disciplined versification, translations mostly obscure the subtlety with which a state of mind is here delineated through discreet tonal coloration. Mozart breathes life into the words 'Non trovo pace notte nè di: ma pur mi piace languir così'; a literal translation of the second half would run 'yet it pleases me to languish thus'. The two verbs 'piacere' and 'languire', treading on one another's heels, give the impression of having received the full musical value of their emotive diversity, 'pleases' as a seventh chord, 'languish' as a diminished seventh chord.

Since Cherubino has only the Count to fear as his sole 'rival', still feels enormous respect for his godmother the Countess, and evidently much enjoys disappearing into Barbarina's room or kissing Susanna, one can easily forget that he is in fact an aristocrat and in no way belongs to the downtrodden who one fine revolutionary day will bring 'the servants' hall into the drawing-room'. His aristocratic self-assurance may help to explain the *opera buffa* circumstance that he dares almost heedlessly to disregard a distinct order by Almaviva.

At a particularly strange moment the young man, curiously enough, anticipates fairly accurately the details of his death as Act II, Scene 1 of *A Mother's Guilt* will describe it. In *The Marriage of Figaro* he makes sheep's eyes at the Countess, but he is incapable of declaring himself. In Act II (shortly before the Count pounds on the door) he bursts into tears at now having to obey his orders and leave. 'O heavens! Why is death not permitted? Perhaps, when indeed my last moment is near . . . this mouth would then dare . . .'. The Countess reproves his death-fantasy with 'Be sensible now, what is this folly?'. Then Cherubino is quick to demonstrate that he has not just been showing off. To help his idol, he is brave enough to jump out of the window: 'Before I harm her, I'd leap into fire'.

The last part of Beaumarchais's *Figaro* trilogy, first performed after Mozart's death, reveals what subsequently happened. Cherubino did succeed in seducing the Countess in her husband's castle. She became pregnant, banished him from her presence, and thereafter devoted her life exemplarily to repentance. Cherubino behaved not unworthily and sought death abroad (a death for love reminiscent of *Isoldes Liebestod*). From a field of battle he wrote to his eternally beloved, 'Since I may no longer see you, life is hateful to me and I shall with pleasure lose it in the assault for which I have volunteered'. The letter has a postscript, blood-stained and touching: 'Mortally wounded, I open this letter once more and inscribe with my blood this painful, lasting farewell . . .'. The rest is blurred by tears.

Da Ponte and Mozart knew nothing of all this. Nevertheless the Cherubino to whom they introduce us is so fiery, has so many facets, and for all his forthrightness is so imbued with infinite longing that even this melodramatic severance of the tie between him and his Countess might already be suspected.

THE COMMENDATORE

⌣

Bass. Wants to protect Donna Anna, his daughter, against the masked Don Giovanni; forces him to fight a duel, and is killed. Returns to earth in the shape of a marble statue as an emissary of the supernatural. His acceptance of Don Giovanni's invitation to supper does not make the miscreant change his ways, but brings about Don Giovanni's descent to hell.

in *Don Giovanni*

At the beginning, as long as he is alive, the Commendatore is an old father whom the seducer hardly takes seriously. In accordance with convention, he is out to avenge his daughter's honour. Triads, in a vigorous minor key without any outstanding or chromatic feature, constitute his idiom. In the trio with Don Giovanni and Leporello his tones, even when dying, are the most neutral, whereas Leporello is reduced by the situation to his typically excited, chattering chant and Don Giovanni, aware that the deed has been witnessed and that he is the guilty party, is momentarily, at least, shaken into some capacity for emotion. However, when the Commendatore returns from the realm of the dead to punish the living, he has put aside his shadowy, conventional character. In sonorous tones louder than life he proclaims the power of the supernatural.

There could scarcely be a greater dramatic contrast than between the Commendatore's first and final scenes. At the start we see an over-zealous father forcing a young, superior, initially even reluctant opponent to fight an obviously hopeless duel. It would have been more sensible, though less bold, to await the help of his servants and Don Ottavio, but the honour of a Spanish officer requires him to fight. This initial appearance is musically divided into three parts of approximately equal length: the heroic challenge, the rapid duel and the tight-lipped mortal agony. Here, with its accompanying quaver triplets alla breve and andante, we have the trio which Beethoven copied out and clearly used as his model for the first movement of the Moonlight Sonata.

In the final scene, prefaced by no more than a few mystically admonitory chorale notes as well as the statue's nod and 'Yea' in the graveyard encounter, the Commendatore is invested with an irresistible, distinctive and dauntless resonance. His 'Stay! Earthly food can no longer sustain him who has tasted of pleasures immortal' needs only slight ingenuity to be heard as a concealed anticipation of the twelve-tone row, without detracting from the power of his utterance. 'Pleasures immortal' likewise reverberates loftily to intervals of two or three whole tones, disquietingly brought together regardless of scale. The gigantic leaps and changes of register are intimidating and majestic, as though transcending human limitations. The Commendatore, who in life preferred petty tonal gradations – he only uttered one octave, and its significance is not apparent until later – now thunders in tenths.

None the less, the first and the last of his scenes demonstrate in their contrasts a certain identity. On his reappearance the Commendatore has undergone a metamorphosis and yet he remains himself. The beginning of the overture, which George Bernard Shaw described as 'D minor and its dominant – a tone of dread titillation to all musicians' – and then the living statue's arrival in Don Giovanni's chamber to the accompaniment of similar chords can serve as a lesson in the technique of progressive variation. The second appearance of the D minor chord and its dominant is characteristically heightened. Forte becomes fortissimo. Trombones add their weight. Analogously the Commendatore's accentuated, octave-spanning challenge in the opening scene ('Battiti!' – 'face me, Sir!') re-emerges, several times too, in the scene of final reckoning ('Pentiti!' – 'repent you!'). The last scene, moreover, reminds us of Don Giovanni's original atrocity by recalling the earlier, swiftly concluded passage of arms precisely at the moment when he struggles to escape from the Commendatore's grip (bars 527–47, Scene 17, correspond to bars 166–73, Scene 1).

Pleasures immortal have infinitely increased the Commendatore's presence and authority. A commonplace, feeble parent has become a supernatural apparition. Don Giovanni can oppose it only with his courage, and that blazes brightly in this meeting with the unearthly visitant.

At the outset, we may conclude, the Commendatore is less than a full human being; he merely performs the functions of a nobleman and a brave but helpless guardian. We do not see inside him. At the end he is definitely more than a man, a spectral apparition enveloped in celestial (or infernal?) light. But if one were to sum up this figure as a childish blend of morality and legend, needing a good dose of sturdy common sense, and if one went on to claim that 'verisimilitude' or even psychological analysis were needed for the end of the opera to make sense – then one would be too clever by half for *Don Giovanni*. Or a little too stupid. For one would be failing to sense the uncompromising seriousness with which Mozart's music underwrites a moral and metaphysical process. Canny reinterpretation would violate a mighty musical creation. Unfortunately sinful producers of that kind, unlike stage villains, generally get away scot-free.

CONSTANZE

Soprano. A prisoner, she must endure the wooing of the noble Pasha Selim, who is not noble enough to refrain from mentioning that he could put her steadfastness to the test with torments of all kinds. But her love for Belmonte is unshakable, and despair seems to render her stouter-hearted rather than more yielding.

in *The Abduction*

Believing herself to be alone (stage direction: 'she does not observe Blondie'), Constanze expresses her sorrow in her only aria in a minor key. She meditates on how her life is wasting away. Not even to the breezes, let alone Pasha Selim, can she speak of her deep suffering. She rebuffs Blondie's attempt to comfort her. 'One who always flatters herself with hope and at the last sees herself deceived has nothing left but despair.' And now, in this frame of mind, she makes the situation perfectly clear to Pasha Selim. She will no longer ward him off, play delaying tactics, tell petty lies. She will never love him. This unhappy girl has reached the nadir of her life's expectations. She rejects easy optimism. For her 'master over life and death' she has, though still unaware of Belmonte's arrival, only gall and wormwood to offer, even if this means losing his favour. At this point he threatens her with torture.

Constanze reacts as though she had passed beyond utter despair and been strengthened by the energy of some impersonal system of values. Consider her C major concertante: 'Martern aller Arten mögen mich erwarten, ich verlache Qual und Pein' ('torments the most varied may be lying in store for me, how I scorn them you shall see').

We know from Mozart that he 'sacrificed Constanze's aria a little to the flexible throat of Mlle Cavallieri'.[6] (The specific reference in the letter dated 26 September 1781 is in fact to Constanze's first and virtuoso B flat aria, 'Ach ich liebte, war so glücklich . . . Doch wie schnell schwand meine Freude' – 'how I loved and was so happy . . . Yet, oh, how brief was my delight'). The 'flexible throat' is of course often cited in connection with 'Martern aller Arten' too; otherwise it would be very hard to explain this sparkling aria in a major key.

So, did Mozart, the 'character dramatist' (Hermann Abert), admit that one of his arias lacked both dramatic and emotional veracity because he had 'sacrificed' it to the virtuosity of a prima donna? Even if this sentence in his letter is accepted literally, his self-criticism should still not be taken at face value. Mozart would be perfectly capable of turning a pure piece of *bravura* into a depiction of character that was far from trivial. But Mozart can be defended less laboriously. He wrote that he had 'sacrificed' the aria 'a little'; the greater part of it, therefore, represents his artistic intent rather than a sacrifice.

In 'Martern aller Arten' Constanze, undismayed by her terrible predicament, barricades herself behind a concerto form. The long introduction conforms to the tonality scheme in the first movement of a Mozart instrumental concerto. In the introduction the main theme and subsidiary theme are in the tonic, as they are in this aria. When the soloist joins in, after the extraneous introduction, the customary sonata form begins, meaning that the subsidiary theme shifts to the dominant.

That is the case here. In bar 24 of 'Martern aller Arten' the flute, oboe, violin and cello introduce the second theme in C major. When the exposition is repeated with Constanze as soloist, we meet the second theme in G major (beginning in bar 93, just before 'Lass dich bewegen, verschone mich, des Himmels Segen belohne dich' – 'let your heart be moved, have forbearance, Heaven's blessing be your recompense'). There follows a sort of development. The recapitulation begins with the second theme which, as the rules demand, is again in the tonic. One can even descry a cadenza ending on a trill, immediately followed by an allegro assai coda derived from the 'development'. What we have, then, is a concerto movement for soprano solo and orchestra (plus four solo instruments).

This glittering concerto performance could also amount to a formal demonstration which does indeed alarm Pasha Selim: 'How has she suddenly the courage to behave towards me in this manner?'. At an earlier stage she had concealed her misery: 'Selbst der Luft darf ich nicht sagen meiner Seele bittern Schmerz' ('even the breezes may not know the bitter pain that fills my heart'). Utterly alone and depressed, that had been the burden of her G minor aria. Then she rejected consolation. Now she has a courage which inspires her like a suddenly revealed sublime truth and whirls her to a climax where an agonizing death on love's behalf is indistinguishable from bliss. In her first solo passage of 'Martern aller Arten' she changes indicatively into a minor key: 'Nichts, nichts, nichts soll mich erschüttern' ('naught, naught, naught shall rend my valour'). She does not wholly blind herself to the danger of the situation, but for her the most dreadful thing would be the possibility of being forced into unfaithfulness to Belmonte. The possibility leads to a gloriously persuasive plea to Pasha Selim to exercise forbearance in return for celestial blessings. But here, on earth, do not torments and afflictions await her if Pasha Selim should rant and rave? Maybe; but 'zuletzt befreit mich doch der Tod' ('death at last will set me free'). This 'zuletzt befreit mich-doch-der-Tod' sounds a little different from the remainder of the aria's brilliant sweep, and it is striking that only at 'Nichts-nichts-nichts' and 'zuletzt befreit mich doch der Tod' does Mozart disjoin the cantilena with rests. Apart from this, his composition constitutes without exception a closely bound legato. Only at 'zuletzt be-freit . . . mich . . . doch . . . der . . . Tod' can we hear for an instant how her voice falters, pauses, and utters a sigh, which is like an awful presentiment, swiftly brushed away, of what 'zuletzt' may portend.

In her first aria – 'Ach, ich liebte, war so glücklich' ('ah, I loved him and was happy') – Constanze refrained from expressing deep sorrow in Pasha Selim's presence. The 'true faith' that she vowed her beloved was twice invoked in the affirmative E flat major (bars 5–6 of the adagio introduction). She also sang in lively major key of quickly transient pleasure (although the subject is pleasure's absence rather than its presence). Remarkably enough the orchestra (from bar 45 of the allegro onward, particularly in the passage 'kannte nicht der Liebe Schmerz' – 'did not know the pain of love') lets on more in this aria about Constanze's grief than her cantilena does. She keeps her deep sorrow to herself until her lonely G minor soliloquy. In her first aria the sorrow that overwhelms her barely obtains musical confirmation. One could leap to the somewhat too psychological conclusion that she would like to engage the dear Pasha's kind and compassionate sympathy without seeming too piteous in the eyes of one whose very male reaction to womanly affliction is, 'Her anguish, her tears . . . enchant my heart ever more'.

After her decision to endure 'torments the most varied' she appears to be beyond all despair. In Act III she has no solo aria. In the recitative duet following the lovers' arrest (they must expect a martyr's death), it is left to Belmonte to bemoan cruel fortune. That is not Constanze's concern. Her own fate, she assures her lover, is of complete indifference to her: 'Let yourself not be troubled. What is death? A transition to peace and then, at your side, the foretaste of blessedness.' She is so carried away as to welcome death as 'delight'. To remain alone in this world would be 'pain'. But, since they can now sacrifice their lives for each other (each claims responsibility for the other's death), 'beatific rapture' prevails. 'Mit wonnevollen Blicken verlässt man da die Welt' ('with blissful, loving gazes the world is left behind').

What a noble graph of sentiment Constanze describes from the first aria sung to Pasha Selim, her lonely affirmation of sorrow, and her ecstatic 'Martern aller Arten' to her joyous, selfless vision of death for love. Is it plausible, probable, realistic? Such objections would be an insult to Constanze's spiritual nobility. As to whether this nobility is desirable, rousing and beautiful, that is a question to which Mozart's music is serenely equal. We are concerned with the existence and strength of values and feelings which the heart of a young woman, who is at first despairing, then in a state of exaltation, resolutely embraces. Mozart, shortly before marrying his own Constanze, created an immaculately loving, ideal human being surpassing terrestrial standards.

DON CURZIO

Tenor. A judge. Stutters and is slightly flustered by the quick turn of events in Marcellina's suit against Figaro.

in *The Marriage of Figaro*

The bounden duty of someone who in the world of *opera buffa* personifies the law is to stutter. This need not be a sign of senility or idiocy; it means that lawyers are not healthy individuals imbued with the joy of life but old fossils condemned to the clumsy repetition of unintelligible jargon. More refined opera-goers do not care for jokes about physical defects, but this is a sentimental mistake, for in principle comedy has licence to laugh at everything.

Yet isn't it terribly old hat to make such crude mockery of a stutter, a limp, a constant little cough or a bent back? Of course, but old hat meticulously performed can be glorious; and in this instance Mozart probably had a specific reason for turning Don Curzio into a stutterer. Michael O'Kelley, who sang the part in the original performance (he left an interesting, although rather conceited and inaccurate account of the rehearsals), also played Basilio, which rendered it appropriate to draw a sharp distinction between the two figures by giving one of them a stutter.

Don Curzio twice gives a crucial verdict. On the first occasion he sentences Figaro to marry Marcellina. 'Either he pays her' (which Figaro, who did sign such a bond, cannot do) 'or he marries her.' It is the worst blow that Figaro's and Susanna's happiness has suffered so far. Seconds later this same Don Curzio establishes: 'He [Doctor Bartolo] the father; she [Marcellina] the mother. The marriage [between Figaro and Marcellina] cannot take place.'

The way is paved for the happy ending, and Don Curzio is even allowed to introduce a minor third-fourth motif in Act III's sextet. Here, after all, is some excuse for his existence; here too his tenor sharpens the Count's sourness against the Susanna-Figaro-Marcellina-Bartolo group and he departs together with Almaviva, to whom he would undoubtedly have been glad to have been of service. Still, irrefutable and palpable proofs have made an impact on this judge. He does not break the law, he pronounces it. And in the ensemble he turns the Count's words against his lordship: 'He quivers, he is beside himself with rage'.

DESPINA

Coloratura soubrette. So familiar with facts of life that her nimble, down-to-earth mind has long ago shed all its illusions. Chamber-maid with abysmal depths.

in *Così fan tutte*

Money and pleasure are what count; hardly anything else matters to this hard-headed girl. Despina makes no effort to disguise her meaning in sentimental or euphemistic language. Consider the following: Dorabella has just sung her distraught 'Eumenides' aria and Fiordiligi explains the reason for this outburst of grief – their sweethearts have had to go to the wars. Despina's cool conclusion is twofold. If they return loaded with honours, fine. If they are killed, what then? Her answer: all the better for you, my ladies. You lose two, but all the rest remain. She shows quick-witted cynicism and glib callousness in one and the same instant.

Despina knows precisely how men should be handled. At fifteen, it seems, she was already a past-mistress in the art. Experience has taught her that love is a simple matter: the main thing is to make sure of pleasure and to see to it that no emotional costs are incurred. From elderly gentlemen this charmer does not expect much, unless they plunge into real expense on her behalf.

This shrewd little bawd plays a part in the seduction scenario which is deeply sinister for her mistresses. She utters her loose maxims in such a way that the ladies, with their high-minded principles, cannot help feeling slightly silly. Once (in 'A girl at fifteen already', bar 88) there is a sudden break so that the ladies can add how foolish are those who act less craftily. The violins stop short as though inviting them to guess Despina's unspoken thoughts; 'Is it further instruction you care for . . .', the wily creature then teases them.

She originates in *opera buffa*, a type at whom nobody can, should, or ever will take offence. The trouble is that she takes her heedless pandering to desperate lengths. She leaps into the breach when the

Albanians are struck dumb by a dim apprehension of what they are letting themselves in for and the mischief they are on the verge of creating. She oils the wheels of intrigue with Mephistophelean enjoyment. 'And if', Despina promises Don Alfonso, the Albanians do everything that she requires of them, 'your friends on the morrow will celebrate victory; they will have the pleasure and I shall have the glory.' Evidently she intrigues not only for the sake of money, but also for pleasure and the sense of triumph. She rallies to the side of those who want to ruin a couple of incorruptibles and to win a wager. Yet Despina's venality, toughness, irresistible gaiety and so on need not be judged morally, for in *opera buffa* such conduct has a different function and value from its real-life counterpart.

In the Act I recitative following Ferrando's aria Despina mentions 'diavolo', the Devil, and Fiordiligi at the beginning of Act II scolds her as 'che diavolo!' ('you little demon!'). Satan frequently recurs in Despina's speech and song. Once this has caught one's attention, it is astonishing how the Devil haunts this setting, whether in the words of Despina and Don Alfonso during the presto in the quartet no. 20 or in the guise of 'satanas' by whose name Despina swears; similarly, Dorabella is appalled at an 'infernal' notion of her maid's. May it not be that Despina, whose melodic pattern has been described as 'snakily coiling', has rather more to do with the Foul Fiend than is apparent at a first amused glance? She is a cheerful demon whose actions effect evil and whose amorality leaves the sisters with hardly a chance of escape. The demonic element need not always make its presence felt in D minor, accompanied by trombones or infernal choirs. Despina, scarcely aware of her evil nature and proud of her brilliant dexterity, certainly bears little resemblance to the Prince of Darkness; yet she has absorbed something of the irresistible power of evil. Devil knows that she could not do more harm if hers were to be listed as a satanic role. There just happen to be some sly she-devils in a major key who are more than a match for innocent ladies and even for rich men. Our Despina, though, seems to be only slightly tainted with devilishness; otherwise she would not make the embarrassed admission at the end of the opera that she too has been hoaxed and led astray – something she resents, although it renders her more human and sympathetic.

DORABELLA

Mezzo-soprano. She is the more ebullient, and therefore the more easily seduced, of the two Neapolitan sisters who fall victim to a male bet.

in *Così fan tutte*

Dorabella's panic knows no bounds when Don Alfonso prepares the ground for his bad news. Horrified, she immediately assumes the worst, something that the more restrained Fiordiligi would never venture to formulate so crudely: 'Can my lover be dead?'. We hear Dorabella's agitated outburst long before Fiordiligi reacts to the situation with her 'Come scoglio' ('like massive rock') solo. Her tempestuous recitative is followed by the 'Eumenides' aria which goes at breakneck speed. At the end – to the accompaniment of ever more stabbing discords – she repeats her E flat tone in crescendo no less than twelve times in succession, as though fixed on a note of desperation. A more direct and passionate example of agitation occurs nowhere in *Così* and very rarely elsewhere in Mozartian opera. Dorabella's suffering is of the utmost intensity.

But it is not pleasurable extroversion that makes her work herself up into a stunning eruption; after all, she believes in the disaster of this separation from Ferrando. She is unaware of what the amused audience has heard and what the men, initially at least, find so hilarious. Nothing leads her to suspect a wager and deceit. Her exalted maidenly affliction may indeed strike those in the know as having an element of parody (in the theatre, violent outbursts often tend to be parodies of themselves). Dorabella's suffering, though, has a thoroughly realistic, subjective reason about which the conspirators and onlookers chuckle because objectively it is untrue. As a manifestation of genuine horror, however, her aria is far from a caricature, but a piece of musical creation.

At the outset we meet, in a garden by the shore of the Gulf of Naples, a pair of carefree sisters who go into ingenuous and delightful raptures about their lovers. When they protest that Cupid may punish them with endless torment if ever they prove unfaithful, it all sounds very lyrical and charming. ('Infinite pain', though long drawn out, is enunciated quite gaily, vivaciously and by no means woefully. In fact, it sounds perfectly cheerful.) In the andante duet, for all its gentle good temper, Dorabella's cantilena is accompanied by vigorous movement in the violins; such demisemiquaver staccatos never once occur in Fiordiligi's soulful singing. It is Dorabella, too, who introduces the first telling switch to a minor key. All this indicates certain differences of character which cannot be dismissed as 'accidental'. There is method at work and the distinctions are being drawn by Mozart.

The two ladies – like their beaux and sometimes the wire-pullers Don Alfonso and Despina – often appear as a pair and sing together a good deal: for this Walter Dirks has hit on the delicious formula 'sisterly terzetto'. These overtly symmetrical groupings have misled many observers into seeing the sisters as ballet- or puppet-like figures rather than rounded characters. But is there any reason for figures who often act and react in pairs, who enjoy and endure more or less the same things, to be delineated less colourfully, more limply, less individually? Must they be devised more musically, so to speak, than dramatically? The Queen of the Night and her daughter Pamina or Don Giovanni and Don Ottavio are certainly easier to distinguish than are Dorabella and Fiordiligi. That need not imply that the characters in *Così* are less plainly distinct. The matter can be put the other way round. If two figures suffer the same fate and we are able to watch how in analogous circumstances they do or do not cope with their destiny, the similarity of the challenge they face encourages us, indeed compels us, to compare them as characters. Within the framework of the same situation, distinctive differences in their respective behaviour will stand out quite precisely and comparably. In *Così* we are spared the labour of contrasting two completely different quantities: two sisters and two young officers are put on a par in the selfsame experiment.

We go through the phases of a precise dramatic process. When will the women's power of resistance break down? How and by what means will they become more amenable, more interested, more venturesome, 'more unfaithful'? As for the men, at what point in the 'game' will they start to get carried away? When and why do they gradually exert themselves, not just as part of the game but in anger and determination, to win the bout against their brides? (Friedrich Dürrenmatt once refashioned August Strindberg's *Dance of Death* into *Play Strindberg*, portraying Strindberg's matrimonial struggle as a 'boxing match with shorter and shorter rounds'. In *Così* it would be possible after each scene or round to act the referee and to award points to the males according to how far they had succeeded in storming the female bastions and to what extent they themselves had perhaps been smitten.)

Part of the vicious game played in this opera is that the men announce their departure with a gloating, merciless pleasure. They are no more than amused by the heartfelt expressions of despair elicited from their deceived womenfolk. The singularity of the disguised lovers' unhesitating pretence of suicide, a damnably crude tactic, may be part of it too. One can sympathize with the ladies, who never imagine that they may be victims of deceit, for being shattered by such behaviour. The gentlemen should not simply be conceded the right to bluff with such stakes.

Granted, the *Così* struggle does not start as sentimentally and innocuously as the first scenes seem to suggest. The music hushes up what the ladies in their *secco* recitative unashamedly babble. Fiordiligi states how ready she is for fun on this fine morning; Dorabella does not mince matters. She longs to be married as soon as possible and there is nothing Platonic about her hot-blooded feelings. It can hardly be put more plainly: she has 'Hymen's altar' in mind.

From the outset the ladies are (I choose a discreet word) excited. Dorabella seems even more so than her sister. In their duet hers is the shriller accompaniment, and she is the first to switch into a minor key. Hers is the great dramatic aria whose searing glow need only once have been conveyed by Teresa Berganza or, even better, Agnes Baltsa in order to cure the spectator for ever of any notion that parody, cunning caricature, or affectation prevail here over real emotion.

One can perhaps learn how the music fuses the two women's unalloyed pain at parting and their erotic excitability by listening carefully to a lyrical highlight in the work, the subdued terzettino 'Blow gently, ye breezes'. It is remarkable, indeed inexplicable, that such magically deceptive cadence harmonies should appear at the word 'desir', wish or yearning, which is certainly applied here in an entirely straightforward context yet lingers with strange persistence in the memory.

Dorabella is the more spontaneous and the swifter of the two women. She is in love with love, as it were. She certainly does not miss the chorus's celebration of the liberty that the soldier's life offers. Despina proclaims the lesson too: just as men have their fun, so should women, especially when such rich, handsome, new, enamoured suitors are on hand. What a fortunate dispensation that they are not really strangers, but friends of Don Alfonso.

The suicidal poison works – if not in the veins of the cheats, then in the souls of the ladies cheated. They lose their composure and their reserve to the rhythm and the discords (Act I finale, from bar 112 onward) already heard in *Don Giovanni* when, after the murder of her father, Donna Anna is so beside herself that she hardly recognizes her fiancé, Don Ottavio. Here, however, pity for the 'suicides' blends – as the crafty gentlemen rightly hope – with a feeling that can potentially swing round into love. Not that the thought of love ever crosses Dorabella's mind: it is completely out of the question. And yet the emotional hot and cold showers of Act I cannot suddenly give way to emptiness and melancholy. Diversion is no sin. One is not being the least bit inconstant if one seeks a little entertainment so as not to die of depression.

The persuasive suicide attempt by the artful 'Albanians' and Despina's 'infernal' efforts to disparage virtue's straight and narrow path have, in other words, altered Dorabella's perspective on the subject. Why not enjoy the company of these agreeable admirers when there is nothing to the matter at all and the lady's maid can be trusted to keep the neighbours from gossiping by saying that the visitors are her friends? It does seem a little odd that Dorabella should be less concerned about the tricky business itself than about how best to keep it secret. And even while she is thinking up an alibi, her womanly pride bridles: who would believe, asks Mistress Dorabella, that the Albanians had come to call on Miss Despina? Why not? Despina is not bad at weaving a net of deception. No, that is not the reason. Men who enter a house where a Dorabella lives must naturally want to see Dorabella, not her maid. That is Dorabella's opinion, and who can fail to share her conviction?

Is she deceiving herself with the repeated assertion that it is only entertainment she is after? This high-spirited individual is less flippant than resolute, prompt of decision. When the sisters plan the allocation of their new beaux (no harm in getting things straight) and Fiordiligi still hesitates, Dorabella has long made up her mind: 'I shall take the dark one'. Her firmness is attested by the staccato military rhythm of her singing as supported by the orchestra. This duet no. 20 at the beginning of Act II, however, brings something more to light. The text merely talks of 'diletto', pleasure, but the music invokes a state of profound emotion, for Mozart's favourite sequence expressive of pure happiness is allowed to emerge in bars 52 and 53. Known to us from the sextet in Act III of *The Marriage of Figaro*, it is supposed to have had a special place in its composer's affections.

The *Così* experiment is approaching its close. Dorabella, previously the more unrestrained in her lamentations, now loves all the more uninhibitedly. She does not, however, fall prey to Guglielmo's wooing without some momentary delay. Guglielmo resorts to the same old story, attempting to extort pity by claiming in the recitative before the crucial duet that he is so desperate that death alone is left for him. The trick's repetition briefly awakens Dorabella's suspicion: 'nientissimo' – nothing whatsoever – shall he have. (Does her unconscious admonish her that the Albanians' suicide attempt in Act I, which so effectively aroused the ladies' sympathy, should not perhaps have been taken so seriously either?) The critical impulse passes. She even leaves it open whether she may not be teasing (a suspicion at one point indignantly stated by her new lover). Erotic ardour suffuses her, their two hearts beat in unison. During the garden party Dorabella is not only the first to give this lover her arm, but also the first to surrender unconditionally. Gaily and confidently, she carols of her new love.

So the impression she leaves is of an ingenuous personality who acts before she thinks, straightforward in her vivacity, with a capacity for passionate sorrow and a blazing eagerness for love, which is why the often-repeated argument that Dorabella is 'strictly speaking' better suited to her fresh partner, the polished and gallant Guglielmo, than to her actual fiancé, the more poetic, sensitive Ferrando, remains unconvincing. This bundle of emotions is closer to the unmistakably rapturous tenor Ferrando than to the flawless cavalier Guglielmo.

Hence the sadness suddenly felt at the end of *Così* does not derive from the 'wrong' pairs being conjoined. It is rather because an innocently ideal notion of 'eternal love' has had to yield to the cynical, worldly-wise realization that a lady's 'no' means 'yes' and that men, even if they only want to win an argument, will not think twice about playing a nasty game with the emotions of the women they think they love. In this process Mozart's melodies leave so-called 'individual love' gracefully behind in the far distance.

ELECTRA

Soprano. Daughter of Agamemnon and sister of Orestes. After he murdered their mother, Electra had to flee from Argos and came to Crete. There she fell in love with Idamante whose father, the King, seems to encourage a union between this princess and his son.

in Idomeneo, King of Crete

From the outset Electra leaves us in no doubt that she is proud, jealous, vengeful, and equally ready either to insist imperiously on having her own way or to accept her own tragic annihilation. With intemperate rage she accuses Idamante of insulting the whole of Greece by wanting to give the Trojans and Ilia their freedom. She is furious that a prisoner and slave (even if Ilia is the daughter of the once mighty King Priam) should have any chance to vie with her for the Prince's affections.

She behaves with an unbridled lack of self-control of which the gentler Ilia (deported from her home, intimidated by unhappiness) would hardly be capable. She tends, moreover, to be egocentric. The news of Idomeneo's death fails to strike in her any spark of sorrow or pity for his son. Her sole consideration is that Idamante, now fatherless, is free to decide for himself on a bride and that she now lacks the support of the King.

Is Electra, harried by the Furies, by pangs of jealousy and thoughts of vengeance, no more than a typical figure of *opera seria*? To see her like that is to reduce her to a group of unwavering emotional traits, which makes it impossible to appreciate her personality in full and to take her seriously; for everything that is no longer 'typical' must then fall, as Hermann Abert rules, 'outside the framework of her character'.[7] In her closely reasoned work on the Mozart operas Anna Amalie Abert takes matters a step further. 'It is strange that between these two passionate outbursts [i.e., arias nos. 4 and 29] there intervenes her dreamy, textually and musically conventional love aria no. 13, "Idol mio, se ritroso", the composer's clearest indication that in this work he was not interested in consistent characterization, but always had in mind only the immediate situation.'[8]

Must we really conclude that Mozart was not interested in consistent characterization if the proud and vengeful Electra occasionally shows a yielding, dreamy craving for happiness? Even in a state of fury (such as the last bars, 58–64, of the recitative before her first aria where she wildly laments 'O disgrace! O jealousy! O anguish! ... I am overcome') she can still light on overwhelmingly delicate, sorrowful chromatic tones which also do not quite fit into the mould of vindictive passion. At those moments where she seems to express herself tenderly, dreamily or happily, was Mozart really concerned only to depict the passing situation, and not a human being? Her savage pride is connected with her partly imperious, partly modest and fervent desire for felicity in love. These traits are certainly not inter-related with much psychological subtlety, but they can be fitted together within a single personality.

Electra does not always behave like a termagant; she tries also to escape from her fatal background of Atrides family history, to be normal and happy. She hopes to find contentment in her life by marrying Idamante. When the King has issued the order, so pleasing to her ear, for his son and Electra to leave Crete as fast as may be, she asks blissfully, 'Chi mai del mio provò piacer più dolce?' ('who at any time felt sweeter joy than I?'). At the word 'dolce' a caressing touch among the strings intimates a soaring, enchanted sensation of happiness. The same touch is significantly echoed in the following aria, 'Idol mio', at the precise moment when, humble rather than proud, she tries to persuade herself that by remaining near him with her love, she will be able to oust Idamante's feelings for her distant rival.

At the beginning of Act III Ilia sings the delicately restrained 'Zeffiretti lusinghieri' ('cajoling breezes') aria. Shortly beforehand Electra too has appealed to the breezes, but how differently, how much more solemnly: we would not expect her to address the winds by an affectionate diminutive. She appeals to them when she and her beloved are about to embark. The chorus (Act II, no. 15) has intoned its 'Placido è il mar' ('placid is the sea'). Electra follows with the second verse, 'Soavi Zeffiri' ('O clement zephyr, swell the limpid sails, assuage the north wind's icy anger . . .'). Her invocation is not confined to a conventional, pleasantly fanciful melodic flow: her cantilena (bars 23–47) is Mozart at a very high level. This descendant of Atreus must not be reduced to the stereotype of the vengeful, intriguing or jealous woman. On occasion she also has a dream of harmony entirely

66

consistent with her forceful spirit; but it is her fate not to be granted either peace or happiness, and that is when her savagery shows. Sometimes it seems as though the ill-starred princess has a presentiment of the calamity in store for her. Similarly, and still more mysteriously, she may at the end be regarded as welcoming her doom with tragic arrogance.

Her astringency stands in contrast to the chivalrous sensitivity which encompasses Ilia and Idamante; this can be plausibly substantiated, if not proved, by the ensembles. In the quartet no. 21 the voices of Ilia and Idamante at the crucial moment are delicately poised against the greater severity of Electra and Idomeneo. One can go so far as to assert that in the trio no. 16 Electra wants to match the tone of her beloved Idamante, but that her cantilena has a different accompaniment (and consequently characterization) from his. Her beginning is accompanied by punctuated staccato violin tones which in his part did not occur in that way.

Has she a foreboding that something dreadful will happen? There would be no discrepancy between that and her yearning for happiness. When she knows herself to be alone – during her first aria – she is full of a cold, uncanny fury. And even when fortune appears to be on her side, her voice dropping to a minor third, in the prevailing key she murmurs, movingly although for no evident reason, 'O gods! What will be now?' (Act II, no. 16, bars 58–60). Then, however, the oracle not only proclaims Idamante's deliverance and Idomeneo's deposition, but announces that Ilia is to marry Idamante. Electra is the sole protagonist to lose out completely. Were she to accept that with a shrug of the shoulders or polite regret she would not be Agamemnon's daughter. The only issue in her final aria is the manner of her death. 'Vipers and serpents or a dagger shall end my suffering.'

Mozart cut this aria (no. 29a) before the first Munich performance because he thought the last Act too long; he also regarded it as clumsy from a dramatic point of view to leave the rest of the cast standing about on the stage while Electra sang her despairing effusion. In its stead he composed a short recitative which allows her an outburst of feeling in a thundering D major (allegro assai). Thereafter her music alternates between major and minor, ending in a vague minor without the glistening major being obliterated. The impression that it conveys is the same as that produced by certain staccato passages at the close of the (eliminated) despair aria. They go against the grain because in the passages following from C can be heard a shrill laughter which corresponds to the demented-sounding D major in the recitative, and they are doubly irritating because elsewhere the Electra role has hardly any coloraturas at all.

The daughter of the Atrides does not break down when her terrible end arrives: with the maniacal arrogance of a tragic heroine, she rejoices in her downfall.

DONNA ELVIRA

Soprano. Fierily determined to avenge herself on Don Giovanni, who promised marriage but deserted her after three days – unless he should return to her after all.

in *Don Giovanni*

In Donna Elvira hatred of his perfidy mingles, in spite of all, with passionate sentiments for Don Giovanni. Initially, being more active and more self-reliant than Donna Anna, she is his fiercest pursuer. In Act II, notably in the sextet, she makes a less aggressive impression. She still loves the man, despite her better judgement. At the close her pity and self-denial make her willing to renounce her claims on Don Giovanni, if only she can induce a change of heart in him and thus save his soul. His mocking rejection of these desperate pleas revives her former ferocity. After he has gone to hell, she enters a convent.

Donna Elvira is not in the least a pathetic, submissive, petty or old-maidish figure. Her outstanding qualities are nobility of character and an ardent strength of mind. This young woman loves intensely and makes intense efforts to hate. She struggles wholeheartedly for the man she loves against the reprobate to whose misdeeds she wants to put a stop. Particularly in Act I, she not only looks like Don Giovanni's true opponent, but seems to be the antithesis of Donna Anna. She manifests the vehemence of her love and of her hate openly and unambiguously (whereas in the case of the Commendatore's daughter much remains concealed, which may explain her hesitations).

Donna Elvira neither hides nor overplays anything. During the adventurous pursuit in Act I she neither loses control of herself nor suffers absences of mind or near-lapses into unconsciousness. From the start she makes no secret of the fact that in certain circumstances she is prepared to forgive the sinner. 'Ah, let me but find the traitor and if he does not return to me', then, her opening aria avows, she will indeed inflict dire punishment on him. This angel, too, would prefer the transgressor, provided he does penance, to ninety-nine just men.

At the outset, Don Giovanni and his servant Leporello so mercilessly deride the noble young woman in word (the Catalogue aria) and deed (Don Giovanni bolts shamelessly and later accuses her of 'madness') that Donna Elvira has no choice but to hound them with fanatical hatred. Ironically and monstrously, Leporello's Catalogue aria humiliates the high-mindedness of Donna Elvira, who thinks she is something 'special' and now finds herself degraded to a mere item in the list. Nevertheless, she is not always a victim: she succeeds over and over again in making Don Giovanni look a fool. How neatly the ruffian would have his way with Zerlina if the watchful Donna Elvira did not keep intervening like a celestial constable!

She does not, however, seem equal to the emotional strain of relentless pursuit, for she cannot suppress her pity for the beloved scoundrel. In the finale of Act I, so perilous for Don Giovanni, she is at the head of his pursuers. (Attila Csampai, in his essay 'Mythos und historischer Augenblick in Mozarts "Don Giovanni"', underlines Donna Elvira's dominant role at this point.)[9] But at the beginning of Act II she is heard telling herself in a dreamy, gentle soliloquy that her heart must not beat so strongly because compassion for the beast would be sin. The music, though, proves that this apparent inner conflict has long been resolved. A major's tender resonance intimates that Donna Elvira's loving heart altogether rejects Donna Elvira's vengeful head; Don Giovanni and Leporello do not at any rate have much difficulty in fanning the embers of her love into flame. Evidently, too, it is her own notion of Don Giovanni rather than his reality which prevails with the proud lady, for she promptly lets herself be duped by Leporello's impersonation of his master. The servant's contemptuous comment on her stirrings of forgiveness is, 'Look now at this crazy woman, once more she will give him credence'.

Yet, when the henchman is unmasked and the repulsively humiliating deceit is discovered, Donna Elvira is remarkably silent in the face of this ignominious insult. Tones or coloraturas reflecting consternation, pain and hatred are few. In the important sextet – likewise at the close when the farce is over – the far more eloquent Donna Anna is the outstanding personality. Donna Elvira's intensive vengefulness has evidently melted. Her E flat major aria reveals only that she is torn between wrath and pity. She is the only surviving character for whom Don Giovanni's descent to hell is not a sheer triumph. The others return to everyday life cheerfully, hopefully, and with relief, while she announces (in E minor, the larghetto of the final scene, bars 740–42) her decision to retire to a convent.

Something 'special' marks Donna Elvira out from the start. Even when exposed to the cruellest humiliations – deserted, despairing, dissolved in tears, taxed with mental derangement – she retains an 'aspetto nobile', a noble look about her. No wonder that Don Giovanni had to be, and was, prepared to invest more trouble in her and in her conquest than in that of his other victims: he not only invaded her chamber, flattered and swore fidelity with well-practised skill, but he promised marriage and thereafter lived with her – although for three days only. All right, it was not even half a week. But it was certainly a far longer time than he needed for any of his other targets.

This special individual treats her misfortune unconventionally. Deserted, she does not slink away in shamefaced silence, but takes to the road in quest of the deserter. Although her pursuit seems a hopeless project, she can hazard a guess where, for instance, her 'spouse' has a country seat. She feels no embarrassment at announcing her misfortune and presenting herself openly as betrayed and calumniated. Don Giovanni supposes of course that the tiresome woman will baulk at causing a stir, uttering vociferous accusations, and provoking a scandal; but he underestimates Donna Elvira. He little knows her. She shows no scrap of discretion, of modest reserve, of wise precaution: 'Your guilt and my condition I shall publicly to all display'.

Where does she get the energy that makes her simultaneously loving and dangerously savage?

Her manner of speech differs from all the rest of the *Don Giovanni* figures. She is surrounded by the secure atmosphere of an older, archaic age. Her archaistic modulation seems not only to be a method applied by Mozart to describe one or another of her traits, but is evidently a fundamental and constantly recurrent mode of expression. There is no mistaking the much-discussed fact that the famous admonitory aria addressed to Zerlina, vehement and in dotted rhythms throughout, sounds extremely 'baroque', set somewhere between a French overture, a Bach orchestra suite, and Handel. Mozart did not however employ this aria no. 8 simply as a stylistic exercise. Vigorously accentuated dotted rhythms and baroque sequences had already put their stamp on Donna Elvira's entrance aria (no. 3, bars 30–34, 42–5, for example) and surely also – if one's hearing is sufficiently alert – on the melody with which Donna Elvira begins quartet no. 9

At the outset, then, there is something baroque about Donna Elvira. This unusual trait is evidently connected with her 'special' character –

her readiness for self-sacrifice, her fiery courage, and the frantic determination which is reminiscent of *opera seria*. It lends the baroque tone a convincing naturalness and is in turn confirmed by the archaic quality. When Donna Elvira proclaims her intention of retiring to a convent, if not before, it becomes obvious that her archaic-baroque quality has at the same time been a symbol for her deep religiosity.

There is no need to seek a metaphysical explanation for the stubbornness of heart and mind which allows Donna Elvira to run so wildly amok, as well as to hope and believe to the point of plain absurdity that Don Giovanni may yet mend his ways and love her again. It could well be a matter of womanly pride. After all, only a short time has passed since she fascinated him and brought him to the brink of matrimony. Her femininity, her 'fragrance' clearly still excite him, her figure still exercises its attraction. As long as he supposes her to be some unhappy beauty, he is briskly ready to 'console' her. What Donna Elvira's pride does not realize is that a woman whom he has once possessed no longer has the slightest interest for Don Giovanni, just as she appears entirely lacking in a definite conception of the real man whom she loved and lost, loves and hates, pursues and wants to save. That, however, need not prevent a religious and fanatical young Spanish lady from displaying vast passion and determination – quite the contrary.

During the 1970s Julia Varady and Kiri Te Kanawa succeeded in embodying and rehabilitating the youth, the nobility, the seriousness, and the fiery eccentricity of Donna Elvira in admirable, unforgettable ways. They moulded a character who could not but end with retirement to a convent after the world had held out so much promise for her ardent temperament and had disappointed her so bitterly.

In his subsequently composed E flat major aria, with its accompanied recitative (no. 21b), Mozart comes to a sad conclusion about Donna Elvira. The recitative resembles a psychic profile. Again and again a fierce outburst is followed by loving, gentle sighing. And the aria, with its changing hues and enharmonic transformations (only the chosen few can sing them quite clearly), is far removed from the baroque self-assurance and vigour of Act I, mirroring the change in Donna Elvira herself. What follows is a last attempt, ending in supplication on her side and disdain on his, to save her beloved, and the melancholy decision to retire to the solitude of a convent.

FERRANDO

Tenor. Sprightly young officer, rapturously in love. Flares up if anyone casts ironic doubts on his beloved or her fidelity.

in *Così fan tutte*

Ferrando's impulsive spontaneity leads straight to the conflict. In response to Don Alfonso's scepticism, he is the first to paint in glowing colours how highly he thinks of his betrothed. Where Dorabella's love is concerned, this gay young man will stand no nonsense. Barely has Don Alfonso made his complacent joke about the phoenix in remote Arabia and hardly has he begun laughing at the officers' confidence in female affirmations as well as their belief in amorous sighings, before Ferrando's self-control and patience snap. He cannot endure such mockery for an instant.

The young officer's inexorable conviction, which he is not prepared to have questioned or mocked, is responsible for the wager. Ferrando's faith in his Dorabella comes close to idolatry. Long after his sweetheart has been trapped by Guglielmo's wooing, genuine doubt remains far from his mind. On the brink of learning an unpleasant lesson, he continues to speak 'with rapture' about how well he knows the sublimity of Dorabella's soul.

This irrepressible enthusiast clearly loathes derision. When he does realize the harm that has been done, his instinct is to kill both his beloved and himself. Yet he realizes that, in spite of the 'shame' he is suffering, he has not stopped loving his unfaithful lady. Does that make him ridiculous, imprudent, or just plain silly?

No, merely very much in love and not the least bit cynical. The males in *Così* have incurred guilt by entering into any such farcical bet and letting their fiancées endure bitter pangs of parting, not to speak of deliberately imposing distress on them, but Ferrando's culpability is somewhat mitigated by the exuberant momentum of his faith and by his incapacity for harbouring distrust or adopting the blasé, sour common sense of a Don Alfonso.

He starts out with the radiant declaration that he will arrange a splendid serenade for his beloved with the winnings from his sweep. Does he not here display just the same *brio* as we see in Dorabella when she sings her 'Eumenides' aria? To Ferrando is allotted the most cloudless, pure, noble and forceful love song in the whole opera. While his friend shows concern over the prospect of missing a meal, he declaims what 'the breath of love' means to him. No dissimulation or irony, not a hint of artifice, qualifies his andante cantabile. His glowingly tender acknowledgment breaks the bounds of the *buffa* framework; that is why it is glaringly wrong, as occasionally happens, to transfer this aria to a later stage in the plot.

No figure in *Così* – if anything has to be cut – normally suffers more amputation than does Ferrando. His comparatively feeble duettino no. 7 (with Guglielmo) and his big B flat aria in Act II are often dropped. Is this pure coincidence? The duettino, without adding much, retards the swift development of the action. (The two officers, believed by the unhappy ladies to have been given their marching orders, harmlessly console them.) But from bar 28 onward a melodic sequence evinces a certain resemblance to one in Mozart's D major string quintet, K. 593. This work was composed in December 1790; *Così* was completed in January 1791. So the quintet was produced during the composition of the opera. How very much richer and more beautiful, though, is the sequence's treatment by the first violin and the viola in the repetition of the quintet's larghetto introduction (starting fourteen bars before the end of the first movement and lasting for five bars) than is its handling in *Così*. Evidently Mozart was unable here to bring out the same depth of despondency. The result was a somewhat conventional piece frequently omitted in performance.

The lack of sensitivity disclosed by the duet has to do with Ferrando's character. His liveliness and dash are obvious. It is equally clear that he is passionately and rapturously in love, without any qualification. When, however, in his Albanian skin he is supposed to sham infatuation with Fiordiligi, he is somewhat out of his depth. As an eighteenth-century Italian officer, he is perfectly prepared to perform the occasional comedy. But when it comes to simulating sentiment, he remains a little stilted. He needs to have been tumbled from his pedestal of assurance and to be thoroughly distressed, humiliated and furious (as well as jealous of the luckier Guglielmo, whose beloved seems more reliable) for his courting cantilena to achieve that sensuous A major exuberance which put its stamp on 'un' aura amorosa' ('a breath of love') and which in the A major duet no. 29 could bring archangels, as well as Fiordiligi, to his feet. After Ferrando's 'very caressive' larghetto 'Volgi a me' ('turn now your beloved gaze on me') Fiordiligi begins to tremble. Seconds later she is vanquished. Ferrando has his revenge for the raillery to which Guglielmo so recently submitted him, and he reminds his friend with satisfaction and exact quotation of the humiliation to which he had been subjected.

When he 'blithely' launches into his first seduction aria the faithful fiancé, believing that his faith is unassailable, certainly does not yet emit any such incandescent tones. ('A breath of love' does not count, for it is a contemplative solo effusion.) At the next point however, in no. 24, Act II, Ferrando is face to face with Fiordiligi, breathing sighs and casting glances. At the start it sounds as though he is smoothly discharging a burden imposed by the wager. He has promised, he is doing his best, but his persuasiveness is distinctly limited. Then it sounds as though he is getting a little more into his stride. The music gains briefly in urgency. Less turbulent, more supplicating passages initially have only a violin accompaniment, but subsequently the more vividly sensual clarinet introduces a languishing, yearning tone. Nevertheless this aria is not really moving or heartfelt, and it still sounds so much like a musical exercise – so cold, in fact – that Mozart himself noted in the original manuscript that aria no. 24 could be omitted.

Ferrando the ardent lover is no spoilsport, but if anything more than witty, good-humoured dissimulation is required, he is not very good at it. His emotional depths remain concealed until he has suffered a major shock; distress and the threat to his romance then render him rhetorical. Humiliation and the wish to sour his friend's triumph inspire him with a gently seductive fervour. Of *Così*'s three males he is the least wily and overweening, and the most likeable.

FIGARO

⌣

Bass. Manservant of Count Almaviva, to whom he was once of assistance. Now his master's adversary because Almaviva wants to delay his marriage to Susanna in order to enjoy the 'droit de seigneur' with her. In the first two Acts the strategist Figaro skilfully sows confusion – an ironic chorus of tribute to his lordship's morality and an anonymous libel against Countess Almaviva which finds its way into her husband's hands. Almaviva is to be made to fret and to find no time to prevent Figaro's wedding. In Act IV Figaro is in turn the victim because the Countess and Susanna have thought it superfluous to let him into the secret of their own intrigue. His imperturbability is not unshakable.

in The Marriage of Figaro

'Keep up your courage, my sweetheart', is Figaro's parting admonition to Susanna after she has told him in the first scene of what is brewing. 'And you, use your head', she replies. Does this mean that she is inclined to be nervous, while he is rather slow-witted?

Certainly, Susanna is sometimes faster on the uptake than Figaro. For here he is not a Jack-of-all-trades constantly dashing hither and thither, no hothead, no factotum for one and all. If he were an excitable, noisy troublemaker, who flares up and cools down with equal speed, he would be an easier opponent for Almaviva. Instead, Figaro – not a tenor, but a character bass or baritone – is wary and reserved by nature. It takes a remarkably long time for anger to rouse him to a forte. When it does, however, it is not a flash in the pan, but a stubborn, determined emotion that lasts.

At the beginning Susanna has some trouble in enlightening Figaro as to the Count's true motives, which she has at once fathomed, for giving them the most comfortable room in the castle. He is busy carefully measuring its dimensions and repeating them aloud; she asks him to look at her and her new bonnet. When the bell summons Figaro on an errand, the room's situation means that a certain event could happen very easily; but this is something that the young woman has to expound in detail and G minor to her dearest future spouse. He had suspected nothing, and had not even noticed that the Count was after Susanna. His eyes are gradually opened. At that point, in grim and slow major key, he wants to hear the full story.

Alone, he suddenly breaks into a clattering forte. That first bar of the *secco* recitative, followed by 'Se vuol ballare, Signor Contino' ('if it is fun you seek, most gracious lord'), comes as a shock, a shock that is always forgotten till it recurs at the next performance. For in this forte bar there obtrudes a parallel minor; such a tone is new and surprising in connection with Figaro, and it suddenly brings home to us how dangerous this manservant could prove to be. The cavatina confirms it. A foil of superficial innocence – allegretto, F major, triple time – seems during the course of the song to begin to glow and crackle with passionate fury. A vivid example of his inflexible tenacity comes from his malevolently corroborative repetition of the syllable 'sì' from bar 16 onward. The cavatina then echoes those breathless seconds, characteristic of the *Figaro* cosmos, with which the overture starts. The bell rings menacingly.

Figaro is not only shrewd but also educated. At the moment of his greatest humiliation he can call on classical mythology for comparison. He takes his time to become excited, to raise his voice to forte, to turn fierce. Not that he seems at all lethargic or insensitive; but he finds it easiest to adopt an aggressive forte when he is engaged in pretence or mimicry: imagining a duel with Almaviva, for instance, in the cavatina, or in the finale of Act I where he portrays the lustre, the glory and the misery of military life.

He is a mature man, calm, watchful, not missing a trick in the game of dissimulation, and with no trace of turgid sentiment. He knows what he wants and is cheerfully determined to get it. His relaxed realism goes so far as to allow him, as long as he has no cause for fear, to find the Count's desire for Susanna entirely 'natural'. In Schiller's *Kabale und Liebe*, written, like *The Marriage of Figaro*, in the 1780s, and one of German literature's greatest revolutionary dramas, the middle-class musician Miller views the aristocratic lust of a young lord just as imperturbably. Although the relationship between his daughter and Ferdinand does not suit him at all, he concedes 'I don't blame him. A man is a man. I ought to know.'

Figaro can rely on his presence of mind. Although not fast as lightning, it works at any rate quickly enough to cope with a situation such as occurs in the finale of Act II. After a slight hesitation he follows the hints of the two hard-pressed women so successfully as to leave the embittered Almaviva unable to prove the deceit that he surmises. In the finale of Act III he feels sufficiently safe to offer Susanna his arm for a dance despite the increasingly explosive situation. He even goes so far as to fit the clumsy Cherubino, who already has several black marks against him, into an intrigue. In the finale of Act II he is moreover confident enough to term his dangerous antagonists, with the law weighing in their favour – Marcellina, Dr Bartolo and Basilio – 'fools'.

This clever man, fond of a joke, loses his head completely, though, when he fears that he has cause to distrust Susanna. The realism needed to put up with so dire a reality (about which earlier he had still speculated *scherzando*) is in the event beyond a Figaro in love. It does not cross his mind to have a little faith in Susanna, regardless of appearances, as even Marcellina recommends. Lacerated by jealousy, he laughs at his misfortune with the bitterness of a Rigoletto. Did he not smilingly observe the Count being invited to a rendezvous by way of a letter, sealed with a pin, and not suspect that it had come from Susanna, of all people? He loses his grip on himself. Passing a spot where the Count asks in a disguised voice 'Who goes there?', he replies savagely 'People go here', as though deprived of his individual identity. And his behaviour, when in the Countess's presence he accuses Susanna of adultery with her ladyship's husband, is anything but gallant.

Mozart's music diminishes Figaro's verbal fury. The aria 'Aprite un po' quegli occhi, uomini incauti, e sciocchi' ('open a little your eyes, reckless and thick-headed men') in E flat major and moderato undoubtedly qualifies as a typical *opera buffa* tirade against women. It vents all his anger in an evocatively clowning, graphic, elegant manner. The phrase 'Il resto nol dico, già ognuno lo sa' ('the rest we'll leave open, for everyone knows it') seems to be savoured by a connoisseur. It is not at all the kind of wildly emotional outburst that the Queen of the Night, Dorabella, or Osmin sometimes produce.

What is it, then? Well, instead of straightforward wrath it could more likely be yet another example of Figaro's talent for burlesque. Just as he knows how to parody the alarums of war and bad pay, a duel, and the six-eight tempo talk of the drunken gardener, so now he imitates the elegant superficiality of a deceitful female world. It leaves him practically no room for the enunciation of his own passionate hurt, although at the end this becomes unmistakably manifest through the repetitions in bars 68–70 – whereupon the horns pitilessly mock the supposed cuckold.

Pig-headed Figaro deserves the slaps which in the last Act he receives. Cuffs and orgies of abuse for the other sex have from time immemorial been staples of comedy and, once the innocence of his infuriated sweetheart has become clear to him, Figaro gladly lets his ears be boxed. Nothing can afford him greater pleasure.

The music, however, distinguishes mere horseplay from what has deeper meaning. Uttering the mischievously cheerful verdict that his curiosity has earned Figaro a fine wage (i.e. a box on the ears by the Count, meant in reality for Cherubino), all the participants join in four-part harmony with lofty chords and solemn chromaticism (Act IV, Scene 12, bars 40–44). The noble music declines to partake in the laughter. It is a reminder of something else – how severely Figaro has sinned against his beloved. The notes are not concerned with a comedy of errors gone astray; their message is chastened self-accusation.

FIORDILIGI

Dramatic coloratura. With more strength of character, and conceived on a more heroic 'Amazonian' scale, than her impulsive sister Dorabella, she is able to put up somewhat more resistance to the tempter's melodic wooing, though she eventually succumbs. Her despairing and bewildered courage arouses our sympathy. Of all the characters in this opera, she has the greatest emotional depth.

in *Così fan tutte*

'The withered oak stands firm against the storm, / The healthy one is hurled to the ground / Because the storm can grasp it by the crown.' That is how Heinrich von Kleist sums up the fate of his tragic heroine Penthesilea. If the storm had not been mentioned, these lines could scarcely be applied to the case of Fiordiligi. Yet in her first major solo – the difficult aria 'Come scoglio' ('like massive rock in ocean founded, though the tempests may surge around it') – Fiordiligi intuitively anticipates something she cannot really know: that she too is threatened by an approaching storm, in the shape of a stormy Mozartian suitor. This aria, beginning as andante maestoso and accelerating via allegro to più allegro, has as much to do with the *buffa* character of the comic opera *Così* as does Constanze's 'Tortures past endurance' with a *Singspiel* – that is, very little. As always when Mozart presses beyond the supposed limitations of a genre and writes a hybrid composition, it is reasonably obvious to suggest that Fiordiligi's paean on feminine determination exemplifies a parody of an *opera seria* number. The young woman, who in any case will soon land in the arms of a new beau, appears to be exaggerating ludicrously and, whether unconsciously or because she enjoys her own heady overstatements, to be adopting an idiom whose solemn emotional starchiness sounds amusingly out of place. Our sturdy feminist is promptly taken down a peg or two without becoming downright comic.

A rock looms out of the sea – providing Neapolitan girls with a constant object lesson – and opposes its imperturbable strength to the forces of nature. Fiordiligi gives the audience to understand how much firmness underlies her feelings, how unshakable is her resolve. In operatic literature there are few passages where major grandiloquent leaps stretching over one octave, on occasion even to two octaves, play such an important role. There is nothing petty, confined or finicky here. The high C is heard. Yet Mozart is clearly anxious to prevent the slightest suggestion of serene coloratura warbling. For whole stages of this aria he therefore pitches Fiordiligi's voice remarkably low. To ensure that this depth is recognized in all its firmness and characteristic unshakability, he contrasts her deep mezzo-cantilenas with strikingly high-pitched violins (running in unison with the clarinets and violas).

Fiordiligi has a touch of sublimity. Her spiritual compass, though (to borrow a formula from the violinist Gidon Kremer), is not confined to this one extreme. In the last four bars of the farewell quintet (Act I, Scene 5) her utterances are of an agonized sincerity which carries her sorrow far beyond anything her sister and the two fiancés can express. And does not the adagio portion in her E major rondo indicate what a profound sense of guilt brings her back to reason, as it were, in the middle of the seduction merry-go-round, and makes her beg 'forgiveness' from her supposedly distant betrothed?

Fiordiligi is a young woman of deep feeling and great sincerity. An easy-going attitude is not natural to her, though she learns it quickly enough, especially here in Naples, should the day begin with 'a certain strange prickling in my veins'. The seducers in *Così* do not bruise an innocent wayside flower. They crush a steadfast character.

Fiordiligi is not pliable and she needs rather longer than the spontaneous Dorabella to stifle fears or to take decisions. Or is she simply more frigid than Dorabella, who is quicker to take fright or become inflamed? Is she perhaps more timid, more conventional, and does she need longer to come round?

Dorabella is the first to panic – after Don Alfonso has hinted at undisclosed fears – in case their lovers could be dead. Fiordiligi only echoes her. When however she recognizes that their parting is truly inevitable, she reacts all the more vigorously, declaring that she will take her own life with her lover's sword. Dorabella would doubtless consider this somewhat crude and melodramatic, for in her opinion the pain itself is enough to kill.

Constantin Floros, in his *Mozart-Studien*, has plausibly demonstrated to what degree Lorenzo da Ponte's text in the *opera-seria*-like arias may have been meant as parody, although Mozart's music displays no such bent.[10] Like so many producers, however, Floros regards the basic situation as harmless. The 'mere fact' that a fiancé has left cannot in his opinion account for the 'extravagant outburst of anguish'. Such observations reveal a widespread error of perspective. The audience is in its seats, the music begins in C major, and we expect an *opera buffa* in which nothing can go wrong. Why such a lot of fuss over a comedy of errors tinged with absurdity? Fiordiligi and Dorabella, though, are not sitting in the house; they are not even aware of being prima donnas. Just as little do they suspect that they will be the victims of a deception, a wager; but they certainly receive its full impact. They are indeed artificial creations, but that makes them neither better informed nor less sensitive. And the end of the story is completely unknown to them. Each time, for as long as there are opera houses in which *Così* is performed, they suffer an identical scenic moment of intense pain at parting, and fear that the military campaign may prove fatal for their lovers.

This means that the situation, however cunningly arranged, is real and menacing for them; which in turn signifies that in *Così* we observe the progressive phases in a struggle and are in a sense referees in an erotic context. Dorabella and Fiordiligi are hard hit. Their wish is to remain faithful. The gallants put on acts to which a wager and Don Alfonso force them. At what point and to what degree do the ladies show themselves to be affected? When is their imperturbability shaken? When do they decide to have a bit of fun? Where does flirtatiousness stop and sincerity begin? That can be established with some precision. The same goes for the gentlemen: when do they anxiously note that the ladies are attending to their pleas? When do they become incensed by the behaviour of their deceived fiancées? At what precise moment do they experience rage and torment?

Fiordiligi, even if quite unostentatiously, first becomes accessible, ready to lend an ear, after Don Alfonso has hoodwinked her with the truth. The two 'Albanians' have appeared. The two virtuous young women have cold-shouldered them, regarding their very presence as an impertinence. Here Don Alfonso takes advantage of the fact that Fiordiligi and Dorabella know him as a friend of their fiancés. He exploits their familiar confidence in him to argue on the newcomers' behalf: 'If you will be but amiable. . . . And they are gallant men whom in esteem I hold as friends of mine'. Fiordiligi lets herself be impressed by his assurances. What, she asks, can it be that these well-recommended strangers have to tell them? By a tactical breach of confidence and disloyalty to the spirit of friendship, Don Alfonso has now penetrated Fiordiligi's armour.

Her defences are penetrated a second time as the result of a crude and unscrupulous trick. When their love is spurned, these gallants, these friends of Don Alfonso, pretend to be on the point of suicide, and thus inspire pity in the shaken ladies. Their legitimate question, in C minor, is whether 'compassion can turn into love'. Fiordiligi's fond heart offers prolonged resistance. She would not like to be the cause of misfortune. Her sister, however, opens up a dangerously easy path leading, let us hope, only to some pleasantly harmless entertainment. Dorabella knows full well what she wants and whom she wants: she wants amusement, and, with care, nothing will happen anyway. She has already made her selection although Fiordiligi still hesitates. After Dorabella's 'I shall take the dark one' Fiordiligi is obliged to accept (not select) the other. We see Dorabella falling in love and Fiordiligi slithering into her love affair. And yet she, although the more restrained, the more emotional of the two, may end up even more aflame with passion.

Initially Fiordiligi succumbs not so much to the seduction of a particular individual as to happiness – the seductive feeling of how pleasant it is to be in good spirits. Her duet no. 2 not only speaks much of enjoyment, joking, delight and laughter, but the music (in bars 51–5, for example) also echoes sequences similar to those in the Act III sextet of *Figaro*. There they signify a pattern of pure happiness, and the ensemble is believed to have been one of Mozart's favourite pieces.

Pleasure mingled with deep emotion, and yet founded on a hoax, is a somewhat repulsive combination which occurs so inescapably only in Kleist's play *Amphitryon*. (Petty, unscrupulous trickery would be morally inferior, but less painful for its actors and for its spectators.) Fiordiligi is almost alone in battling with misgivings and pangs of conscience. She is wheedled into a state of emotional distress which reflects no credit upon the wire-pullers. Her sister is already leaning on the arm of her new beau while Fiordiligi, still coy or embarrassed, retreats with Ferrando into the darker of the garden paths. Her bad conscience grows in proportion to the danger. Instead of surrendering to her new passion with complete abandon, she looks back, and before her inner eye there arises again the vision of her old, genuine relationship. Assailed by repentance and confusion, she comes close to regaining her good sense amidst the beautiful nightmare. She wants to flee, to join her lover as a soldier, to avoid satanic temptation. But again, though more than ready for flight, she is swayed by her suitor's threat of suicide. ('If your strength to do the deed does fail, I shall guide your hand myself', sings Ferrando with psychological slyness.) Their cantilenas are woven into one. This is not a shallow, cheerful melody glibly pretending to some slight feeling: it is an authentic, slow Mozart cantilena full of heart-stirring tones and profound emotion which finally vanquishes the trembling victim.

Not only our heroine, but also the voyeurs in the audience fall victim to the logic of increasing weakness, the gravitation that pulls Fiordiligi towards that dulcet capitulation of 'You have won'. Yet even before she proffers her heart – and she eventually does it like a defeated animal holding its throat ready for the victor's lethal bite – the music divulges that Fiordiligi and Ferrando are at one, indeed almost identical. In their C major duet allegro, just before the ultimate breakdown of Fiordiligi's resistance, the flow of the lover's consummate singing complements that of his beloved. All differences have melted away.

This unity of sentiment is something new. When Ferrando, who is clearly fond of this reliable trick, intones 'I am left alone to die', Fiordiligi utters the discordant cry (duet no. 29, bar 21) 'Do not taunt me, I implore you'. It is a wrong note, a jaggedly discordant F in an E minor chord, totally out of keeping with what precedes it. It symbolizes fright and resistance.

At this point Fiordiligi is in the grip of violent emotion. Seconds earlier she had been demanding sabres, helmets and cloaks, her wits apparently wandering, but in reality on the brink of regaining her senses. Though her character makes her slow to react, it produces resolutely forceful action, or at least the capacity for action. But when her new love has transformed her resistance into submission, then Despina, whom Fiordiligi had earlier, and quite rightly, reviled as a she-devil, becomes her cherished ally. So, at the most nightmarish moment, while the uncannily speedy preparations for the sham wedding are proceeding – the bribed bridal chorus wishes 'prolific offspring be their blessing' – Despina is no longer the intriguer, but her precious little Despina, 'cara Despinetta'. These kind words show how far Fiordiligi has become estranged from her true self.

An evil game has been played with the strong feelings of a serious-minded girl. It is as though, after many efforts to escape (which would never have occurred to Dorabella), her emotional strength finally betrays her. What conquers her is not frivolity or weakness, but her natural inclination to feel sincere emotion and listen earnestly to people's pleas.

Fiordiligi's development provokes one last reflection. It all happens in a day, albeit a sharply divided theatrical day where the sun, high in Act I, is already setting in Act II. We know instinctively that the graph of such a day's events cannot be equated with twenty-four hours of real experience: a much longer period of emotional development has been compressed into two Acts. Just as on the stage we see historical dramas spanning greater periods of time concentrated into a few hours, yet are in no doubt that months have elapsed before our eyes, so, with the graph of Fiordiligi's feelings and development in mind, we must expand the events of this Neapolitan summer's day into a much fuller tale. Fiordiligi's breach of faith thus becomes a much more gradual process, and hence easier to forgive.

DON GIOVANNI

Baritone. Young Spanish nobleman with a passion for pursuing and conquering women. The most famous and most discussed hero of eighteenth-century opera, he has become almost unrecognizable behind a mountain of interpretation and fascination.

in *Don Giovanni*

Essential to Don Giovanni's personality and life-style are sensuality, glamour, and pace. As Mozart and da Ponte present him, he can also behave quite undiabolically: he is not, for example, above bothering about ices for his guests. He knows what fear is, and in dangerous situations he turns pale or blushes, which renders his enormous courage and love of adventure the more impressive. He is witty, can be well-behaved, treats his servant familiarly at one moment and brutally the next. He breaks oaths when they become inconvenient, and ignores warnings. As a suitor his wooing is not always recklessly daring. Provided it promises quick success he can adopt a tender approach and make himself irresistible.

At the outset he kills (in a duel which he would have preferred to avoid) the over-haughty Commendatore, whose daughter he intended to ravish. During the action Donna Elvira, whom he promised to marry but then abandoned, intervenes several times between him and his (willing) victim. Finally hell claims this man who is prepared neither to repent nor to mend his ways.

'They have written so much about me that I no longer know who I am', says Paul Valéry's Faust. Most of us have a similar feeling about Mozart's Don Giovanni. Countless musicians, philosophers, professors and desk-bound people have apparently derived satisfaction from speculations about his demonic nature, his genius for sensuality, his relationship or non-relationship with the opposite sex, his triumphant eroticism or his frustrated masculinity. Hence it has become well nigh impossible not to confuse the Don Giovanni defined by Mozart's music and da Ponte's text with his literary, academic and journalistic reincarnations. Is this young, adventurous Don Giovanni really a Don Juan? Concept and character can become hopelessly separate. After all, Wolfgang Böhm, the literary scholar, once described Faust as 'un-Faustian'. (A note for piano fans: the witty pianist Moritz Rosenthal, after listening to a recital by the inordinately admired Ignacy Paderewski, remarked, 'He is undoubtedly a good pianist, but no Paderewski'.)

An unmarried man who takes a fancy to spending one night with an unmarried, respectable woman has to look after her for the rest of his life and to make an honest woman of her by marriage. This is demanded by Christian and bourgeois ethics, which are always concerned with preserving the system as a whole and not with satisfying the subjective needs of the individual.

Don Giovanni opposes such ethics. It does not enter his hot-tempered mind to accept responsibility, to keep a promise, to take any consequences into account. For his temperament, only the moment counts: he chases women and drops them once he has enjoyed them. What attracts him is the sexual conquest, and presumably too the confirmation of his male self-esteem. His servant is not alone in maintaining the tally of victims as conscientiously as a bookkeeper: Don Giovanni himself concludes his misnamed 'Champagne' aria with the prophecy 'Ah, in the morning my list I'll be extending by ten more names, I do declare' (he is preparing a banquet in order to sap female resistance). Clearly, he has no time for the emotions of 'individual love'. Splendidly endowed with the physiological and social prerequisites, Don Giovanni enjoys his libertinism and hunts recklessly for pleasure. As a result he becomes – as a sexual criminal, marriage swindler, villain – the nightmare of those whose social life is based on freedom from evil and anarchy.

The moral freedom to which Donna Anna, Donna Elvira and Don Ottavio lend their vengeful support and the sensual freedom which Don Giovanni practises are both acclaimed in the finale of Act I as 'libertà'. This is a grand moment, clear-cut yet suspiciously ambiguous, when the principal figures, Leporello not excepted, chant together in C major 'Viva la libertà'.

Don Giovanni sees things from a definite standpoint, to put it mildly: no modifying considerations undermine his determination to be as he is. No caution interrupts his adventurous course, even when prudence is required because too many of his dupes or their kin are in pursuit. He neither sees nor feels the sufferings he causes. Indeed, he himself seems strangely incapable of pain – hounds don't weep – not that he is incapable of anger, moroseness, irony, and momentary fright. But when something irritates him or threatens to have nasty consequences, he simply brushes it aside and cries 'Bravo'. In the cemetery he ignores the mystic force of the Commendatore's adagio threats, although three trombones render them sinister and piercing to every ear. Don Giovanni, however, is deaf to metaphysical sound. He reacts 'indifferently and with contempt'. At least he does not shout 'Bravo', right away but he dismisses the uncanny with a facile rationalization: 'There must be someone outside having a joke at our expense'.

On the one occasion when he shows something resembling compassion for the laments of a 'poor soul' (whom he has not as yet recognized as Donna Elvira), he can utter a simple, almost gentle 'Poverina, poverina' ('poor young lady, poor young lady') in a C minor key far removed from irony or hauteur. On hearing him continue 'Let me seek to give her consolation in her torment', one might fancy that he is a philanthropist; but if one were tempted for a single instant to respond sentimentally to his civility one would be taken in, for Leporello's comment is 'That is how he has consoled eighteen hundred more'.

What does this extreme predatory urge – not forgetting the desperate consequences for the victims who fall under his spell – signify to Don Giovanni himself?

His unsuccessful attempt to ravish Donna Anna is followed by the fatal duel. (Secretly and softly he had forced his way also into Donna Elvira's house, seduced her, and she fell in love with him; but this simple plan of attack seems liable to go wrong if the victim is as aggressive as Donna Anna.) After these goings-on Leporello attempts to give his master a good talking-to, once the latter has sworn not to fly into a rage. 'Sir, you are my master, but the life that you lead is that of a rogue, Sir.' Don Giovanni promptly becomes incensed. 'And the oath that you gave?' 'I know nothing of an oath. Silence, or else!' A master can indeed easily stifle troublesome warnings from his subordinates.

Admittedly, he deceives himself without realizing it. That he has no intimate, never commits himself, is interested only in the conquest and never in the prey are matters which he rationalizes by the naive assertion that he would be wasted on one woman and belongs in a manner of speaking to the whole female world – as though any woman would want to share him so liberally! The truth of the matter, as he himself says, is that Don Giovanni's urge to pursue women is as elemental as his need to eat and to breathe. His primal eroticism is disclosed far more clearly in the presto tempo, the irresistible breakneck pace of the so-called 'Champagne' aria, than in its text, which would suit any crafty marriage-swindler.

It is also worth noting that with 'Finch'han del vino / Calda la testa' ('now that the bottle heats up the noddle') da Ponte quite plainly prescribes a musical programme – 'Take to the dance now! Some shall minuet, some trip the follia, some the German step' – that should really have provoked the composer into characteristic compositions. Don Giovanni, however, has no time to supply cues for minuets, folías and Allemandes: the demon of his libido is in a prestissimo hurry. He is again summoned to mend his ways – not by his servant, but by Donna Elvira – in the Act II finale when the shadow of the Commendatore has crept into Don Giovanni's and Leporello's lives. Again he reacts with nothing more than politeness, ironic applause, and eventually a not altogether unintelligible rebuff, 'Do let me eat now'.

Ultimately it is Heaven itself, in the shape of the Commendatore, which tries to make the hero change his ways and repent. Don Giovanni, his hand gripped by the statue, utters a scream: its clasp must be hideously cold. Nevertheless, he yields not an inch. He abuses his torturer, harbinger of death, with 'No, never, preposterous dotard'. He cannot change his way of life, despite a remarkable paranormal experience. He is as he is, and in that cause he will accept every form of trouble, fright, torment, indictment. The elemental sexual drive has become flesh in the form of a Spanish nobleman.

Some ingenious amateur psychologists have commented that any-thing so straightforward cannot really be so. Perhaps he is over-compensating for impotence; perhaps his compulsive philandering, like the macho behaviour of heroes in the Wild West, conceals homosexuality; perhaps the hero without ties (one thousand women and three are less, and less strenuous too, than only one) is really a poor isolated devil covering up for his failures?

Don Giovanni has no partner and his only true opposite number is death: there is at least poetic force in this contention of Luigi Dallapiccola's, who notes that at the beginning and at the end of the opera, both in D minor, the Commendatore appears as the symbol of death. But initially the Commendatore does not represent death at all: he is a proud old father who insists on fighting a duel. Nor does he appear only at the beginning and at the end, but also during the scene in the cemetery which is followed by Donna Anna's aria and only then the finale. Dallapiccola's ingenious argument is thus difficult to uphold. Leporello, in his wretched master-menial relationship with Don Giovanni, could qualify just as well. Sometimes, if he is too timid to obey orders, Don Giovanni bullies him mercilessly; at other times Don Giovanni will cajole him with familiar gossip and tolerate being aped by his servant (who therefore cannot really be too terrified of him).

The music in no way supports psychoanalytic speculations. Not being a literary man, Don Giovanni never ponders why he should chase women, except when he is challenged on the subject. Nor is he likely to set forth his attitude to life or his emotional state in detailed confessional arias. The seduction numbers aside, this Spanish gentleman neither presents his views on life in prolonged monologues (his name is not Sarastro), nor does he express his desire for amorous fulfilment in fits of exasperated fury (his name is not Almaviva). Don Giovanni and the pursuit of women are a single whole, one and the same thing. This sexual offender need not use his arias for reflections or misgivings, to examine his conscience or to worry about morality. (As an operatic character this does not lose him the audience's sympathy, although it deprives him of some rewarding solos from which, as an operatic character, he might have benefited.)

'Quiet, it seems to me that I catch the scent of woman here.' Let Don Giovanni sense that there is something female in the air and the hunter in him is aroused. He becomes unswerving in stalking his quarry. He is in love, at least, with being in love, which makes him utter beguiling melodies. An expert at seduction is at work.

For Donna Elvira's maid, all he needs is a rather conventional, precisely calculated mandolin canzonetta coupled with a reference to suicide in case of refusal. Zerlina's heart is won with an A major cantilena whose impact is so overwhelming that, although she claims to be still wavering, she is hypnotized from the very first note. With Donna Elvira, closer to his own social level, he has to take greater pains. In the andantino trio utterly irresistible turns of phrase and modulations occur to him. His gloriously persuasive 'Come down, precious fair one', lushly descending from E major to C major, is undoubtedly one of the most captivating moments in the whole trio. (With such music for his procurer, any 'villain' would have an easy conquest.)

So Don Giovanni is endowed with an absolute, totally unqualified urge to seduce. He can also transform his genius for sensuality into an overpowering musical wooing. If a seduction attempt miscarries, the reason will be less that the victim has no wish to 'hear' him than that third parties intervene. His abortive attack on Donna Anna may be reckoned an extreme exception. Finally he is endowed with the anarchic courage that keeps him steadfast even when threatened with torments by Heaven. Does that make him something other than human, a sensual monster?

The facts of life and the conventions to which the other characters in *Don Giovanni* subscribe seem to hold good for him too. This libertine still talks about God and the Devil. He is no insuperable superman. During his first relatively harmless meeting with Don Ottavio and Donna Anna, Mozart and da Ponte depict him as a hypocrite who, suddenly driven into a corner, turns pale with fright and laboriously tries to brazen things out. The argument that at such junctures it is the old *opera buffa* pattern shining through, while his true character is disclosed in the major dramatic scenes, would mean drawing an arbitrary distinction between the parts of the score that are meant to be taken seriously and the merely conventional parts. Composer and author have moreover attached such importance to the quartet in question (Act I, no. 9) as to arrange tiny textual differences even in homophonic ensemble moments. Donna Anna and Don Ottavio remark on a stirring of hidden torments ('d'ignoto tormento') in Donna Elvira; Don Giovanni, keeping a cooler head, sings in the same second of hidden fears ('d'ignoto spavento'). Thus he is always characterized with deliberate care. In this quartet, as in the preceding recitative, his situation is an awkward one and he himself is disconcerted. Afraid that Donna Anna has detected something, he calms down a little, but changes colour suspiciously when Donna Elvira levels her accusation. Later Masetto's presence – just when he is about to lull Zerlina into the right mood and her bridegroom becomes visible lurking in a niche – very naturally upsets him. At the end of the first finale, with his back to the wall, his wits are 'in disarray'. A few uneasy instants pass before he regains courage.

At the moment of his destruction he will heroically defy the supernatural. How frightened of it he is, though, can be observed in the cemetery scene, for a few bars after the Commendatore's statue has given its sudden and horrifying nod, he sings exactly the same notes as Leporello, whose knees have from first to last been knocking together with terror.

Don Giovanni is no Siegfried who has yet to learn the meaning of fear (by encountering a sleeping woman!), but a gentleman capable of feeling dread yet quick to master this weakness. He could not live according to his form of 'libertà' if it were not closely linked to strength and daring, not to mention contempt for people, death, and God too. His abrupt 'belief' in the Devil who has his hand in the game or his invocation of God at the moment of greatest danger could be figures of speech rather than deeply felt convictions: to say 'O God!' does not necessarily entail believing in God.

In association with his social equals he is well-bred, otherwise Don Ottavio would not greet him as an old acquaintance. He rises when a lady enters the room, and likewise he will – ironically – kneel to her, provided that she has already knelt to him when pleading for his soul in an ecstasy of tears and despair.

None the less his occasional display of good manners can hardly hide his lack of magnanimity. He enjoys tormenting Leporello, leaving him to experience hunger or fright until at last he throws him a sop. Is it really necessary that in his last scene he should, more than once, tell the musicians to play up because he wants value for his money? Such behaviour seems singularly vulgar. The scoundrel deserves to eat on his own (even if at the end a few pretty girls should be decoratively lolling about or dancing to the table-music). In opera, lonely meals instead of feasting in gay company are the fate of high-ranking ruffians, as both Don Giovanni and Scarpia illustrate.

This successful rake knows neither sorrow nor tribulation, and never utters weary or downcast tones. He always bounces back after a defeat, and yet, despite his pleasure in the chase and his irresistible potency, he never really seems happy. The great producer Walter Felsenstein, responsible for an intelligent production of *Don Giovanni* and a highly judicious essay on this opera, offered the following explanation: 'Don Giovanni's magic is totally overwhelming, and he takes delight in exercising it. Yet he is driven by an insatiable need to increase it, to vary it, to bring it to consummation.'[11]

If we thus see Don Giovanni as possessed by a craving as insatiable as Macbeth's power-lust, we are seeing him in a very Faustian, German, Romantic perspective. 'His desire', Felsenstein continues, 'derives from his boundless sensual longing, which idealizes each victim and transmutes her into the condition required. In his presence, the woman feels herself freed from reality. She responds to his desire with a passion she has hitherto not known and is never able to forget.' In the light of Don Giovanni's encounter with Donna Elvira, and possibly that with Donna Anna, this is in many ways a fine and appropriate interpretation, although the music assuredly does not intimate 'boundless longing'. Yet if Don Giovanni frees all women from reality, which he certainly succeeds in doing during his first meeting with Zerlina (only unfortunately someone interrupts them), why does she so strongly resist yielding to him in his mansion? Just after he 'almost forces her' away from the company, why does she scream, nine bars later, in obvious terror, instead of pleasure? Why does the blackguard, caught red-handed, have to resort to idiotic accusations against Leporello which no one believes?

Don Giovanni may not be lacking in sensuality and radiant irresistibility. Is it, however, 'longing' and a constant faculty for idealization that inspire him? There is room for doubt. But on occasion, and simply as a means to seduction, his cantilenas contain something which he himself, proud rake, lacks – soul.

GUGLIELMO

Baritone. An officer blithely prepared to bet that his bride will never betray him because he regards himself as irresistibly lovable. Less sensitive than his friend Ferrando, but probably a little more down-to-earth, complacent and aloof.

in *Così fan tutte*

He likes to outdo Ferrando. When the ominous wager is laid, Don Alfonso asks the two young officers for their word of honour that a whole day long they will perform whatever he bids. 'And swear to me', the cunning old misogynist adds, 'that not a sign, not a word, not a hint of all this shall be revealed to your true loves.' Instead, the gentlemen are to obey all his behests without contradiction. 'Tutto' ('all right'), says Ferrando. 'Tuttissimo' ('most all rightest!') is Guglielmo's elaboration. His success in leading Dorabella astray and in enraging her lover Ferrando at first only increases his self-assurance without arousing his concern. In all masculine (im)modesty he imagines that no woman could ever forget Guglielmo. In the *secco* recitative following Ferrando's cavatina no. 27 he analyzes the difference between his friend and himself with enviable clarity. 'In all things, dear friend, fine differences must be observed. Is it conceivable that a betrothed could ever forget a Guglielmo? Not that I wish to extol myself, but, if you compare the two of us, then perhaps I merit rather the more. . . .' It is not that he wants to pat himself on the back, but only that he is rather a conceited ass. Just punishment swiftly catches up with him, for Ferrando exerts all his tender persuasiveness to secure for his friend precisely the fate which the latter has afforded him.

What did the two of them have in mind when they accepted the wager? How did Guglielmo come to utter his radiantly confident 'Tuttissimo'? The question is legitimate, but there is probably no definite answer. He may have thought that through some masquerade or prank, his lady-love would be put to the test and her unwavering loyalty be brought to light. When he cried 'Tuttissimo', did Guglielmo really foresee that his friend Ferrando, likewise in disguise, would use every trick in the book to test Fiordiligi? Assuredly not. The exchange of partners, however, is implicit in the logic of Don Alfonso's idea of disguise. If only to avoid being seen through, the two men in their Albanian costume, after being treated as no more than a pair of impudent intruders who can scarcely be told apart, do not turn to their own fiancées, but each addresses the other, her sister.

Indeed, the ladies also decide crosswise, although, despite a widely held view to the contrary, the two pairs (the lyrically fiery Ferrando and the impulsive Dorabella, Guglielmo with his polish and intelligence and Fiordiligi with her strength of character) are better matched at the outset.

Ferrando's betrothed is the first to succumb. Guglielmo not merely fancies that nothing of the kind could ever happen to him, but with a snobbishly blasé air waves aside his friend's agitated, despairing resolution. 'Are you demented? Will you indeed rush to ruin on behalf of a lady not worth two soldi?'

Guglielmo's underlying attitude reminds me nostalgically of the witty, complacent arrogance that used to be typical of the Baltic nobility (alas, they exist no more). Omitting the geographical gloss, Guglielmo's reactions evince a nicely aristocratic cynicism. That is how conceited baritone gallants behave. It is consistent that, when the two are still certain of victory, and are planning how to spend the money which they cannot fail to win, the more sincere and impetuous tenor proclaims, 'A fine serenade will be brought to play unto my lady-love'. Guglielmo's mind runs on more material pleasures. He wants not only to sing, but also to eat: 'I, in honour of my beauty, a dinner-party shall arrange'. And when Don Alfonso is busy with tactical instructions about the seduction attempts ('Proceed ahead and await me awhile there in the garden. In that place your further orders from me you shall hear'), Guglielmo's appetite gets the better of him. 'And today we do not eat?' he inquires anxiously. For Ferrando this aspect is not so tragic. Food can come later; the main thing is for the breath of love to nourish the soul.

Guglielmo's attitude during the wager is self-assured but not stupid, cool but not malicious. He is perfectly capable, as his word of honour requires, of pretending to be enamoured as long as the experiment is running, even though he observes uneasily that his bride is beginning to enjoy the company of his fellow-Albanian.

It still seems unlikely, indeed impossible, that a cavalier of his calibre should begin this comedy of dissimulation by committing himself passionately and with clear erotic allusions. Mozart originally composed for Guglielmo the no. 15 aria 'Revolgete' ('turn now to him'), but he had to replace it at the original performance with the far less ardent and less witty G major air 'Oh be not so demure'. The deleted 'Rivolgete' aria is indubitably a brilliant inspiration. Alfred Einstein called it 'the most remarkable *buffa* aria ever written'.[12] Wolfgang Hildesheimer thinks that it belongs 'in musical terms to the most important of all *buffa* arias' conceived by Mozart, transforming a ridiculous gallant into a real man.[13] Yet in this particular context, sung by the blasé Guglielmo, it is simply too 'direct', too 'committed'. He commends himself and his friend by boasting in unmistakable, almost offensive terms of their virility: 'If my fires with sighs aglowing, my love hard as bronze compelling . . . Many a matter still to mention, but for that too great the tension.' Even if Guglielmo does not express himself quite nakedly, the Neapolitan ladies are left in no doubt as to what the saucy fellow means. Their reaction, according to the original stage direction, shows how clearly they do understand: 'The girls leave in a fury', *con collera*.

Such provocative behaviour accords ill with what we have so far seen of Guglielmo's character. Until now he may have allowed himself smart jokes, but no smutty cracks. Instead of militantly infusing into the game a richly rhythmic, rousing D major piece, in Mozart's final version he sings a small-scale and fairly innocuous G major aria. Its andantino restraint amounts to little more than the self-advertisement that the wager requires of him: 'From head to foot in limb well-shaped, ornamental, well-behaved'. He even draws attention to their absurd moustaches and false noses, thus rendering their masquerade utterly ridiculous.

Hereupon the ladies do not 'leave in a fury', but as likely as not merely shaking their heads. There is no stage direction to tell us. Guglielmo's nonchalant G major ditty has certainly not attacked anyone's steadfastness; this explains why he bursts into laughter as soon as he is left on his own. Aren't the ladies admirably coy, and isn't the wager going well? In a broadcast talk Ivan Nagel put forward the persuasive suggestion that the 'Rivolgete' aria makes obvious the sultry, direct sensuality which in fact lies behind the *Così* jests, and that, since such open eroticism was all too flagrant a breach of the conventions, Mozart had to replace it with something less naughty. A look at Guglielmo's character as a whole, though, gives some support to a less exciting argument. The need to make him a consistent character, fulfilling his task in the manner appropriate to this early stage of the affair prompted the substitution and led to the G major andantino.

At the moment of this first Guglielmo aria the scene is peopled by two blameless women, curious but reserved; two panders (Despina, Don Alfonso) who so far have achieved little; and two spirited young men performing a fancy-dress frolic. When does the situation change, as far as Guglielmo is concerned, and why? As a matter of convenience, so it seems, the two ladies, reluctantly impressed by the suicide attempt and its awe-inspiring 'magnetic' cure, take a crucial step away from their state of reserve during the interval.

When in Act II the gentlemen first come on-stage, surrounded by attendants 'in rich liveries', and sing their duet and chorus, Guglielmo and Ferrando have no idea that their fiancées have meanwhile planned to venture on some harmless amusement. Nor does the music give any sign of knowing. Neither tingling nor 'spicy', it is restrained, like a serenade, strikes an E flat major beatific chord, and is possibly a little too lush and limp. Then it happens. A queasy feeling befalls the disguised beaux. 'Cupid cripples true lovers' limbs', Guglielmo confesses. He is suddenly at a loss for seductive speech, so that Don Alfonso has to guide the conversation. Even the ladies have to request the strangers – so forward a moment earlier – to impart their wishes.

Guglielmo's conduct now becomes increasingly schizophrenic. On the one hand, he realizes that his love (Ferrando is 'taking care' of her) is not unimpressed. 'Alas', he groans. On the other, he is man enough to make a sophisticated approach to Dorabella. His self-control, his cynicism, and his sovereign attitude are at any rate sufficient to enable him to maintain this gentlemanly schizophrenia – trembling on his unhappy bride's behalf, but bringing his friend's bride to happy trembling – to the end of the piece without manifest loss of composure. In the larghetto of the nightmare marriage ceremony at the close of the work, with Albania and Naples being united in wedlock, Ferrando becomes absorbed in the lovely passages he utters, but the cooler-headed Guglielmo remains master even of this absurd situation. His venomous parlando, 'Ah, I wish 'twere poison in the cup that would choke this vixen pack', upsets the harmony of the A flat major quartet.

Guglielmo is capable of a certain aloofness, as well as the irony which he uses, with carefully concealed malice, to inform Ferrando that the latter's beloved has been the first to 'fall': 'None the less a little doubt could do no harm' and 'In this world some suspicion is always as well'.

Perhaps his pity is genuine. Perhaps he really does not want to distress the poor deceived lover. Not as yet involved himself, he goes on to chant his *buffo* attack on women in a gabbling manner resembling Monostatos – 'That's the way, girls, that you always behave'. He does it, so to speak, on behalf of men in general since he can hardly imagine that the same fate is in store for him.

Though a moment earlier his self-assurance seemed unassailable, Guglielmo is cut to the quick and declares an immoderate contempt for women – 'Satan's bride! Traitress, thief, bitch!' – when his predictable fate is fulfilled. Of course Guglielmo finds his way back to Fiordiligi, but now and forever after we may expect some arrogant irony to be blended with his geniality.

HIGH PRIEST

Tenor. As Neptune's high priest, urges Idomeneo to fulfil his vow.

in *Idomeneo, King of Crete*

Should there be a spark of obduracy still flickering in Idomeneo, should the King still be considering any way of escaping the consequence of his vow, such as sacrificing himself in place of his son, then Neptune's high priest in his recitative (Act III, no. 23) would quench such glimmers of resistance with the utmost severity. He forces Idomeneo to understand the dreadful truth and to recognize the harm already done by his evasiveness. The zealous priest lays it on thick, describing how he has seen thousands upon thousands die, and how the roads of Crete are running with blood as the murderous monster becomes more and more ravenous.

The priest sternly confronts the King with the facts for which he is responsible because of his refusal to fulfil his promise to Neptune. He draws the logical conclusion that, after all this, the King can no longer procrastinate. 'To the temple, to the temple!' Render unto Neptune what is Neptune's.

In response to the ardent, severe, dogmatic and unimpeachable diatribe of the peremptory priest, volubly underlined by the orchestra, Idomeneo's emotional answer reveals the composer's pity, for it sounds like the harrowed reply of a man driven into a corner. Instead of resisting the priest's harsh demands, he can only attract more sympathy, and appear more human, than does his priestly opponent, obsessed with collecting the sacrifice at all costs.

Yet Idomeneo's paternal suffering does not leave the high priest altogether unimpressed. In the first verse of no. 24 the chorus, deeply moved, bewails the King's frightful vow, and in the second verse the priest himself, solo, utters a charitable plea – the son is innocent, may Heaven hold back the hand, ready to lunge, of the devout father prepared to offer the sacrifice. The impulse seems to be no more than momentary, mere rhetorical pity with no practical consequence. For, as though he had never uttered his appeal, his last words are at once followed by those triplets and those choral harmonies, appropriate to horror and to death respectively, that had resounded earlier when Idomeneo had confessed that it was none other than his son whom he owed to Neptune.

IDAMANTE

Castrato role. (Mozart altered the part to that of a tenor for a Vienna concert performance. If the original Munich version is chosen for production, a mezzo-soprano must take over.) Son of Idomeneo. Innocent victim of events. It is painful for him to have to wait so long before he learns that Ilia returns his love. Not until Act III is he told why his father so cruelly repudiated him at the beginning.

in *Idomeneo, King of Crete*

An air of gentle melancholy surrounds this young man, particularly when the part is entrusted to a lyrical female voice. Though entirely innocent, he is the victim of a vow by his father. If he takes any initiative of his own, it is to do good, kind deeds. His release of the Trojan prisoners, for instance, is humane and magnanimous though doubtless helped by the fact that they are Ilia's compatriots. Another example is his compassionate treatment of a shipwreck victim long before the stranger turns out to be his father. Later, when the King orders him to leave his country as quickly as possible in the company of Electra, he is badly upset on Ilia's account, but he does not refuse to obey. It would scarcely cross his mind to offer serious resistance to the authority of the king or the gods. Idomeneo is much more refractory and embittered in his response to the gods' demands, and Electra flies into a rage. Idamante is a lyrical man of sorrows who only occasionally utters a few harsher expressions: not a particularly exciting princely personality.

Yet although he neither curses, violently bemoans his fate, nor intrigues, he still has a decisive will of his own and can transpose his warm feelings into heartfelt cantilenas. He is certainly not weak or cowardly. When the situation gets beyond him, he goes off in the hope of finding death in battle with the sea monster that is a mortal threat to his countrymen; in fact he kills the loathsome creature and has to continue living, his love affair and exile problems unresolved.

Ilia's 'ironic' treatment of him at the outset neither disturbs his equanimity nor alters his good intentions towards the Trojans. Indeed, he even compares her ardently with the most famous woman of antiquity: 'Helen roused all Greece and Asia to arms. Now this young heroine, loveliest and most beautiful princess, disarms and unites Greece and Asia.' There could hardly be a greater compliment than that; at this stage, however, Ilia's misery prevents her from appreciating it. Idamante's gloriously ascendant expression of longing, 'Ma me'l dica il labbro almeno' ('a word coming from your lips' – aria no. 2), shows the purity of his soul. He certainly does not lack temperament, although it may initially seem so subdued. We must bear in mind his princely shyness and also, of course, the pain caused to him by his father's repudiation, which overshadows his life and his love.

His frank and open feelings are totally unable to cope with the obscure, catastrophic events in which he becomes involved although, heaven knows, he is in no way to blame for them. He is 'deeply grieved'. Quiet and yet heart-breaking are the pauses as he exclaims 'Well, then, I shall depart . . . But whither? O Ilia! O Father!'. These spiritless syllables trickle forth and die away just before the quartet in Act III. Under the baton of Nikolaus Harnoncourt they were so touchingly despondent, so inconsolably melancholy, particularly the question 'But whither?', that a few pianissimo minor bars became an unforgettable Mozartian experience. So great is the capacity for sorrow of Idamante, who only wants everything to turn out well. As he begins to realize that his love for Ilia is reciprocated, he is allowed a few instants of unalloyed lyrical contentment, although without effusion. Actually the statement that he makes at the start of the A major duet sounds more rapturous than his tender, but certainly not gushing, cantilena, for his reply to Ilia's admission of her love runs, 'S'io non moro a questi accenti, non è ver, che amor uccida' ('if delight at these tidings does not kill, 'tis not true that love is deadly').

He is a proper prince, full of pure sentiments. When he learns that he has been promised by his father for sacrifice to Neptune, this young martyr is not so much downcast as relieved. Now at last he sees confirmed that he has given his father no cause for wrath and knows why Idomeneo has behaved so strangely, hurtfully and coldly. There is one moment of gloom, of brief tremolo consternation, when the son, expecting his father's embrace, is instead ordered to depart forthwith. He feels his senses reeling and he moans 'O cruel gods!'. The whole role is a question of proportion. It is because the other *Idomeneo* figures are much more passionate in expression, much more deeply torn by grief, much more emotional in the utterance of their sufferings and their dismay that Idamante, even when he is at his unhappiest, seems unshakable, a steadfast prince – and an endearing martyr.

IDOMENEO

Tenor. King of Crete. In distress at sea and in mortal fear, he vowed that if he were saved he would sacrifice to the god Neptune the first person he met after his rescue; and that was his son. Now the King can think of nothing but self-reproaches for his vow, railing against his fate, and schemes for possible escape (like sending his son abroad in the hope that eventually the god will become pacified). The unhappy ruler does not tell his son why he shuns him. Only the dire reaction by the god whom he tries to cheat renders Idomeneo ready for a despairing attempt to fulfil his promise.

in *Idomeneo, King of Crete*

Several times Mozart says in his letters that he would have composed the part of Idomeneo differently if he had been offered a singer other than the fairly aged tenor Anton Raaff.

Raaff is the best and most honest fellow in the world, but so tied to old-fashioned routine that flesh and blood cannot stand it. Consequently it is very difficult to compose for him . . . as, for instance, the first aria 'Vedròmi intorno'. When you hear it, you will say it is good and beautiful – but if I had written it for Zonca [another Munich singer] it would have suited the words much better.

(27 December 1780).[14]

And some months later, discussing the project, unfortunately not implemented, for a translation of the work to be performed at Vienna, 'I would gladly have given him my Munich opera to translate. I would have altered the part of Idomeneo completely and changed it to a bass part for Fischer.'[15] In other words, Mozart was neither altogether satisfied with what he could ask of Raaff nor with having to entrust the role to a tenor. Many scholars have made the most of Mozart's twofold dissatisfaction, and the secondary literature has awarded innumerable bad marks to Idomeneo's music. After all, don't Mozart's own critical remarks provide some sanction for this sort of mild carping?

But when some external circumstance has compelled a genius to rack his brains and sweat blood in search of a solution, it is pointless for his interpreters to persist in claiming that the hard-won solution 'doesn't count'. It is more pleasant and rewarding to examine the solution itself.

Idomeneo is the central figure in a drama of catastrophe where there is nothing for him really to do except perform the almost impossible sacrifice. Before the opera begins, mortal terror has wrung from him a momentous vow, the victim of which his son is destined to become. The King is dejected and embittered. Where there is no escape (at best, evasion), maybe delay can help. Idomeneo's recitative is full of gloom, but he is not prepared tamely to accept Neptune's cruelty. In contrast to his son, who is ready to face the consequences with almost martyr-like docility, he rails against fate with curses and outbursts of horror. He knows now that Arbace's scheme cannot prevail against the sea god's claim. His brief euphoria is over, but not his angry remonstrance against Neptune's will. His mental process now cannot be described in psychological terms alone. As he realizes that neither flight nor imprecations can help, only submission, he has to come to terms intuitively with the divine order of things. At the end of Act II, ever ready to sacrifice himself, he is still arguing, 'Regard me as guilty, cruel god! I alone erred, punish me alone. . . . Yet you demand another victim in my stead. An innocent one I cannot give you. If you none the less demand it . . . you are unjust, and you cannot exact it.' In Act III he retracts this royal sophistry as to what a god is entitled to require or not. It is his own son who gives him the necessary strength, and now Idomeneo acquiesces in the fulfilment of his promise and of the inevitable, whereupon it can be forgone.

Giambattista Varesco's text does not spell out this mental process; the course of the action, however, conveys it laboriously but un-mistakably. But what kind of music did Mozart assign to the central figure and its vacillations? (A singer's weakness, the absence of requisite strength and depth, means that the composer may have to adopt a different method of conveying what is of importance to him.)

In his recitatives the King's lamentations are not marked by wild excess. Uttered slowly and harrowingly, they reflect the awareness of a man who knows that he is responsible for his own misfortune as well as that he now, in ominous circumstances, proposes to perform an ominous action. When, in his first aria, he meditates how the blood spilt on account of his vow will rise in accusation against him, the long-drawn orchestral accompaniment illuminates his pain. Here is the despair engendered by a bad conscience obsessed with its guilt. Even in the allegro molto the oboe echoes on a distinctly fiercer, more stabbing note his elegiac C minor phrase, 'Di tormento questo core, quante volte morirà' ('how often will this heart from torments yet die a thousand deaths', cf. aria no. 6, bars 62–6 and the oboe repetition in bars 67–9). And at once, as he sees someone approaching, he bursts out, in the recitative, 'Brutal, unjust gods! Loathsome altars!'. (Since he has not discerned that the newcomer is his son, his anguish proves that his goodness encompasses humanity in general, not simply his own family circle.)

Idomeneo's despair and bitterness are so great that he not only seeks counsel as to how he may avoid fulfilling the vow, but tries to act on the advice immediately – not that he fails to realize, with distress, what this means for those concerned, Ilia and Idamante, who love each other and must be parted. It leads him to repeat (Act II, Scene 3, bars 1–3) a tender phrase that has just been heard from Ilia. Being inwardly tormented, however, his repetition of the phrase darkens into a subdued minor key. He and Electra are, as the psychological con-struction of the quartet in Act III corroborates, the embittered, remonstrant pair as against the gentler, more submissive, more lyrically suffering couple, Idamante and Ilia.

The dreadful ravages of Neptune's sea monster among his people and the imperious admonitions of the god's high priest in Act III make their impact on the King. He is prepared to sacrifice not only his own life (which does not interest the divinity), but to slay his son. 'You shall see, O gods, how the father opens the veins of his own offspring!' He appears suddenly overcome by a fatalistic frenzy. What is, properly speaking, the painful context of his surgingly melodic F major cavatina, 'Receive now our sacrifice, O Monarch of the Sea', is invested by the violins' brilliant pizzicato accompaniment with a glittering, vibrantly vital quality. Raaff could hardly have managed to sing that. Here as elsewhere Mozart took this into consideration and availed himself of the orchestra's resources. Idomeneo's determination, however, is short-lived. In a recitative marked by strikingly numerous tempo changes the unhappy father's burst of vigour is utterly spent: 'My strength abandons me in every fibre and sombre night overshadows my eyes' light . . . O my son . . .'. Mozart ensures that we notice the King's irregular pulse and realize that he is close to fainting. Even in the sight of the terrible gods, it is clear that Idomeneo has now suffered sufficiently for his egotistic vow and for his desire to escape its fulfilment. The oracle proclaims his son's deliverance and elevation to the sovereignty which the father relinquishes. Idomeneo's last words, 'Oh, what happiness!', obviously come straight from the heart.

ILIA

Soprano. Trojan princess. After the fall of Troy she was brought as a prisoner, along with some of her compatriots, to Crete. Idamante, son of the Cretan King, loves her and as a sign of his feelings sets free the other Trojan captives. Gradually Ilia returns his love. At the end, when the innocent Prince is in greatest danger, she is even prepared to sacrifice herself on his behalf.

in *Idomeneo, King of Crete*

Just as Verdi's Aida, an Ethiopian princess at the Egyptian court, loves the young general Radames and has to endure the rivalry of the high-spirited Egyptian princess Amneris, so after initial hesitation the exiled Ilia loves Idamante, the King's son, and has to endure the rivalry of the tempestuous, proud and jealous Electra, descendant of the Atrides dynasty. Ilia, homeless, fatherless, carried off to a foreign country, is enveloped by an aura of tremulous, sombre suffering. When she comes gradually to love Idamante, her affection is as restrained as her despair. Being a captive in an alien world, reticence behoves her rather than vehemence.

She is not, however, always borne down or passive.

In Ilia's heart and mind the most various feelings and ideas conflict with one another – her innate virginal shyness, respect for the King, grief at her fate . . . and finally love for Idamante. Gluck would have reduced everything to the simplest formula, as he did elsewhere. Mozart, on the other hand, did justice to all the emotions and, unlike the economical Gluck, he employed an abundance of motives which often succeed each other within the shortest space. It is a constant interplay and mingling of the most diverse emotional forces.[16]

So Hermann Abert, in his Mozart biography, describes this fascinating personality.

Ilia's aura of suffering is therefore something complex, transformed by longing and heartfelt love into throbbing restlessness. An unhappy girl's distress acquires energy from a gentle, hopeful disquiet. Her words and feelings are restrained, but she never seems puny or passive. She is a figure enhanced by the richness of her melancholy, lofty feeling.

How thoroughly Ilia is suited to the wholly noble Idamante, incapable of selfish or aggressive sentiment, Mozart demonstrates in the carefully delineated E flat major quartet (no. 21). Idomeneo and Electra belong together there as more forceful and defiant characters: Ilia and Idamante are meeker. While the King ('Is there none who will slay me?') and Electra ('When shall I have my vengeance?') inveigh against fate, Ilia and Idamante complement them with gentle thirds. They use (as from bar 34) the same words – begging the King to let light into his gloom – and the music declares them to be a couple, united by deep emotional affinity.

At the outset, however, Ilia is unaware of this. She only surmises it 'somehow', as in her first recitative when she admits in some perplexity that at the sight of Idamante she is unable to maintain her patriotic hatred of the enemy nation responsible for her father's death. (The violins comment on her contradictory feelings with sharp forte and piano contrasts.) She tells herself that Idamante is said to love the princess Electra from Argos, but the disquiet she experiences renders her unhappy. A sustained phrase (bars 39–40 in her first scene recitative, which Beethoven was to use again in his F major Violin Romance) intimates her agitation. In her G minor aria, acknowledging to herself that she cannot as yet abhor the sight of Idamante ('Ma quel sembiante, O Dei! Odiare ancor non so'), the words are initially sung as a yearning syncopated sequence in B flat. On their repetition, chromatic passing-notes in the (initially neutral) second violins add a grieving and rhapsodic minor dimension, reflecting her rapturous state of mind.

She works herself up, delicately, insistently, but not demonstratively, into a dismayed feeling compounded of pain and happiness. At the beginning she still has the strength to answer the Prince ironically ('con ironia'). He need not fear that the gods would do anything to Greece – 'the gods' entire wrath fell upon Troy'. This moment of rebelliousness, though, remains unobtrusive, restrained. Even the vigorously dotted forte just before the frank admission of her love shrinks back twice into a hesitant piano declaration (the andante of Act III, Scene 2, bars 15–18). Ilia is not a flamboyant heroine.

Her three arias never violate the bounds of noble self-control in order to make emotional impact. Within these limits they possess a wonderfully glowing, elegiac strength. For the sake of their profusion the youthful Mozart was ready, if necessary, to throw aside the text. 'I should prefer an uninterrupted aria', he wrote on 8 November 1780 to his father, '. . . as I have not got to contend with difficulties arising from the words, I can go on composing quite easily; for we have agreed to introduce here an aria andantino with obbligato for four wind instruments, that is, a flute, oboe, horn and bassoon.'[17] Precisely this is Ilia's E flat major aria (andante, with four solo wind instruments), where the text asserts 'Or più non rammento l'angoscie, gli affani' ('no longer I ponder agonies and distress'). Her cantilena, however, is far superior to such platitudes. Even the first time she rises to a gravely expressive minor sixth followed by a sad chromatic descent. But when the passage, harmonically intensified, is repeated, then it intimates a range of mental agony which is really quite irrelevant to the utterance 'No longer I ponder'. For all this she remains touchingly simple. In this aria (no. 11), so heedless of its text, there hovers (bar 27 onward) a B flat theme in the wind instruments. It is when Idomeneo, who has overheard Ilia, broodingly and gloomily takes up the same theme at the beginning of his recitative that we realize how innocent it was when sung by Ilia.

Her lyrical and graceful 'Zeffiretti' aria, urging the cajoling breezes to hurry to her beloved, in reality deals also with the pain of impeded love, although it is in a gently restrained major key (a reference to her wishes, not to her worries) that she sings. Yet to try to make such a precise distinction between baroque musical description (of the breezes) and emotional delineation (of Ilia's worry), which is voiced in the more astringent central portion of the aria, would be pedantic and unworthy of the emotional wisdom in Mozart's music for Ilia. Now that she is no longer so terribly alone, the music sometimes blurs the distinction between love's *felicity* and the *infelicity* of love.

We can best understand her robustly steadfast purity of feeling from the scene where, although her love for Idamante is now as manifest as Electra's jealousy, she turns at the most critical moment to her rival to beseech relief ('Woe is me! Merciful princess, oh solace me!', whereupon Electra understandably suspects that she is being mocked). No wonder, then, that while the second violins play a vehement tremolo and the first violins interpose diffuse quaver passages, she is almost intoxicated by the prospect of self-sacrifice, rushes between Idamante and Idomeneo, kneels before the high priest, and pleads to be sacrificed in her beloved's stead.

KLAAS

Speaking part. Boatman in the service of Belmonte.

in *The Abduction*

No emotional outpourings need be expected from the excellent, taciturn Klaas, who regards himself as quite an expert on abductions. Even the anticipated reward in gold cannot elicit more than a dry joke from him. He urges haste and carries ladders without contributing anything else to the success of the operation. Why should he sing?

FIRST LADY

Soprano. Top voice in a female trio on whom the Queen of the Night has imposed a quasi-Valkyrie task, although in a traditionally fairy-tale Viennese way.

in *The Magic Flute*

She would like to appear alone but she is never allowed to. For instance, when she sees Prince Tamino stretched before her in a delicious faint, and instantly finds him so handsome, she tries to establish whether she is the leader of her trio by sending the other two away: 'So geht und sagt es ihr, ich bleib indessen hier' ('go now and tell her all, while I do meanwhile stay'). But her authority is too feeble, so that her clever companions see through the scheme and annoyingly decline to depart. For form's sake she is permitted to be the last to sing 'Ich sollte fort' ('I should be gone'), even though that is hardly more than an admission that she is unable to achieve anything else.

For the rest she laughs maliciously when she punishes poor Papageno with water instead of the wine he had hoped to receive, and appears to have rather a frivolous personality. She also enjoys repeating venomous rumours. Nor should she have too good an opinion of herself just because her exposed register allows her to perform more solo cantilenas than the partners to whom, from start to finish, she is joined as though they were Siamese triplets. Otherwise, she is a genuine, charming and fairly egocentric Viennese.

SECOND LADY

Mezzo-soprano. Middle figure in a female trio acting at the behest of the Queen of the Night.

in *The Magic Flute*

It is difficult for her to stick her neck out or to make any mark, since any characteristic qualities seem to have been allocated to her colleagues. On one occasion she brashly interrupts the First Lady, but after her mini-sentence the Third Lady straightaway chips in. She has no chance of acting independently, though she needs to be reliable. She should be pleasing in appearance because her part, though never prominent, is quite extensive.

THIRD LADY

Contralto. Deepest voice in a female trio. Subordinate only to the
Queen of the Night, certainly not to the First Lady.

in The Magic Flute

The Third Lady seems to be the most serious of the Three Ladies. She
tells Tamino who his liberators were. She encourages him: 'Zittre
nicht' ('be not afraid'). On the Queen's instruction she hands him the
portrait of Pamina, which he must have, if only because of the
'Bildnisarie' (portrait aria).

When she is just about to describe how Sarastro, in disguise,
abducted Pamina, the First Lady unfortunately interrupts her, otherwise we would know the whole story. Her contralto, on a flexible basis,
always imaginatively fills the acoustical space of the trio and serves as
its foundation.

LEPORELLO

Bass. Servant of Don Giovanni. Constantly wants to quit the service in which he has a lot to endure, but also a good deal of fun from time to time.

in *Don Giovanni*

There are only two arguments which this vulgar fellow finds difficult to answer: naked force and money. If his master uses curse or cudgel to make him commit a villainy or hold his tongue, Leporello obeys. If Don Giovanni opens his purse, Leporello will get on with the job.

Not that he lets his reluctance and resistance be overcome without a fuss, however. He boasts that, unlike Don Giovanni's female victims, he is not to be seduced with money. 'No, no, no, no, no, no, no, no, no, no, no, no!' He chants his 'no' as fiercely to Don Giovanni's face as his master will later hurl his 'NO' at that of the Commendatore. True, the servant's refusal to continue obeying his master is no more than an anticipatory parody of Don Giovanni's later portentous and irrevocable decision. And although Leporello's excited 'no' in G major allegro (duet no. 15 at the beginning of Act II) may be meant in earnest, yet the earnestness will not stand up to four doubloons: all right, just this once he will help out again, but it is, positively, the very last time, and so on.

So Leporello is dependent on his far from lavish master and on the latter's purse. Still, that does not automatically make him a mere shadow, a non-person, a negative reflection. Nor does his occasional air of being Don Giovanni's 'plebeian imitator' (Hans Mayer) reveal much about his individual character – or even whether he has any.

A dependant, he necessarily acts dependently, but he does not think like one. When he sees how his master behaves and how the women put up with it, he has harsh things to say. Don Giovanni strikes Leporello as a blackguard, a killer, a rapist, while Donna Elvira is off her head.

In confidence the servant calls his master a scoundrel. This suggests that, no matter how vile the actions which Leporello obediently performs, he still retains, or at least displays, a more conventional, more moral view of life than his master does. In the performance of his 'duty' he is coarse, but not completely hardened. In the final scene Don Giovanni's behaviour is too extreme in every way for the mortally frightened Leporello. The audience may well be surprised to notice that he even pities Donna Elvira. A few scenes earlier, in the guise of Don Giovanni, he had held the lady, afire with love, in an embrace ('This jest is not unpleasing', he remarked). Now his reaction is humane and compassionate. No touch of irony spoils his 'The woman brings me close to tears'. What he means is: 'If her suffering does not move my master, he has a heart of stone or none at all!'.

Since Leporello has to conspire with Don Giovanni in joint operations (the master needs his servant), they inevitably become accomplices. It speaks either for Don Giovanni's easy-going tolerance (arising from indifference) or for Leporello's courage as an accessory (arising from sulky defiance), or for both, that Leporello is not content simply to mimic Don Giovanni, but mimics him ironically, even allowing himself a teasing word-play with his master's name. 'O Leporello mio, va tutto bene!' ('O my dear Leporello, all is going well'), says Don Giovanni with wicked optimism. 'Don Giovannino mio, va tutto male!' ('my dear Giovannino, all is going badly'), replies Leporello in a flash, using for his master's name a (hopefully) endearing diminutive. He is just as capable of that as of the ironic repetition of Don Giovanni's 'Bravo, bravo, 'pon my conscience'.

He is hardly a strong, intrepid character, but he is a tough one. In a rebellious mood he may let himself be put down, but he quickly returns to the charge. He always bounces back. Humiliations and dangers may rain down on his head, causing him to tremble and moan, but neither cunning nor his gift for observation ever abandon him. When the vengeful visitant from hell drives him, terrified, howling, teeth chattering, under a table, that is more natural than Don Giovanni's courage. Only exceptional individuals stand the test of exceptional situations.

In a truly dangerous situation, albeit not one ablaze with supernatural flames, Leporello shows the fibre he is made of. His position is anything but enviable. His disgraceful masquerade has come to light, and since Don Giovanni is out of reach, the reprobate's pursuers compensate by venting their rage violently upon his servant. There is nothing for it but to abase himself and plead for mercy with knocking knees in aria no. 20 when, the sextet over, his treacherous conduct has become obvious and awful punishment approaches. 'Let us slay him, we three, at once', suggests Masetto.

Mercy, mercy, he implores, a musical picture of wildly whining woe. Only for twenty bars, though, because suddenly there awaken in him, at first just for a moment, then more and more vigorously, his animal spirits, his animal will to live. For he has Donna Elvira (grievously affronted, God knows) as an alibi to prove that it cannot have been he who thrashed Masetto; and while he is still producing this alibi, though it scarcely makes him innocent, he senses a possibility of escape. The orchestra intimates as much. Sparkling and sprightly violin passages tell the audience of his resurrected will to live. Trills among the violas, like impish jokes, emphasize the development. Eventually he reaches the door on which he has had his eye for so long, and off he goes.

Does this puppet bass really bear such a close resemblance to Don Giovanni, the cavalier baritone? Attila Csampai writes:

> As square pegs in round holes, as outsiders, they are chained to one another. Leporello is the common man's Don Giovanni just as Giovanni could be called the Leporello, the one who opts out, among the aristocrats. The close relationship between them has undoubtedly redounded to Leporello's advantage.[18]

'Redounded to his advantage'? Csampai takes that line because his loyalty to Don Giovanni leads him to conclude that for Leporello there can be no other 'such straightforwardly human' master as Don Giovanni.[19]

Da Ponte and Mozart, however, present Leporello as constantly whining and grousing about 'that scoundrel'; not that this prevents him indulging in a certain camaraderie, looking around for ladies, and conscientiously keeping the tally of his master's conquests. During their joint operations Mozart underlines Don Giovanni's sovereign courage (which seldom wavers, and then only briefly) by letting Leporello always appear in a comic light as the more afraid. He talks faster, more tremulously and more breathlessly. The extent of his devoted collaboration is fairly limited. At the beginning, with Donna Anna on Don Giovanni's heels, he still feels allegiance – 'Il padron in nuovi guai' ('master's in a mess again'). When the situation becomes more precarious, he is his own best friend – 'In the end I shall be the one who will pay for his skulduggery'. He gets a severe fright, and, both then and a little later, upbraids his employer accordingly. Thus he is distinctly timorous, although a number of his master's adventures leave a few pickings for the subordinate. He has quickly learned to assure young women of his 'protection'. After declaring that he is tired of escapades, a minute later he cannot but laugh heartily at how easy women are to deceive. He even ventures, though in a mask, to flirt demonstratively with Donna Elvira.

How does all this fit together? Da Ponte affords no psychological explanation, but Mozart delivers a musical one. The fast, though not unduly terrified, quavers which convey his fear and which distinguish Leporello from Don Giovanni, change swiftly from rapid babbling to cheerful chatter that shows that Leporello has recovered his spirits.

Leporello neither conceals nor suppresses his thoughts, unless he is brusquely muzzled. Should that happen, his is at any rate not the mulish repression which we see in that other dependant, Masetto. Right in the introduction, where he is seen keeping a look-out, his discontented soliloquy contains the most violent reproaches against his master (in whose shoes he would like to be). He does not, though, do it only in unalloyed molto allegro F major, but in a tone of sprightly heartiness. His gamut is wide-ranging, far greater than in any half-stifled, miserable monologue, and his 'no, no, no, non voglio servir' has about it something of familiar *opera buffa* patter – even here, in the middle of the night, on the verge of catastrophic events.

Leporello is robust, agile, not particularly complex, and his anger and indeed his fear, even when deeply felt, are remarkably akin to the merry, often ironic garrulity which he manages so well. Irony, in its coarse form, stripped of all subtlety, is often a safety valve for dependants who have independent trains of thought. In addition to all this, Leporello has something of the clown, Papageno and Merry Andrew, the *buffo* who informs the audience of his troubles when he is at his wits' end to know how to deal with his master: 'I must at all costs abandon for ever this fine madman! There he is, and look with what indifference he steps along.'

It is not just funny when this puppet, at times so violently maltreated by Don Giovanni, keeps getting caught in his parlando gabblings. What repulsive, class-conscious effrontery does Don Giovanni display when he describes how he has just snared one of Leporello's sweethearts. 'But suppose that this woman had been my wife?', says Leporello, disconcerted. Don Giovanni, laughing very loudly: 'Even better!'. Faced with such shamelessness Heaven is simply bound to intervene, and it does so in the next bar.

His jabbering does not even leave him – and this is humour on a

Shakespearian scale – when, at the fastest possible pace, he says that he cannot say anything (because he is still completely stunned by the shock of Don Giovanni's descent to hell). On one occasion the orchestra is called upon to join in and to embellish Leporello's frivolous, uncontrolled volubility. In the A major trio, intended gently and irresistibly to tell of the suitor's wooing, he blathers rapturously about the mean comedy of the situation: 'If you don't stop, I shall start laughing, laughing, laughing, laughing, laughing, laughing, laughing, laughing, laughing, laughing'. Mozart's woodwinds wrap this daft hilarity in their modulatory aura to prevent it from spoiling the scene and damaging the power of the music.

During the cemetery duet Leporello's babbling – an expression of shock and quivering fear – points up a dramatic contrast. The orchestra enriches the interludes by progressive variation. The contrast is between Leporello's calmly composed invitation formula 'O statua gentilissima' ('O statue so fine and so handsome') and his trembling 'non posso terminar' ('I don't think I can finish') to Don Giovanni. Don Giovanni's behaviour now becomes fairly repugnant. He threatens his servant with his sword, forces him to address the statue, and is obviously inspired by the sadistic wish to make him shudder. Finally, though, the scare caused by the statue's acceptance induces both Don Giovanni and Leporello to react, for a few bars, with the same frozen terror, followed by Leporello's customary babbling, to the effect that they must leave this spot.

Leporello is a realistic *buffo*, incapable of learning from bitter experience not to remonstrate and not to say too much. He unsentimentally delivers girls into his master's hands, records his successes like an efficient bureaucrat, yet is not quite happy with his function, even if he fares quite well when his master is not being odious or domineering.

'Let him go', is Leporello's humanitarian advice to the agitated Donna Elvira, 'he merits not another thought on your part', whereupon he pulls out his little book and the audience settles down to enjoy the 'Catalogue' aria. Sparkling with wit, spiteful glee and cruel operatic brilliance, this aria, if one listens carefully, evolves in a curious way. Leporello begins in something of a recitative parlando manner, with numerous tone repetitions and a suggestion of a litany. The wit, the sparkle, the wicked glee are long held in check until the mention of the 'mille e tre' ('one thousand and three') Spanish ladies, entirely to the orchestra, with the violins sneering and the flutes, the bassoons, and the horns sniggering almost indecently.

Evidently it takes some time for Leporello himself to get into the spiteful mood that has already been displayed by the orchestra and before he effectively joins in the passages of ninths. His slow ending, 'You know full well what he'll do', has by then become neither critical nor ironic nor spiteful. It is a pure, syncopated D major: possibly a symbol of Don Giovanni's universal amorousness. Nor is it Leporello, harbinger of Don Giovanni's treachery, against whom the stricken Donna Elvira bears a grudge, but the reprobate himself. As for Leporello, let us hope that he will eventually find what he wants, a better master. After all, what good did Don Giovanni's 'straightforward humanity' ever do him, seeing that he usually had to put up with its darker, more egocentric side?

MARCELLINA

Contralto. Housekeeper and lady-in-waiting in Count Almaviva's castle and once a domestic in Dr Bartolo's household. Made Figaro a loan which he acknowledged in writing together with a promise of marriage if he should be unable to repay. The contract proves the main impediment to his union with Susanna.

in *The Marriage of Figaro*

At the outset Marcellina, an *opera buffa* type, is unmercifully made into a laughing-stock. She brandishes a marriage contract in the faces of passionate, sensitive people fighting to remove the obstacles to their love; where youth is what counts, she is told with spiteful glee that she is an old frump. 'My old domestic', whispers Dr Bartolo, who would happily see Figaro punished by having to marry her. In the jealousy duet Susanna is of course only too glad to mention Marcellina's advanced age and to deride her opponent as a 'doddering sibyl' and 'decrepit old governess' who pretends to great wisdom because she has read a couple of books. Although she suffers such ridicule, Marcellina's behaviour does not arouse our pity. It is she who at the last moment institutes with Bartolo an intrigue against Figaro, and it is she who in the duet with Susanna is the first to create mischief, so that she ends up being humiliated and failing to have the last word.

A miserable start indeed. Her only solo comes late, in Act IV, and is usually a little unwanted because it holds up the action. Her assertion that all women desire peace and are treated shabbily by men sounds too guilelessly innocent for her to gain any sympathy on her own account – except that a twist in the plot has already been produced by other means.

The creature who initially fusses around like a dignified governess scarcely seems to be human, let alone feminine, but simply to be a comic, derided *buffa* bogey. This impression is a caricature. Marcellina is not necessarily quite as the excited, biased Susanna sees her. Cherubino, for example, holds a somewhat different view; how else would he hit on the idea of wanting to include her in the list of those who can read his canzone? 'Read it', he says, 'to my lady, read it to Barbarina, to Marcellina, read it [with effervescent excitement] to every woman in the castle!'

Thus he counts Marcellina in. She 'belongs'. We can easily explain why she loves Figaro and tries by means of very inept blackmail to steer him into her matrimonial haven. (She is so unskilful that it is only on his wedding day that she makes use of Dr Bartolo's enmity.) Her behaviour is not an eccentric whim, but a distorted echo of the voice of nature. Though for three Acts no one knows it, she is Figaro's mother; he was stolen as a child, and Marcellina appears constantly to be on the brink of suspecting as much. She recognizes him – little Raphael – sooner at any rate than his father does. Her hysteria at the beginning can be read as the bewilderment of a mother who has no idea of this relationship with the man she loves.

From the moment that she knows the truth, Marcellina behaves inoffensively and reacts altogether sensibly. She tries to damp down Figaro's all too confident rage against Susanna and with warm friendliness takes sides on behalf of her prospective daughter-in-law, who is no longer her rival. Finally she is allowed to marry, if not her son Figaro, then at least his father.

MASETTO

Bass. Bridegroom of Zerlina. Neither a class-conscious peasant
nor an utter moron. Inhibited and uncontrollable when enraged.

in *Don Giovanni*

Masetto has enough wits to be able to work out pretty quickly on most
occasions what the game is and what sport is being had with him; but
he is not ingenious, powerful and imaginative enough always to be able
to forestall what he fears. Since his fury does not exactly make him
clairvoyant, it should be accounted bad luck rather than stupidity
when he is taken in by a carefully prepared comedy on the part of Don
Giovanni, masquerading as Leporello. How could he be a match for so
crafty an opponent, so used to disguises, duels and disputes? The
hiding he receives proves no more than that he is a young peasant and
not an old hand at cloak-and-dagger dramas. All the same he is no
simple, charming peasant lad, but from the outset a complex case of
inhibition, even though we should not make too much of the fact that at
his very first entrance he stands in Zerlina's shadow (his singing starts
after her, usually a third below). She is the livelier of the two, but that
means little; Masetto may have other virtues.

The trouble is that Masetto does not seem all that sure about his
good fortune in having Zerlina: he never sings or says that he loves her,
and his rage, his contrariness, his violent reluctance to leave his bride
alone with the domineering aristocrat confirm this conclusion.
Zerlina's wheedling sensuality turns his head, although he has a fair
idea of how shamelessly she could behave, and he admits this to himself
once, almost with embarrassment. Beguiled by her F major aria, he
mutters, 'See now how this witch enraptures me. Mental weakness is
our manly lot.' But he is wrong: it is not in the head that he is soft, for he
sees what is going on, but in the heart. As far as his conscious thoughts
are concerned, he seems neither a happy lover (the day's events hardly
give him cause to be) nor a confident bridegroom.

Whenever Masetto sings, he nearly always strikes the listener as strangely frustrated, skulking and self-conscious. He scarcely ever ventures on larger intervals, Leporello's staccato gabble, or Zerlina's boisterous frills. His tones mostly cling close together. In his aria (no. 6) he mutters through his clenched teeth his 'no, no, no, no, no, no, no, no'; compare that with Leporello's far looser, rebellious 'no, no, no, non voglio servir'. Both pieces are in F major and in fast allegro. But where Leporello requires for his overflowing and furious 'no' an interval of a tenth, blurting the syllables out briefly with pauses between, Masetto sticks doggedly, without the slightest pause for breath, to the smallest of intervals, a second.

There really is something 'strained' about the peasant lad. Is he secretly afraid that Zerlina's temperament will give him a hard time once they are married?

During their first encounter Masetto is not outwitted by Don Giovanni; he is forced to give way at sword's point. No wonder that he grinds out his 'Understood, Sir!' between his teeth, and that such a poor devil does not feel like a cantilena for his vengeance aria. This begins, logically enough, like the fierce aside of a helpless subordinate who has to hold himself back, but who certainly does not wish to connive opportunistically at events or submit to them like a coward. What he altogether lacks is a self-assured, happy medium. In his plight he knows only two extremes: a teeth-gnashing, frustrated, bald statement of the facts and an explosion of towering rage. When that happens, he is out to kill, scalp, massacre, a fate for which in his thirst for revenge he earmarks Leporello as well as Don Giovanni. The aria, though, does not continue as it starts. The ending pours ironic and unbridled derision on his bride: just believe the fine gentleman will make a noble lady of you – you're stupid enough to believe anything. . . .

Driven into a corner, Masetto gives voice literally, not merely by implication, to the apprehensions which he feels on his wedding day about his bride. Hitherto he had repressed his fears, but the wretched situation forces them into the open: 'Wanton traitress, you were always my undoing'. If his outburst were provoked only by immediate circumstances, why should he use the word 'always'?

Masetto whispers his way through the piece. He slinks through Don Giovanni's mansion and startles its owner by coming around corners at inappropriate moments. He behaves like a crafty conspirator; yet he is always the loser, at the mercy of one far mightier than he. The weaker of the two, he is constantly trying to prevent or to save something, but knows no other means than to be ironic, dogged, and gnash his teeth.

He does not let himself be shaken off, and what he has to swallow as bridegroom and lover makes his subsequent explosion all too intelligible. So it is really bad luck rather than his own fault that he remains a figure of fun: a man whose bride runs away on his wedding day gives people plenty to laugh about. And someone genuinely and resolutely determined on vengeance, who lets himself be fooled by the object of his revenge, hands over his weapons, and finally gets piteously thrashed, presents a picture of heartfelt misery which is pitifully comic rather than heroic.

As long as Masetto retains at least some of his vigour, he, the subordinate, who is neither a revolutionary nor a cowardly booby, renounces neither his claim nor his rage. He is no weakling, he is perfectly capable of throwing off Leporello, but he is no match for his bride's tempting and Don Giovanni's wiliness. At any rate he, and he alone, is allowed in the stretta of the Act I finale to sing the crucial deep bass line 'Trema, trema scellerato' ('tremble, tremble, vile seducer'). On his elemental force depends the vengeful glitter of the whole ensemble. He is neither nincompoop nor hero, but a character role.

MONOSTATOS

⌣

Tenor. A Moor. Pamina's jailer, loathed by his underlings.

in *The Magic Flute*

A Moor who feels love, though forbidden to do so? A brusquely rejected victim of the *Singspiel*'s naive racism? The clearest example of Schikaneder's black and white portraiture? His C major aria – 'the careering semiquavers underline the hasty, flurried character of the music' – almost lacking contour, without any minor key opacity, sounds like *opera buffa* gabble set in perpetual motion. 'Alles fühlt der Liebe Freuden, schäbelt, tändelt, herzt und küsst' ('all the world feels joy of love, bills, coos, hugs and kisses'). Then our sympathies are unmistakably focused on Monostatos himself: 'Und ich sollt' die Liebe meiden, weil ein Schwarzer hässlich ist!' ('And I should such love eschew, because a black man's ugly!').

Were this his only aria, the case would be simple. In the days when people thought nothing of cutting Schikaneder's dialogue, Monostatos got off lightly. It neither became clear what his underlings think of him, nor what a vindictive character he is, how sadistic he is when angry, how he fawns to Sarastro yet tries to blackmail the Queen of the Night. Or is this too vehement and puritanical a way of describing the characterization of a jovially lecherous Moor? He is no Shylock. He is not even Osmin, though he does share the latter's habit of spitefully mimicking the words of his victims.

To a large extent the 'evil' Monostatos adapts himself to the natural totality of *The Magic Flute*'s cosmos. He joins cheerfully, like the rest, in the dancing to the chimes and he praises wholeheartedly the love between man and women.

The *Singspiel* does not reproach him for wanting to 'have' the beautiful Pamina: 'attempted debauchery of subordinates' would not be the right judicial category. It is his other designs and deeds that reveal the blackness of his heart. At the outset, for example, he chains

Pamina up and tortures her until she faints, which so moves the attendant slaves that, out of pity for her, they can scarcely bear to watch. Or, as another example, when he catches Pamina and Papageno, he maliciously mimics their frightened quavers, 'nur geschwinde, nur geschwinde, nur geschwinde, nur geschwinde' ('Oh, but quickly'). He taunts his victims and calls for steel, irons, chains and ropes. Of course, Papageno's chimes are of help and in a moment the two captives are laughing again, while Monostatos, still enchanted by the chimes, prances away. But soon he is back, having grabbed Tamino, and now he becomes furious with the Prince's 'impudence' in embracing Pamina.

The seventy-seven bastinado strokes to which Sarastro condemns him would not be inflicted on an innocent victim. Later we find him, although unpunished, still on the prowl after Pamina. As he steals towards her she is asleep, and he sings the aria which has had less effect on audiences than on certain musicologists.

Here Mozart composed one of his most peculiar dramatic characterizations. It has no wild outbursts in the style of Osmin, but remains largely in pianissimo, only the middle section producing a twofold mezzo-forte piano accent. Against this background is deployed a sensual glitter and tingle that causes the listener's blood to run faster through his veins and his nerves to quiver.[20]

(Well, if Hermann Abert is thrown into such excitement by this aria, what happens to such an inflammable professor in *Tristan*?) Having proclaimed his intentions clearly, Monostatos approaches 'slowly and softly', but now Pamina's mother comes between him and his intended victim and incites her to kill Sarastro.

Having overheard the planning of the 'murder', Monostatos uses his information to put Pamina under duress. 'You have but one way to save yourself and your mother.' 'What is that?' 'To love me.' What could be clearer? But as Pamina defies death and refuses to yield to compulsion, Monostatos is just raising his dagger when Sarastro intervenes – and lets him run away. Monostatos will join forces with the Queen of the Night.

He is a black-hearted villain, then, a comic lecher. The *Singspiel* reproaches him, not for pursuing Pamina, but for his choice of methods.

This characterization of Monostatos, as standing for the duskiness in a black and white world, could suffice if it were not for a mysterious stage direction preceding his C major aria: 'Everything is sung and played piano as though the music were far off'. What does this mean?

How can it be interpreted? To Rainer Riehn it presents no difficulty. The direction indicates that 'this scene is not real. It is not actually Monostatos who sings this aria, but as we know that Pamina is asleep, what we hear is her desires, projected on to Monostatos.'[21] So Pamina, the 'prude', has a subconscious (a pretty masochistic one after all the torments he has inflicted on her) which longs for Monostatos' embrace. Can one really infer all this from the direction 'as though the music were far off'? Considering how openly Pamina reacts to Papageno's desire for love and how unconditionally she loves Tamino, there is really nothing to support Riehn's fantastic interpretation.

All the same, why 'far off'? It could be a metaphor for caution, so as not to awaken the sleeping girl. It might then be a dream on the part of Monostatos, able to imagine the equal union of black and white only as a distant ideal.

This interpretation may seem a little far-fetched too, but is it entirely unacceptable? From where – this is a notion that Götz Friedrich tried to follow up in the 1960–61 edition of the *Jahrbuch der Komischen Oper*[22] – did Monostatos come before joining the initiates? How did he gain the confidence of Sarastro, who made him jailer of a 'delightful' young girl? Friedrich quotes Walter Felsenstein, who suspected Monostatos of having been 'a Nubian prince'. Having joined the initiates, he first appeared trustworthy, but then, under sexual pressure, turned into a villain.

'Lieber guter Mond vergebe, eine Weisse nahm mich ein' ('beloved moon, so good, forgive, a white girl has my heart'). For Monostatos to ask the moon's forgiveness because he has fallen in love with a white girl is less an intimation of unscrupulousness than of a conscience vanquished. And since he does not state his obvious intentions with clamorous drollery, but quite softly, as from far off, in a restrained or even inhibited tone, we may conclude that Monostatos is neither a naive comic figure nor a deeply depraved character, but a human being somewhere between these extremes.

OSMIN

Bass. Overseer on the country estate of Pasha Selim. Boorish and conscientious. Dreams of sadistic punishments for culprits caught in the act. His weakness is that he loves Blondie, but despite his strong-arm tactics he cannot handle the young woman. In Act III he foils the abduction. The outcome is however a happy ending, not the penal tribunal of his hopes, and he retires in a towering rage.

in The Abduction

Osmin takes his profession as overseer of Pasha Selim's harem with exemplary seriousness. His xenophobia would be hard to match. Europeans whom his master has in his employ are no exception; in the case of Pedrillo jealousy is also at work, because Osmin loves his girlfriend Blondie. At his first encounter with Belmonte, who is apparently on a harmless visit to the estate and is introduced as an architect, he chases him away too. A sadist would relish the number of times Osmin talks about bastinados, whippings, tortures, and the varieties of horrid death which he would have imposed long ago if he had had his way.

Osmin's seething distrust is not entirely misplaced, however. Belmonte does want to 'steal pretty girls', as Osmin, with bitter derision, tells him to his face at their very first encounter. And he sees through the Pedrillo-Belmonte connection: 'I don't need to look twice to see that he is one of your gang and that you have cooked it up between you to outwit us', he flares up at Pedrillo. He may be unfriendly, but he is not far wrong; and he also has a highly delicate nose for scenting abduction plots. His ill-humoured intimation that Pasha Selim, 'soft as butter', lacks thoroughness in dealing with them is, as the humane ending to the *Singspiel* proves, fully justified. 'Ich hab' auch Verstand' ('I am clever too'), his initial aria (no. 3) lets him confidently proclaim, and the oboes, first in unison, then in assertive thirds, giggle their confirmation.

Watchful suspicion, choleric xenophobia, fanatical faith in Draconian punishments, and a complete failure to understand the rights of women – these are the main features of this comic villain, a by no means harmless character who fortunately has his weaknesses. He likes to invoke Allah resonantly, but sometimes he exercises a certain latitude in interpreting the Prophet's ban on alcohol. He may be as strong as an ox and ready to have people whipped at a moment's notice, but where Blondie is concerned he himself fears blows, and she even threatens to scratch his eyes out if he lays a finger on her.

If there were nothing more to Osmin, he would be an amusing, transparent personality whom we would soon tire of. But he has some additional facets which are not easy to interpret.

He makes his entrance, he sings three verses of a sad song and he thereby unexpectedly poses a riddle. The song's text tells how a lover must always, particularly on moonlit nights, keep meticulous watch on his sweetheart: 'Oft lauscht da ein junges Herrchen, kirrt und lockt das kleine Närrchen' ('oft another little gander waits, lures and tempts the little goose with baits'). It is as though he had a presentiment of the abduction, though it has not yet got off the ground.

Anyhow, the portly Osmin takes pleasure in singing at his work. Understandably enough, he is unwilling to be interrupted by an inquisitive stranger. It is hardly remarkable that the verses of such a folk-song should end in a difference of accent: 'Trallaléra ... trallálera', with very subtle rhythmic differentiation, the whole in G minor. Osmin, however, does not merely declaim the verses with a characteristically varied accompaniment. Each time he reaches 'trallalera', this high-strung ending becomes more dissonant, more richly harmonized. At the close of the last verse the violins, till now in conformity with the melody, soar in an astringent contrary motion. A bombastic gesture in a minor key, and an 'exotic' minor at that. In the rage of 'dann Treue, gute Nacht' ('then loyal love good night'), which still resounds in the 'trallalera', the convention of the strophic song is wittily and brilliantly consummated and burst asunder at the same time.

What has this wealth of idiom to do with the song and with Osmin? Bernhard Paumgartner hears in it the 'demonic element in this bearish monster', overflowing with 'sultry sensuality'. Hermann Abert thinks that 'there is something sultry, uncanny in the lumbering chant . . . and finally the colossal upswing into the 'trallalera' where suddenly the fellow's fanatical viciousness erupts with elemental force'. Can a chromatically intensified G minor be interpreted like this? On 26 September 1781 Mozart wrote: 'in the original libretto Osmin has only this short song and nothing else to sing, except in the trio and the finale'.[23] On 13 October, also in a letter to his father, he said, 'Now as to the libretto of the opera . . . still, the poetry is perfectly in keeping with the character of stupid, surly, malicious Osmin. I am well aware that the verse is not of the best, but it fitted in and agreed so well with the ideas which were already buzzing in my head, that it could not fail to please me.'[24]

The two passages help to solve the Osmin riddle. Mozart admittedly merely speaks of the 'short song' and calls Osmin simply 'stupid, surly, malicious'. Yet does he not likewise say that the notions he employs were earlier already buzzing in his head, i.e. before he received the libretto? This could explain what makes Osmin so fascinating – his latent superabundance of musical energy, variety and profusion. Mozart had 'already' had these inspirations, but he now assigned them to the overseer in whose character comic stupidity merges with musical variety, producing the brilliance rather than the banality of evil.

Mozart was in a generous mood when he characterized this fellow with such grandiose vitality. Much of it has a directly comic effect – the cumulative fury behind the prolonged tones of 'Solche hergelauf'ne Laffen' ('such vagrant worthless jackanapes') which suddenly breaks into passages, the pigheaded but profound anger that is conveyed by the seconds rubbing up against each other in 'uns auf den Dienst zu passen' ('to spy upon our duties'). This musical characterization makes an immediate impact. Here is a fanatical character, heavily built and yet enormously agile too, devout and yet thoroughly prepared to do mischief, cunningly watchful and yet (almost) succumbing to a sleeping pill, fundamentally honest and yet not wholly wedded to the truth.

Moreover, there is that wealth, that superabundance which has no simple psychological solution unless one reinterprets all Osmin's characteristics as rigidly and reductively as those exegetists who promptly detected in the beautiful, expressive ending of his song a love mired in 'crude concupiscence and carnality'.

At one particular moment – in the vengeance aria 'Ha, wie will ich triumphieren' ('ah, how shall I be exultant') – the Osmin composition becomes almost mystical. 'Schleicht nur säuberlich und leise, ihr verdammten Haremsmäuse, unser Ohr entdeckt euch schon' ('slink on tiptoe, softly, softly, wretched harem mice too crafty, but my ear shall hear you yet'). About the setting of 'unser Ohr entdeckt euch schon' there is nothing to hold the attention. But in 'Schleicht nur säuberlich und leise', especially on its repetition when the octave motif, as though in *stretto*, first makes its appearance in the orchestra, the lofty musical inspiration leaves the naive text far behind. It is an inspiration which could well have its place in Mozart's Mass in C Minor, K. 427, or issue from Sarastro's mouth. Yet here it is Osmin singing; and that is part of his mystery, and of the superabundance vested in him.

To try to separate out the music that simply portrays Osmin's character and the music that serves a further purpose would not just be pedantic and psychologically over-ingenious; it would be downright wrong. Osmin has something which may not seem appropriate to him at first glance. His vitality cannot be fitted into any facile theory or convenient set of adjectives. It includes, triumphantly, an excess of revenge-fantasies which gush from him to the point of absurdity (e.g. in the sequence 'first beheaded, then strung up'), and an excess both of mulish xenophobia and of clumsy, helpless infatuation which is plainly expressed in his soliloquy ('Poison and poniards on the girl! By Muhammad, she drives me mad. And yet I love the rogue').

Osmin, who seems to be getting on in years, cannot cope with his constitution. He suffers from an explosive temper, especially when affairs fail to take the direction which his rough-and-ready sense of justice demands. However, when he wants to make an impression with well-chosen phrases, he produces expressive quasi-leitmotifs of an appropriately serious, bass-like nature. Slow tonal sequences eliciting respect, such as 'bis du zu gehorchen mir schwörst' ('until to obey me you swear') to Blondie, 'Das heiss ich, dass heiss ich gewagt' ('that I call, that I call daring') to Pedrillo in the adagio portion of the drinking duet, or 'Denn nun hab ich von euch Ruh'' ('for now I am rid of you') in the vengeance aria.

His intemperate excess of energy mars the *Singspiel*'s closing reconciliation. The successful overseer is so appalled by the generosity of his master, who gives the Christians (including his beloved Blondie) their freedom, that he refuses to accept gracefully that things have gone wrong for him. In the *Singspiel*, music forms the essential link between the individuals who love or afflict one another. In the finale they are united in a blissfully happy ending. Osmin, though, wants to have no part in the reconciliation, and spoils the harmony by running off, cursing. Could it be that, well beyond the *Singspiel* confines, he is not so far removed from the pedantically vengeful Jew Shylock, who, ruined by a Christian court, took his leave early, alone and in despair? Or Beckmesser who, in *The Mastersingers*, unable to bear the finale jubilation at his exposure, hastily retires and leaves the rest to rejoice all the merrier after his sacrifice?' Osmin's excess of temperament invites speculation.

DON OTTAVIO

Tenor. Engaged to Donna Anna. Sincerely in love, he tries to soothe his fiancée's distress, and relies on good sense to heal her trauma. Mozart's music seems to treat him (and make him behave) somewhat differently from the rest of the dramatis personae.

in *Don Giovanni*

'Passion', wrote Arnold Schönberg in 1914 to Hermann Scherchen, 'is something that everyone is capable of. But sincerity, the chastely higher form of feeling, seems denied to most. This is fairly understandable, for the sensation underlying it must be genuinely felt and not simply exhibited. That is why all actors have passion, only very few sincerity.'[25]

In the world of *Don Giovanni* it is Don Ottavio who embodies the lustre and the limitations of sincerity. His love is sincere. Nothing is more important to him than his fiancée's happiness and peace of mind: Donna Anna's distress and agitation cause him pain. When Schönberg defined sincerity, he praised it as the 'chastely' higher form of feeling ('chastity' does not signify lack of sensuality). That is why, surrounded by sensual, impulsive, vengeful and eccentric personalities, Don Ottavio seems too restrained, too admirably mild. He is all too lacking in uncompromising passion. If his noble sincerity of feeling happens to be expressed with a touch less strength and intensity than Mozart intended, Don Ottavio will come across, not only as an individual with positive and negative qualities, but as a dry pedantic character who seems comically out of place amid such torrid action. Among psychopaths the rational man looks silly.

But doesn't Don Ottavio's unalloyed sincerity demand as much courage as ecstatic passion? This enlightened eighteenth-century gentleman who tries to think for himself deserves far more respect than a merely spiritless pedant.

His first solo comes after scenes in which he has had little

131

opportunity for emphasizing his own character because the others have been more distressed and more dynamic. Donna Anna is almost out of her senses, and Don Ottavio's main concern is therefore to help her recover her peace of mind. That, very naturally, means even more to him than investigating the assault on her, though, like a rationalistic detective, he still proposes to do so. His initial aria (added by Mozart for the Vienna production) sets a pure nobility of utterance to consummately pure music. (To make him 'sophisticated' would have been too easy.) It is a plea, almost a prayer, for the tranquillity of a human, no, two human souls. 'Dalla sua pace, la mia dipende' ('on her peace and pleasure is all mine dependent, what commands her gladness is the breath of life to me, that which pains her stabs deep into my heart').

Before Don Ottavio utters this virtually static miracle in G major, most of the action has been fast and furious – the assault on Donna Anna, her father's mortal duel with Don Giovanni, her terrible mental anguish, Don Ottavio's shock at her failure to recognize him, succeeded by clamour for revenge, the meeting with the allegedly demented Donna Elvira, the encounter with Don Giovanni. And finally there is Donna Anna's intuitive flash of recognition – Don Giovanni was the criminal! – which is divulged in her tremendous recitative and aria, crowned by infallible certainty, to the accompaniment of much tremolo and a trance-like D major instrumentation.

After so much hustle and bustle this is the first time that we find Don Ottavio alone. For a fleeting moment it seems as though everything has been brought to a standstill – time, the drama, the alternation of compulsive hunting and unavoidable vengeance. A man of intense sincerity realizes that his own life is worth living only if his beloved believes hers to be so too. There is no motion in the orchestra. A static G major sound, a string chord in half notes, a slow andante. Don Ottavio's melody resembles a pure G major soliloquy. Perfect fifth, third, tonic; then sixth and perfect fourth. At the start there is no discord or friction that could mar the annunciation of peacefulness. Don Ottavio makes use of the simplest sounds, the bedrock of music.

The effect could be banal. But Mozart composed the simplicity, the ethereal equilibrium of the first five bars with a magical touch. The first soft and simple dissonance, the plain dominant seventh in the sixth bar, becomes almost lovelier. After what has gone before, this delicate tension conveys the riches of a tender soul. Woe to the singer who, failing to sense this, fancies that not much is happening, and rushes heedlessly over hallowed ground. We are permitted to overhear a prayer for peace of mind. After all that has occurred and that has resounded, here is an oasis, an island of tranquillity, sought and imagined in all sincerity.

That is what Don Ottavio's G major aria stands for. Not that Donna Anna's betrothed remains unaffected and impassive in the face of preceding events. When he recalls her suffering, her rage and her tears, his aria shifts to a minor, although so to speak regular, key (G minor in a G major aria). Although this is intelligible and predictable, the next development comes unexpectedly. Not only is Don Ottavio's entire sympathy engaged, but as well as being sad and concerned he seems bewildered. On reaching 'E non ho bene, s'ella non l'ha ('I call not my own what she does not have'), something strange supervenes. The music 'flounders . . . away from its key, improvises an enharmonic change, and lands in B minor' (Oswald Jonas) as if his tormenting unrest had thrown even this rational-minded man off course.[26]

His other big aria, which seems so gracefully buoyant, urging the others to look after the exhausted Donna Anna while he makes arrangements for Don Giovanni's apprehension, likewise evinces despite its andante coloraturas and the decisiveness of its dotted notes, a temperament which is peaceable, restrained, gentle, rather than forceful and strong-willed. The difficult coloraturas in bars 43–8 of 'Il mio tesoro', astoundingly but characteristically, form a ritardando. In this aria, which is intended to make a strong impression but must never be allowed to degenerate into mere *bravura*, the brilliance gradually becomes lyrical and soothing. Only the quasi-heroic aria ending – with Don Ottavio swearing to return with tidings of bloodshed and death – shows that for him, once all doubts are resolved, 'essentials' do exist. He is sincere, he feels sincerely, but he does not make sincerity into a comfortable cult that would spare him any exertion.

Why is it then that the role of this sincere, modest and devoted personality, far from being popular, is generally regarded as that of a slight, tame figure overshadowed by Don Giovanni?

During the course of the opera Don Ottavio suffers a series of rebuffs arising either from the plot or from the character of his partner. He cannot help the former, and he should not be blamed for the latter. His very first entrance, with drawn sword and a noble declaration of his readiness to stand by the Commendatore and send the villain packing, is as valiant as it is futile. He is marvellously ready for battle, but he turns up much too late. We know all that has happened in the meantime, but he does not. His immensely well-meant offer of aid seems a trifle superfluous. Is that his fault? He himself is not ridiculous, but the situation makes him so.

Mozartian heroes can suffer set-backs (we need only recall the reversals sustained by Don Giovanni, Count Almaviva, and many another) without deserving to be written off as weaklings. Don Giovanni loses his temper and curses. Count Almaviva is equally reluctant to reconcile himself to mere facts.

Does Don Ottavio strike onlookers as feeble because, instead of cursing, he pleads sensibly and lovingly? Perhaps he takes his quietly conciliatory patience to excess. If so, it is because he realizes that Donna Anna can barely recover a hold on herself, let alone act with due deliberation. How distressed he must be when Donna Anna, recovering from her faint, believes him to be the ruffian who has murdered her father. This twist in the plot, though, is meant to convey Donna Anna's mental state, not to show that Don Ottavio's personality is so nondescript as to be interchangeable. In the first frenzied D minor duet, just after Donna Anna and Don Ottavio find the Commendatore lying in his own blood, it is the despairing Donna Anna who sets the tone. Don Ottavio, however, contributes a single, highly moving theme: 'Leave, beloved, the bitter memory. Friend and father alike I now shall be.'

This theme is glowingly replete with love, concern and longing, certainly not an expression of weakness, and entirely consonant with his noble character. It is most unfair of Donna Anna to force him so ostentatiously to swear vengeance when he has already shown that he was and is ready for anything. Although he feels himself as friend and father alike, he takes the oath, not just superficially, but in chromatic sequence. He swears 'by your eyes', 'by our love'. The latter phrase repeats the former's sequence half a tone higher, something that also happens in *The Abduction* when Belmonte pushes his initial questions to Osmin a tonal degree higher to intimate urgency, or when Lohengrin repeats his 'Nie sollst du mich befragen' ('never shall you ask of me') first in A flat minor and then, more harshly, more surprisingly, in A minor.

What makes Don Ottavio seem feeble is a quality more appropriate to reality than to the operatic stage – his modest, restrained, entirely unironic good sense which dictates that he should investigate matters before jumping to conclusions. Another likeable characteristic is his desire always to assume the best about others and to try to make the best of his and others' troubles. When Don Giovanni declares Donna Elvira to be mad, it is he, not Donna Anna, who resolves in an aside during the quartet, 'I shall not go from here till this business I can clear'. He has no prejudices: he wants to clear matters up in a rational way. Then he has to cope with Donna Anna's monstrous tale and accusation. First appalled, then relieved, he deliberates, 'How can I ever believe a gentleman to be capable of so gruesome a crime? To unveil the truth, I shall use all my means.' And his conclusion is, 'I must undeceive or avenge her'.

Thus even at this stage, after the fiery dramatic recitative and Donna Anna's tumultuous D major aria, Don Ottavio's reactions are not spontaneous or thoughtless, but sensible. Even here he admits that his fiancée may be mistaken, in which case the truth must be explained to her, or else in the right, in which case Don Giovanni must indeed be done away with.

During this recitative he is alone. If Donna Anna were present to hear him pondering so soberly whether she is right or wrong, his investigatory, 'enlightened' attitude would make sense, but nevertheless be hurtful. A man of feeling cannot counter the passionate emotional outburst of his betrothed with such cool argument. His G major aria on the heels of the recitative shows that it is her peace of mind which he has at heart. All the same, while a detective's caution may be justifiable in logical terms, his rational circumspection at this precise moment is difficult to commend as a wise psychological response.

Where suffering and emotions are involved, lack of spontaneity can be a weakness. Don Ottavio does not recognize until the tenth scene of Act II that 'after all these enormities I can no longer doubt that Don Giovanni is the pitiless murderer', and this confirms that his cautious, rational behaviour does make him rather slow off the mark.

He remains logical in the best sense to the very end when, in the sextet after Don Giovanni's death, he invokes Heaven as matchmaker: 'Now, O my beloved, that we are by Heaven avenged, extend to me fresh strength and let suffering no longer be my lot'.

The slight air of absurdity which sometimes encompasses Don Ottavio does not really result from the deficiencies of a chastely sincere character; it is more like the verdict which opera itself passes on figures whose purity of feeling is admirable, but who lack the vigour of direct emotional impact. For all their capacity for love, it is nearly always their good sense, hesitant rather than gripping, which comes to the fore.

PAMINA

Soprano. Daughter of the Queen of the Night. Kidnapped by
Sarastro in order to remove her from her mother's influence.

in *The Magic Flute*

'Do you no longer love me?' (Tamino sighs.) 'Pagageno, speak, tell me,
what ails my friend?' (Papageno has his mouth full, holds the food with
both hands, gestures to her to go away.) 'What? You too? Explain to me
at least the reason for your silence.' Papageno: 'Shhh!' (He makes signs
urging her to go.)

Yes, Pamina is the only 'positive' figure in *The Magic Flute* who does
not know what a game of tests is being played, with Tamino and
Papageno, at her, Pamina's, emotional expense! Tamino and
Papageno have had the reason for their heroic exertions well drummed
into them, but Pamina is faced with the inexplicable silence of her
beloved and his companion, whom she is fond of: 'du hast ein
gefühlvolles Herz, das sehe ich in jedem deiner Züge' ('you have a
feeling heart, all your features show it'). In beseeching Papageno to
explain the reason for their silence, she is implying both that it is wrong
to make her the victim of some ploy arranged among the men, and that
she herself must be to blame for having somehow caused them suddenly
to treat her in such a cold, stand-offish way.

Pamina, then, is the victim of ritual tests which she does not
understand. It is only after her suicide attempt that the Boys assure her
that the Prince still loves her, despite his unwelcoming behaviour.
Earlier, nobody felt under any obligation to let this young girl, this
young princess, know what was happening. Admittedly, the harshness
required by the plot was sustained more clearly in the dialogue scenes
than in musical numbers such as Pamina's trio, 'Soll ich dich Teurer
nicht mehr sehn?' ('dearest, shall I never see you more?'). For there
Sarastro replied: 'You will meet again in gladness!'. Tamino declared
his love, but did not account for his silence.

The initiates thus do not initiate both the lovers – only the male one. Women are not tested; but this puts Pamina to the worst possible test. For once she knows the purpose of the 'trials', she is every bit as brave as her lord and master – and shows more initiative in opening the singing.

Pamina is not only a victim of the tests that take place in Act II: even in Act I she is a victim, for she has been kidnapped as part of a power game whose meaning she has never learnt. After being taken from her mother and placed in the charge of a hideous guardian, she has been entrusted to a friendly rescuer who now suddenly turns cold towards her.

As the victim of plans that have been devised and agreed on without consulting her, she demands more compassion than any other character in *The Magic Flute*. She can call neither on Sarastro's power and fairy-tale omniscience, nor on Tamino's princely self-assurance and helpful magic flute. Nor does she share the vital egoism that always restores courage to Papageno, the other victim of the intrigue, who is likewise driven to make a suicide attempt which, for him at least, has nothing funny about it. Nor, finally, can Pamina sustain her spirits with the aid of her mother's furious fanaticism.

Pamina's touching sorrow certainly arouses our pity. Yet she is more than an innocent sacrificial lamb, attacked by the wicked wolves of this fairy-tale. She is more than a cry-baby who makes other people cry. She is interesting as well as touching, a human being as well as a victim – the only human being in *The Magic Flute*, perhaps? No, that would be less than fair to Papageno and the Prince. Let us call her the *most* human being in the opera.

In well-cast and intelligently directed performances of *The Magic Flute*, the Speaker and the Queen of the Night can be impressive, Papageno can dominate the stage and Tamino can provide the linchpin of the action. (The best such performances are not necessarily the most brilliant and professional ones: a dose of unaffected simplicity, even some good old-fashioned barnstorming, never does any harm.) But nine times out of ten Pamina is the central character, the one who calls forth the deepest response from the audience and the warmest plaudits from the reviewers; and that cannot be because she is a victim, for everyone knows that evil-doers are more interesting than losers. Well, what is the reason?

It is because Pamina's musical character is a living embodiment of exciting contradictions. She adapts herself lovingly to her various partners, and yet it is usually she who is the more active and decisive. She never speaks badly of her mother, but she suspects that Sarastro is something better than a kidnapper. To Papageno, whom she comforts sympathetically for his pangs of love, she proves a warm friend, but she reveals a princess's proper self-respect when she stands up to Monostatos' vile threats of rape and blackmail. Pamina knows that Sarastro, who kidnapped her, can be 'severe', and Tamino even fancies that she may already have been 'sacrificed'. She certainly thinks it possible that in Sarastro's domains fugitives may suffer an agonizing death in his name, even if not at his hands. 'The agonies of your death would know no limits', she informs Papageno, if the two of them should be caught by Sarastro as they try to flee.

This reveals the emotional and intellectual equipment of the 'timid doe in deadly terror', as the First Slave calls her. But the Third Slave tells us how ingenious she can be. When Monostatos almost had her in his clutches, 'in the moment when he was sure of victory, she uttered Sarastro's name; this terrified the Moor, and he stood stock still in silence . . .'.

So what she pronounced, in the utmost terror, was *not* the name of her much-loved, much-lauded mother, but that of the severe Sarastro! This happens in Act I, and Pamina accounts for it in Act II by explaining that her father thought very highly of the initiates, that Tamino merits love, and that 'Sarastro is no less virtuous'. Indeed, she identifies so closely with the powerful man who holds her captive against her will that she does not try to justify her escape attempt (which does not annoy Sarastro) as self-preservation, but sees her disobedience through the eyes of the person who issued the prohibition: 'Sir, I am indeed a criminal!'. She wants to tell the truth, 'even if it should be a crime'.

She is equally sympathetic to Papageno, who has been sent into the lion's den by the remarkably cautious Prince in order to announce his arrival – surely an excessive formality amid such desperate dangers. When he laments his lack of a girl-friend, Pamina adopts his simple diction to such an extent that, just after their escape from deadly peril, she and Papageno, who lives from moment to moment, laugh and sing the light but heartfelt couplet, 'Könnte jeder brave Mann solche Glöckchen finden . . .' ('if only all good men could find such bells . . .').

Pamina is therefore remarkable for her spontaneity, her ready sympathy, her warmth and her courage. A victim she may be, but far from being a passive female, she is the one who first expresses her feelings on meeting her beloved and thus provides the material developed in the motifs. It is she, too, who initiates the duet 'Bei Männern, welche Liebe fühlen' (men who know what 'tis to love') with Papageno, and finally, before revealing at the crucial moment that the magic flute was carved 'from the deepest root of the thousand-year-old oak', takes Tamino by the hand and sings 'I myself will lead you – love shall be my guide!'.

That shows how strong the trust is that she places in her feelings of love, and how little suited she is to become, as she does, the passive object of masculine rituals. Since her love is unreserved, she is defenceless against these rituals, and their artificial destinies bring her to the verge of madness.

All this can be gathered from the text. But to learn how intense and how deeply human Pamina's sufferings are, one has to listen to the music. Mozart not only encoded his fondness for Pamina's spirited affection in the duets and ensembles, but allowed her overwhelming pain two great solo moments – with a final moment for her overwhelming happiness. Her pain is conveyed in the G minor aria 'Ach ich fühl's' ('Ah, I feel it'), and her suicidal outburst in G minor, when she is close to madness. Her declaration that if Tamino does not love her, she will find peace only in death, has the emotional power we expect from such a spirited girl. Her wildly beating heart, the andante mixture of melody, chromaticism, and coloratura, the great jumps despite her slow pace ('peace in death' is an interval of an octave and a half, like falling into the depths of the grave) – all this amounts to an expressive miracle.

At the beginning of the G minor andante, the bassoon makes a quite inconspicuous contribution. It is not only an accompanying chord, but a hint of counterpoint (bar 4). This detail would scarcely be worth mentioning if the bassoon did not return at the height of Pamina's agony to enhance its expression. This occurs in the moment when she lifts the dagger against her own bosom. 'I can endure no more misery! False youth, fare thee well! You have caused Pamina's death! Let this dagger end my breath!' (about to stab herself). Here, once again, the unmistakable colouring of the bassoon, together with the cellos and double-basses, accompanies the melody as a living counterpoint. In the sphere of *The Magic Flute* this seems to indicate the utmost pain.

We know that Mozart had seen Schikaneder's production of *Hamlet*. Perhaps Schikaneder had Ophelia in mind when he created Pamina, not only because their misfortune drives both young women mad, but because they both suffer a twofold misfortune. Just as Ophelia has lost her beloved (her hope of becoming queen), and also her father, so Pamina is driven beyond endurance by the loss of Tamino's love and by her mother's curse.

Unspeakable misery is followed by unutterable happiness, as is usual in the extremes required by opera and *Singspiel*. Conductors and solo performers tend to worry too much in case something goes wrong in the difficult bits, the top notes, the fatally awkward passages, where every fool can hear every mistake. The transitional chords after 'ist würdig und wird eingeweiht' ('is worthy and will be admitted') – at the point where 'the door opens, Tamino and Pamina embrace' – are perhaps not all that difficult; they only need to sound completely sincere, blissful and pure. (Mozart also introduced them into the slow movement of his B major piano concerto K. 595, which was the last piano concerto he ever wrote.) The dialogue that follows must also be pure, sincere and blissful. 'Tamino's mine! O what happiness!'; 'Pamina's mine! O what happiness!'. The most brilliant singer who concentrates solely on the high notes will be put to shame if such moments lose any of their impact, just because they may not be quite so 'difficult'. They make *The Magic Flute* into a well-loved miracle. This andante dialogue, too, is initiated by none other than – Pamina.

PAPAGENA

Soprano. Papageno's amatory reward.

in *The Magic Flute*

This young lady really differs from Papageno only because of one small detail – the last letter of her name.

For the rest, it is a long time before we have any reason to see Papagena not just as a fairy-tale wish-fulfilment for poor Papageno, but as a human being. Papagena, Papageno's vision of a pleasant love-life, is finally permitted to assume flesh and blood. It is not a god but Papageno who utters her name. He feels like plucking out all his feathers when he thinks 'that Papageno still hasn't got a Papagena'. Later, this projection of his feminine counterpart is allowed to appear in bodily form, though only after Papageno has asked why there has to be such a fuss about tests and torments if 'the gods have sent him a Papagena' in any case.

Why should Papageno, of all people, be an expert on the problems of divine providence and human freedom? Anyhow, his simple but logical question causes the Second Priest some ill-concealed embarrassment: 'Your good sense can answer this inquisitive question'. That is a wholly inadequate and inappropriate reply. If there is one authority that cannot tell Papageno why he had to get mixed up in the adventures of *The Magic Flute*, then it is his good sense.

In order to keep Papageno's wish-fulfilment from being immediately recognizable as such, Papagena first appears disguised as an old woman leaning on a crutch. For lack of better alternatives, and to avoid worse, Papageno lets himself be constrained to a marriage vow. Now the old woman is transformed into a young one. He is, however, the Test Commission fears, 'not worthy as yet': only after his suicide attempt are no bounds imposed on union and procreation. The two withdraw into the seventh heaven. At the close of the festive finale, contrary to all comedy conventions, they have long since left the stage.

Their happy ending can undoubtedly do without any E flat major hymns.

All the same, is Papagena any more than a delightful female reflection of her Papageno?

When still dressed as an old crone, she backs away and demands pledges, she develops a personality. She has to say a few words which are necessary to bring Papageno to the brink. Admittedly she performs the task less of her own free will than as a servant of the test operation. Transformed into 'a young woman dressed just like Papageno', she says nothing more at all, only sings. And what does she sing? Not a solo; simply the duet with Papageno.

Now the character of Papageno comprehends a great deal, from benignity to mendacity, from cowardice to attempted suicide, from naivety to grumpy slyness, from loving procreative bliss to protest against ascetic 'principle'.

There is hardly anything of this in Papagena, except for one thing – she looks forward as keenly as does Papageno to child-begetting and parenthood. Otherwise, though, there is not one minor chord, an unclouded G major key prevails throughout, there are no chromatics, little modulation. Papagena's procreative bliss is radiant, sprightly, amusing, delightful. And even though one cannot help feeling that Papagena mirrors merely one of Papageno's many characteristics and reflects only his carefree G major good humour (his most rollicking rib, if you like), one must still take care to note the differences. Right to the end Papagena is presented as an 'item' in the frolicsome reward ritual: 'Now am I wholly given to you' (not 'Now I want you, now I have you'). But is it not she who intones the cantilena 'es ist das höchste der Gefühle' ('it is the highest of all feelings')? Is she not a good ten years younger than Papageno? No more than eighteen? And if she un-mistakably evolves into a personality on her own account isn't that because she has no personal history, no unhappy past, and is thus able to embody the pure idea of earthly, physical happiness and extort a blissful smile from the spectator? She could not be less problematic.

According to Egon Komorzinsky's great Schikaneder biography, the Austrian National Library at Vienna has a letter from Schikaneder to Mozart which runs as follows:

'Dear Wolfgang,
For the nonce I am returning to you your Pa Pa Pa which suits me pretty well and will fit the bill. This evening we shall be seeing each other at the – you know – Whites.

5.IX. 1790
Your
E. Schikaneder'[27]

This letter has been shown not to be genuine. But if the forgers wanted to show that Mozart must have composed *The Magic Flute*'s most serene number – i.e. the Papageno-Papagena duet – many months before the rest of the score, because above all he was anxious to extol humanity's harmony, then the 'forgery' contains a grain of truth; for *The Magic Flute*'s highest aim is the celebration, not the disparagement, of happiness.

PAPAGENO

Baritone. Bird-catcher who lives in the Queen of the Night's realm. Twenty-eight years old. He is forced to accompany Tamino as his man.

in The Magic Flute

A droll but difficult case, like so much that seems naive, comical and natural. Why do we laugh at Papageno? Because he is a 'child of nature' who is a tough customer, a distant cousin of Sancho Panza (Schikaneder is known to have read Cervantes' novel), and a descendant of Kasperl (the Punch of the Viennese popular theatre)? One could amass much scholarly material on this subject without provoking a smile.

Is Papageno's story really all that funny? He is scared at finding himself near a terrible, freshly killed snake. He does not claim actually to have slain the monster, but he does not mind being thought to have done so. When Tamino assumes that Papageno must have killed it, the latter does not bother to correct this mistake, but is so surprised and flattered that he encourages it. Far from breaking a lance for truth, he is pleased to be thought a hero for once, and to take advantage of his good fortune to indulge in some bragging and to wear some phoney laurels.

A short time later, however, we see him, in mute embarrassment, exposed as a liar. His punishment is disproportionately hard and harsh. He has to accompany the Prince as his man on a perilous mission and has to participate in a rescue operation and an awkward test, even though he has no desire for enlightenment or moral impulse to spur him on. He is consoled by the promise of Papagena, but plans suicide when his hopes seem doomed to disappointment. And all this because he diddled a little, because he is a kind of feudal inferior obliged to follow his master everywhere – in a word, is Papageno.

To look at events in a *Singspiel* in this way is to sentimentalize them too much. Is not Papageno, following ancient stage tradition, meant to be the coarsely realistic counterpart to the Prince's pure idealism? Does

144

he not embody the truth of earthy actuality as against the ethic of sublime self-sacrifice? Or is he too immediate a presence to be summed up in terms of abstract concepts?

In 1974, during the preparations for his great production at the Salzburg Festival which then unhappily proved such a failure, Giorgio Strehler ruminated intensively on the problem of interpreting Papageno. Was he a victim of exploitation? A materialist? An optimist who always bounces back? The symbol of the common man and his timeless virtues? Strehler considered all these possibilities, only to reject them. His conclusion, as tautologic as it is profound, was: 'Papageno is . . . Papageno'.

Papageno stands, in the clearest possible way, for the grace of physical existence which has been bestowed on mankind, in contrast to the tension and hysteria of the intellectual world with its systems and ideologies. While Tamino sighs and flutes, Papageno rejoices gratefully at Sarastro's 'good cooking'. He thinks (and we agree with him), that if one is privileged to be a guest in a four-star restaurant, one should do justice to the dishes as well as the drink ('wine divine!') and neither play the flute nor bewail one's fate. Who can tell what is yet to come? 'Long live the chef and the cellarer!'

Papageno's memory is short. He lives from moment to moment on a wearisome grand tour in which he fibs his way from one stage to the next, learning caution through experience, but not wisdom. The effect is that of elemental comedy and drama. Of course this spontaneous and quick-witted child of nature is just as easy to frighten as to cheer up. Present him with a set of chimes and he forgets his opposition to the detested journey, he is even prepared to be sent ahead by Tamino into the lion's den. Miraculously rescued from a dangerous plight, the next instant he is laughing again. Some slight bother to attain the longed-for wife and the would-be lover hurriedly gives up: 'bachelordom for me'. 'With such perpetual wandering the taste for love could well wear off entirely.' But later he wants to kill himself, because Cupid's dart has pierced him after all: 'Sterben macht der Lieb' ein End', wenn im Herzen noch so brennt' ('death is lovers' funeral pyre, though the heart may be on fire').

Papageno's unconscious, unaffected insistence on man's right to be afraid, to eat well, to be unheroic and to take things a little easy has an irresistible force. That is how exploited servant figures in every theatrical epoch, down to Bert Brecht's Matti, have wittily held their own and saved their skins. That is how peasants and city-dwellers alike have resisted their rulers' demands, not necessarily in the name of any social or proletarian ideology but, like Papageno, from a vague, plebeian sense that their basic human nature must survive all attempts to change it.

Of course, if we impose such a momentous historical destiny on poor Papageno, who derives directly from the Merry Andrew tradition of popular theatre in Vienna and Salzburg, we lose sight of what is peculiar to him. He may be everyman, but with some local colour. Lacking a past and a memory, he scarcely knows who his father was or where his mother is. Perhaps the birds' feathers worn by this 'animalistic' being are more than an oddity or a professional costume. Nowadays fowling is a more popular sport in Italy than in Austria or Germany. But one need only try to envisage Papageno as an Italian *buffo*, as a smart harlequin, to see that such a figure is Austrian through the through. His first entrance cries out for a great Austrian vernacular actor who gives the audience deep satisfaction by making himself at home on the stage and leaving it only occasionally and reluctantly for the rest of the evening. Although the individual Papageno is based on collective, popular strength, as a 'person' the bird-catcher is by no means intimidatingly strong. He is not even an enthusiastic liar. When Tamino thanks him for his courageous slaughter of the snake, his answer is evasive: 'Let's keep mum about that. Let's just be pleased that it's happily over and done with.' We can sympathize with his desire to send Tamino to the devil and to take his leave. He manifests this desire partly in asides, partly without a trace of irony, only to receive from the Three Ladies the pertly ironic answer, 'Dich empfehlen kannst du immer, doch bestimmt die Fürstin dich, mit dem Prinzen ohn' Verweilen nach Sarastros Burg zu eilen' ('your leave you can take any time, but the Queen appoints you now with the Prince to be without delay to Sarastro on your way').

For the rest Papageno identifies himself remarkably quickly with the wishes of his master. He says to Pamina that 'we' are here in order to tell her a thousand agreeable things and to fold her in 'our' arms. Later too he expresses a very masculine satisfaction at how effectively poor Pamina has been rebuffed: 'True, isn't it, Tamino, I can keep my mouth shut too, when necessary. – Yes, indeed, in such a case I am a man [he drinks].'

There is no tragic hauteur about him: he is an innocent, egotistic character with a sly resolve to survive. At first Papageno considers love not as attraction to an individual, but as a powerful impulse which only causes sorrow when it is unfulfilled. Nature and the initiates, however, are on his side. What at first seemed only a yearning projection of Papageno himself, his female image, is actually given him. Hence one can imagine the troubled heroes of *The Magic Flute* feeling just a tiny bit jealous when Papageno can freely look forward to enjoying the sublimest of sensations and diligently helping to propagate the species.

PEDRILLO

Tenor. Servant of Belmonte. In his capacity as a skilful gardener has managed to win the confidence of Pasha Selim, who holds him prisoner. Except during their joint drinking bouts, however, he has not been able to placate the instinctive hatred of Osmin, especially as the powerful overseer has an eye on Pedrillo's sweetheart, Blondie.

in The Abduction

He too would like to resemble the splendid heroes of *Singspiel* in their exultant readiness to defy death and to sacrifice themselves for others. But that would be too much to expect from this thoroughly sensible, cautious manservant with his serious attitude to dangers. When he has to risk his life, he is plain frightened.

As he is aware, this makes him look a little paltry, puny and small of soul in comparison to the enthusiasts. In his aria 'Frisch zum Kampfe! Frisch zum Streite!' ('Bold in action! Bold in combat!') we watch him virtually attempting to persuade himself to be brave. We even hear a trumpet when he tells himself that in a threatening situation he must not merely fight, but must do it 'boldly' and without hanging back. The top A, not to mention B, lustily bellowed, proves that he is doing his heroic tenor's utmost to convince himself. To quiver and quake might be natural, but cowardly and contemptible for all that. No less than eight times Pedrillo reflects 'Nur ein feiger Tropf verzagt' ('only craven fools despond') and at the end of his aria everything is theoretically clear – 'Bold in combat!'. Nevertheless, once the hour for action has come, his clarity of vision is again blurred. 'It's a silly business, valour. Who hasn't any won't achieve it, however hard he tries. How my heart pounds.' Is he a *buffo* who makes himself ridiculous?

And yet his lack of valour, his possession of what is commonly known as fear, does nothing whatever to prevent Pedrillo from assisting in the dangerous abduction operation, with a beating heart, but none the less coolly and punctually. Matters are not easy for him. He is neither well-off nor an enthusiastic 'absolutist'; his sweetheart is under pressure from the imperious overseer. If he were less crafty and hard-headed, he would be in a tight spot. As it is, he cleverly exploits the weakness of Pasha Selim for gardens and architecture, plying his green fingers to improve his position. Thus it occurs to him to introduce Belmonte as an architect, warning the enamoured young man not to imperil the liberation scheme through careless slips caused by emotional pressure.

People like Pedrillo have to have a wary eye for every petty advantage, they have to scrutinize reality closely, for all that that may appear very unmagnanimous, very *buffo*-like, very farcical among those who have no inhibitions. Pedrillo the realist likes to weigh up pros and cons, balancing profit and loss. We should not hold it against him that he praises wine at Blondie's expense when trying to get Osmin drunk: 'I prefer wine to money and girls . . . My bottle pulls no face at me as my girl does when she is not in the mood'. Let us hope that it is merely a tactical manoeuvre when he places 'wine on the tongue' above love and wedlock.

At a later stage he certainly goes a bit too far in his balanced reflections. Before the rescue operation he intimates to his sweetheart in pantomime that he is, after all, risking his neck and that he would feel cheated if Blondie had already succumbed to the amorous clutches of Osmin (whom he has himself not been able to handle). 'That would be a bad buy', the scamp calculates impudently. He gets away cheaply with the ringing box on the ear which this piece of consumer analysis earns him.

To live among high-minded souls and to be a realist is to invite suffering. For the abduction to be successful, it would have been advisable to take Pedrillo's strictures even more seriously. Having rendered Osmin drowsy with drink, he ponders, 'My only fear is that it's still too early. Three hours till midnight. He could easily sleep himself sober by then.' (O his prophetic soul!) He also gives a very sensible reason for giving a signal by means of a song – namely, that he has been in the habit of singing a serenade every evening. And when he does sing it, the content of the romantic ballad is perfectly in keeping with the abduction: 'Glock zwölfe stand der tapfre Ritter da' ('on midnight's stroke the valiant knight stood there').

We may well be surprised, however, by its tones, the melodic delicacy at his command, the harmoniously alternating agitation of the ebbing, enigmatically modulated melody with its folk-song simplicity, to which he accompanies himself on the mandolin. Pedrillo is the worried 'realist', but that certainly does not make him the one unpoetic figure in *The Abduction*.

PUBLIUS

Bass. Prefect. Commander of the Praetorian Guard. His duty is to ensure the safety of Titus and the deep tones of the ensemble.

in *La clemenza di Tito*

When an emperor starts walking in his sleep and displaying a dangerous bent for clemency, there has to be at least one man to give warnings and to see to safety. Likewise there has to be someone to deliver the deep tones otherwise absent among the soloists (four sopranos, one tenor) of *La clemenza*, and that someone is the prefect Publius, a *basso profondo*.

An unflinching civil servant, he sees things as they are, says what he thinks, and scents complications. For example, 'If he suffers so much, then he is still Sextus' friend'. The 'he' is Titus, and that in spite of Sextus appearing so palpably guilty of treason. At one point Publius is, for discretion's sake, sent out of the room: not too far, though. His own aria is unassuming and borders on dullness. With the worldly wisdom of a police chief he declares that anyone who thinks too well of his fellow humans, because he is himself good, will be slow to detect traitors.

This is hardly a complex insight, and so it is suitable for sonorous recital. At the close C major semiquavers come thundering a whole tenth down. They rumble with an unimpeachable assurance which is also imposing, righteous and conventional, like the man himself.

QUEEN OF THE NIGHT

〰️

Soprano. Antagonist of Sarastro because her husband assigned to
him the power associated with the 'Shield of the Sun'

in *The Magic Flute*

'O zittre nicht, mein lieber Sohn' ('be not afraid, beloved son') is the
recitative phrase introducing the Queen of the Night on her first
appearance. The mountains part, revealing her seated on her throne.
Our expectations have already been raised by hearing of her power and
her unapproachability.

On the other hand, the soprano who has to sing this notoriously
difficult role will probably herself be more than a little afraid unless she
resembles an impassive coloratura robot, a condition fraught with
considerable disadvantages. The Queen of the Night is a part
comprising two ruthlessly as well as gruesomely difficult arias. The
coloraturas demand that the voice shall soar to treble F. A slow pace in
the allegro passages is of no help because then their legato performance
proves still more difficult; a rapid pace is no cover because then the
staccato tones cannot be separated and become slurred. In *Ariadne on
Naxos* the orchestra charitably cloaks Zerbinetta, but not here. Mozart
composed these arias in such a manner that the orchestra and the
soloist make it oppressively clear what kind of music must follow – or
should follow. During this moment of truth the singer stands exposed
and utterly alone, dependent wholly on the glibness of her larynx, her
technique, and her nerves. If all this can be managed (and the arias are
manageable), then the house thunders its applause.

It is no accident that vocal techniques should be mentioned here at
the outset. Competitive pressure in the fine arts has created a situation
where opera fans, spoiled by recordings, fancy themselves somehow
entitled to certain top notes – and unfortunately those of the Queen of
the Night are better-known, more popular, and more familiar to even
the veriest amateur than the 'Nile C' in *Aida* or the *stretta* squalls in *Il
Trovatore*. This means that a role rich in human interest is reduced to

half a dozen high tones, a few passages, and something left over.

Why, though, does a singer, if she can, perform coloraturas? For the fun of achieving the almost impossible? For the pleasure to be derived from glittering energy? Because such coloraturas can be taken to stand for exceptional quality and excitement, i.e. for personality and triumph? Such explanations were not enough for Walter Felsenstein. A coloratura soprano, this thorough producer maintained, 'is in no position to adopt the role of the Queen of the Night . . . [it] must be executed by a dramatic singer'. Why? Because the Queen is fundamentally evil. If her first aria makes her seem a 'good' figure, the part has been wrongly interpreted. 'This aria . . . constitutes a totally mendacious masquerade. The Queen of the Night plays at being the saddened, tender mother in order to win over Tamino.'[28]

Felsenstein is mistaken. If any aesthetic question can be resolved, then we can be sure that the elegiac music of the G minor aria 'Zum Leiden bin ich auserkoren, denn meine Tochter fehlet mir' ('suffering is all my lot since of my daughter I have been bereft') was never intended by Mozart to be hypocritical or devious, but to convey affliction and sorrow. And why not? If Pamina later talks to Papageno about her 'loving', 'most loving' mother, to Sarastro even of her 'sweet' mother, then we have no reason to suppose that the Queen of the Night has always been fundamentally wicked and has deceived her (obviously slow-witted) daughter her whole life long.

The role of the Queen of the Night exhibits, as Sarastro aptly says, a 'proud' woman. He is no less proud, but his pride seems justified by the feudal and patriarchal order which he and his followers accept unquestioningly. The Queen of the Night's 'pride', her avidity for power and her fanaticism, must on the other hand be wicked: that goes without saying if you think that a woman's place is in the home.

Highly dramatic heroines – from Beethoven's Leonora via Senta and Isolde to Brünnhilde – seem to have been forerunners of women's emancipation. Did the Queen of the Night start the movement? She furiously resists the overbearing dispositions made by her husband, not to speak of those made by Sarastro. The proud regent suffers because she has been deprived of her beloved daughter. She tries by emotional appeal to enlist Tamino's help as a saviour. And when she sees that nothing can be of help to her, that the *natural* order has assigned women their place, then she responds logically, albeit with fanatical vindictiveness, by destroying *natural* ties – and herself. She is, to exaggerate somewhat, the eccentric victim of her own belief in female equality, which could never be put into practice in a world where men were judged by men, and women could only hope to be acknowledged and initiated if they had enough masculine courage to stand their ground in the face of danger. No wonder the Queen of the Night reacts to this situation with hysterical excitement. It simply shows that the woman is not what she also wants to be – a practical politician. But her habitual 'wickedness' is not proved by the developments into which her husband, his friend Sarastro, her imagined auxiliary Tamino, and her daughter Pamina gradually force her.

Eventually she seeks revenge on them all. Viewed in the most favourable light, she is an early example of a liberated woman; at worst she is a female Michael Kohlhaas who cannot tolerate her maternal rights being usurped so callously.*

And where is the proof that her affliction is genuine? A twice-recurring, compelling sad G minor aria and an expressive bassoon counterpoint represent in *The Magic Flute* the apogee of suffering (this has already been discussed in relation to Pamina's G minor aria and her suicidal outburst). The unmistakable intensification contained in the Queen of the Night's 'noch seh' ich ihr Zittern mit bangem Erschüttern, ihr ängstliches Beben, ihr schüchternes Streben, ich musste sie mir rauben sehen' ('I see still her tremors, her tremulous shudders, her timorous struggles, and could but watch the wolf with his prey') must likewise be accepted as an augmented declaration of her agony without the slightest deviousness or dishonesty. No one who reads the score, listens, and takes in the words has the slightest occasion to dispute the depth of her emotion and to suspect her of lying. One could even perceive thematic analogies between the Queen's 'denn meine Hilfe war zu schwach' ('for my help was all too weak') and the first movement of the C minor piano concerto K. 491, which is certainly not intended as a composition of an ironic or deceptive nature. In her first aria, therefore, the Queen of the Night articulates vehement distress and a hysterical hope of victory and rescue. A temperament of extremes with a range far above two octaves!

Thereafter she experiences deadlock and sees her efforts being frustrated. Her daughter displays a lack of fanaticism which makes her

---

* Michael Kohlhaas, the hero of Heinrich von Kleist's long short story (1810) of the same name, is a sixteenth-century horse-dealer, 'one of the most virtuous and terrifying men of his time', whose inexorable sense of justice causes him to become a robber and a murderer. He ends on the gallows – with full recognition for the integrity of his original motives, and that suffices him. The figure, based on true facts, has in German literature become the epitome for right-headed obstinacy taking a self-destructive wrong turning.

mother exclaim, 'Verdanke es der Gewalt, mit der man dich mich entriss, dass ich noch deine Mutter mich nenne ('thank the force with which you were taken from me that I call myself your mother still'). In other words, because force was used against you and you came under a strong external influence which alienated you from me, I am still prepared to call myself your mother (otherwise I would long ago have repudiated this potential deserter). These statements are more partisan than maternal, but they scarcely show that the mother was doing no more than pretend to be distressed by the abduction of her daughter.

Since, however, her own daughter does not want to take sides and finds good words for the adversary Sarastro, the Queen rebels with seething fanaticism even against nature. This she now sees as a purely patriarchal order of things. 'Zertrümmert sein auf ewig alle Bande der Natur. Verstossen, verlassen und zertrümmert alle Bande der Natur' ('shattered be eternally all the bonds of nature. Cast out, forsaken, shattered be all the bonds of nature'). These are not the chirrupings of an average coloratura, nor should they be sung in sonorous crotchets. They demand ebullient, pungent and overwrought emotion.

The Queen is now completely out of control, and regards the initiates as 'bigots' to be extirpated. In return for Master Monostatos' help she will give him her daughter, just as Tamino would have received her for the same service. The Queen is now a tempestuous character who has put herself beyond the pale. But cold-blooded lies and crafty tactical ploys – no, that is not the Queen of the Night's way.

SARASTRO

Bass. Fairy-tale ruler. Head of the initiates.

in *The Magic Flute*

'Great Sarastro,' says the Speaker at the beginning of Act II, 'the wisdom of your utterances we acknowledge and admire.'

Posterity has been somewhat less reverential about Sarastro who, clad in priestly garments, tends to express himself with pompous solemnity: 'With a clear conscience I tell you that our assembly today is of paramount importance', and 'Touched by the unanimity of your affections, Sarastro thanks you in the name of mankind'.

Sarastro's aim is to enlist the twenty-year-old Prince Tamino in the ranks of the 'initiates' – much as Wagner's Gurnemanz means to do with Parsifal – so as to fortify them with young blood. And he is not prepared to let the Queen of the Night (because she is a woman!) acquire the symbol of power (that is, the 'Shield of the Sun'), nor will he let her, a widow, use her daughter Pamina for her own ambitious purposes.

The 'wisdom' of Sarastro's utterances has met with severe criticism, especially in the 1970s. He has been called a boring, puritanical windbag as well as a contemptible anti-feminist. Attacks on the text of *The Magic Flute*, especially on the figure of Sarastro, by Wolf Rosenberg and others can be read in no. 3 of the *Musik-Konzepte* series, where Emanuel Schikaneder's libretto provoked the issue's title, 'Is The Magic Flute A Mess?'. 'What', asks Rosenberg, 'was he [Mozart] to do with this tedious Sarastro figure, barely capable of illustration in music, a figure lacking in contours, in determinable qualities of character . . .'.[29] A year earlier Wolfgang Hildesheimer, in his book on Mozart, had already voiced an emphatic condemnation: 'The burden of Sarastro's song is not his own experience, but a morality which nobody puts into practice because it cannot be translated into stage action. His role can therefore be neither convincingly acted nor sung without causing involuntary derision.'[30] This is strong language to use of the central figure in one of Mozart's major works. The composer certainly did not create Sarastro in a 'critical' spirit, but the plot and the jubilant choruses plainly indicate that he was intended to be understood, indeed acclaimed, as the picture of a positive, benevolent ruler.

Is it in fact a weakness that he is so positive? The question must be raised, for the scolding earned by Sarastro from the *Magic Flute* critics Hildesheimer, Rosenberg, and Rainer Riehn ('Sarastro's Proverb-Coining')[31] finds indirect support from the terms in which certain *Magic Flute* admirers describe the 'divine sage'. Aloys Greither's praise has an ambiguous ring. 'His absolute excellence almost robs Sarastro as a stage figure of any drama since he has no need to choose between good and evil. What he gains in humanity by his inviolable goodness he loses in dramatic opportunity.'[32] Sarastro's adherents evidently view him as a sublime principle on two legs rather than as a stage personage. The jurist Gustav Radbruch, in his essay 'Penal Law in *The Magic Flute*', went so far as to claim that 'freemasonry's penal concepts' find in the opera's 'words and music their highest, ultimate expression' – Sarastro embodies Plato's ideal of a philosopher-king and is comparable with Shakespeare's Prospero.[33]

He makes a late entrance. Although normally Mozart's protagonists become audible and visible relatively quickly, we do not meet Sarastro till the finale of Act I. Even then he does not appear right at the beginning, but when all the other important figures of *The Magic Flute* (with the exception of Papagena) have long been heard and seen, most of them several times at that.

For the most powerful figure in a drama to appear late is an invariably effective *coup* bordering on the melodramatic. The better an entrance has been prepared, the more exciting it proves, because in the theatre nothing is more boring than mere surprise.

We await Sarastro with excitement and considerable uncertainty. Some people whose integrity we are disinclined to question have been heard to say that he is 'vicious', a 'tiger beast', a demon who can change his shape. Pamina, moreover, whom we know to be angelically good-natured, has spent some time in Sarastro's power, or custody, and should therefore know him a little. She takes it for granted that, if she were to embrace her longed-for Tamino in front of him, it would mean the 'end' of her, in other words, her death. Papageno's 'agonizing death' too, if he was caught, would, she says, be 'interminable'.

Tamino for his part is convinced that Sarastro must be 'a monster, a tyrant'. Yet contrary opinions have also been heard. The Speaker has managed to undermine Tamino's hostility to Sarastro by supplying information honestly and without artful euphemisms. The jubilant choruses with which the sovereign is welcomed – six lions draw his triumphal chariot – sound more like expressions of admiration and love than applause enforced by tyranny. The Speaker, it is true, has intimated that it can be dangerous to life and limb to spread obdurate untruths. 'Wenn du dein Leben liebst, so rede, bleibe da! – Sarastro hassest du?' ('if you value your life, so speak now, and remain! – Do you hate Sarastro?').

The Sarastro whom we finally meet is neither 'tiger beast' nor an enlightened freemason who rejects any notion of violence. His outstanding qualities appear to include unruffled awareness of his patriarchal power, humour (at other people's expense), fatherly amiability, and a sense of responsibility. The text is not unambiguous and the music occasionally pulls in a different direction.

When Pamina sensitively recalls her affection for her mother, Sarastro becomes decidedly irate, and comments: 'Du würdest um dein Glück gebracht, wenn ich dich ihren Händen liesse' ('your happiness would be the cost, were I to leave you in her hands!'). The accompaniment is composed as a jaggedly dotted C minor recitative rising in crescendo to forte; he must be a youngish prince to become so worked up.

How does he react to Monostatos' coarsely sensual attacks on Pamina? His attitude is anything but 'understanding' and he shows himself to be no sanctimonious freemason to whom 'vengeance remains unknown'. The lecherous Monostatos is condemned to a bastinado. On his knees, he wails, 'ach Herr, den Lohn verhofft' ich nicht' ('I had not hoped for this reward') and receives the complacently ironic retort, 'Nicht Dank, es ist ja meine Pflicht!' ('Spare thanks! 'Tis duty, this award!'). This does not quite accord with the oft-quoted 'humanitarian outlook of freemasonry', although later the solemn atmosphere of the purity test means that the sentence of seventy-seven strokes is suspended. In Act II Monostatos remarks, 'Und um einer so geringen Pflanze wegen wollte man meine Fusssohlen behämmern? – Also bloss dem heutigen Tage habe ich's zu verdanken, dass ich noch mit heiler Haut auf die Erde trete' ('For such a wayside flower's sake they meant to cane my soles? – So it is just due to this day's events that I tread the earth unbruised').

Sarastro's loftiness rests primarily on his depth, however paradoxical the assertion may sound. Whoever sings the part must have at his command the low F, and that at the crucial moment when Sarastro sets bounds to his liberality. 'Zur Liebe will ich dich nicht zwingen' ('my wish is not to force your love') proclaims the enlightened potentate, but continues with a qualification dreadful enough in Pamina's ears, 'doch geb' ich dir die Freiheit nicht' ('yet freedom shall not be your lot'). The first time his 'yet' is in a comfortable place; the second time the low F has to be enunciated and held as a half-note. Having achieved that, and breathing heavily, the bass has to repeat this 'yet' for a third time, only more briefly.

The core of Sarastro's limited tolerance is his unquestioned patriarchal rule. Far from being banal, it is incisively ironic where evil is at work, but tempered by benevolence towards what merits affection.

Not for a moment does he doubt that it would be wrong to concede to any woman, let alone an ambitious one, equality of status as a political opponent or even as parent. Speaking of the extent and increase of his power, he becomes solemn and pious. As a royal figure, he is remote from the other characters, but the gap can be bridged by his paternal solicitude. Hence the chorus of priests in 'O Isis and Osiris' only chants a marvellously magical echo of what he has already uttered on his own.

The contrast between what Sarastro says and what he sings is particularly marked in the dialogue preceding the farewell trio and the trio itself. In speech he is severe, especially to Pamina, who does not yet understand that a test is in progress. Oppressed by the awesome silence, she asks, 'Where is my young Prince?' He heightens the girl's fears mercilessly: 'He awaits you to speak his last farewell'.

In the trio he mitigates his severity. Right at the outset of the andante moderato he sings, 'Ihr werdet froh euch wiedersehn!' ('in gladness shall you meet again'); at its close he promises the lovers, 'Wir sehn uns wieder! ('we shall meet again'), at which point his voice achieves a special expressivity. Its tones stretch for a moment an octave below the cellos and the bass line of the orchestra. It is as though he were the primal cause of all the other characters' actions and expectations.

Is it really the case that this mixture of young manhood, reflectiveness, severity, profound charisma and patriarchal joviality cannot, as Hildesheimer contended, be acted and sung without involuntarily arousing derision? Only if Sarastro were a windbag, lacking internal conflict, benevolent but tiresome, then perhaps the critics could be right. It is pointless, of course, to compare the dignity of a fairy-tale prince with a realistic figure like Count Almaviva. But if one compares him with certain regal figures in *opera seria*, one sees what a living human being Mozart has made of Sarastro.

The producer Jean-Pierre Ponnelle has even managed to integrate into the plot Sarastro's prominent and sonorous aria 'In diesen heil'gen Hallen kennt man die Rache nicht' ('within these sacred precincts vengeance remains unknown'), which all too easily deteriorates into an anti-dramatic humanitarian hymn, 'und ist ein Mensch gefallen, führt Liebe ihn zur Pflicht' ('let man be fallen, duty's way will by love be shown'). He has proved that these splendid professions need not consign Sarastro to sublime vacuity. Just before the aria there has been an exchange between Pamina and Sarastro.

Pamina: 'Lord, punish not my mother. The pain caused by my absence . . .'

Sarastro: 'I know all . . . know that she prowls through subterranean chambers of the temple and concocts revenge against me and all humanity. You shall however see how I avenge myself on your mother.'

Immediately afterwards Sarastro intones 'Within these sacred precincts . . .' for the benefit of the Queen of the Night, spectrally roaming in the background, as though to give her pause for thought, divert her from her plans, offer reconciliation. But, being mortally offended, her personal dignity never taken seriously by Sarastro, she will never allow herself to be deflected from her course.

Goethe, in his fragment *Der Zauberflöte Zweyter Theil (The Magic Flute, Part Two)*, was later to intimate that Sarastro also had some sin to atone:

Between these silent walls a man learns to fathom himself and his inmost soul. He prepares to hear the voice of the gods. But Nature's sublime speech and the tones of indigent humanity can become known only to the wanderer who roves the earth's broad realms. Therefore our law demands that each year one among us shall be dispatched into the harsh world . . .

The lot has fallen upon me and I do not hesitate for one moment to submit to its behest. Yes, the warning is fulfilled. The gods remove me from your midst to test you and me. I am summoned at this important moment when the forces of hostile powers are becoming more active.

Sarastro leaves the temple of wisdom and the initiates. Will he some day, like Duke Vincentio in *Measure for Measure*, return in disguise to judge the conduct of those he left behind? Or at least to make his peace with the Queen of the Night? We do not know. Goethe's sequel remained a fragment.

PASHA SELIM

Speaking part. One of the mighty. A convert from Christianity to Islam ('renegade') who holds in his power Constanze, her maid Blondie, and Pedrillo. Seeks by gentle patience to obtain Constanze's love while she keeps asking for deferment. Likewise threatens her with the tortures which he could impose. Finally sets an example of humanity.

in *The Abduction*

What are we to make of someone in a *Singspiel* who does not sing, who does not divulge his inner feelings of love, fear or hatred in sensuous and sonorous tones? Since Pasha Selim only speaks, are we to conclude that he is 'nobler'? No, he is merely more enigmatic. He lacks the music which could have revealed or explained to us something of what goes on inside him. Osmin fancies that he knows his lord: 'The Pasha is soft as butter. You can do with him what you want', he fumes indignantly about his sensitive master, who cannot see through the Christian riff-raff. Osmin is right only with regard to the abduction planned by Belmonte, Pedrillo & Co. As far as Pasha Selim is concerned, the overseer confuses sentimental softness with feebleness: soft-as-butter feebleness is not necessarily the Pasha's outstanding characteristic. Sensitivity and cruelty (as they seem otherwise to be fairly customarily practised on Pasha Selim's country estate) are by no means mutually exclusive.

Constanze's comparatively favourable situation, Pedrillo explains to Belmonte, derives from the Pasha's former Christianity. It imbues him with 'still sufficient delicacy not to force any of his women'. This appears also to prove that Pasha Selim is not all that dangerous. Who can tell, though, whether he has ever yet found it necessary to force anyone?

When Pasha Selim finally reveals himself to be magnanimity personified, releasing the son of his mortal enemy, the beloved Constanze, and their domestics too, it looks as if the statements of

Osmin and Pedrillo are confirmed. The great-hearted man even speaks slightly disparagingly of his good deed: 'Best to be rid of whoever cannot be won over'. And he teasingly consoles Osmin for the departure of the quick-tempered Blondie: 'Are your eyes no longer dear to you, old fellow?' The fact that he has valid travel orders to hand – 'He gives Belmonte a document: "Here is your passport"' – strongly suggests that this is not an unpremeditated gesture, but a well-prepared scene which he has forced himself to go through with.

Indeed, the Pasha has not always behaved so nonchalantly. He tried to put pressure on Constanze by intimating that he could force her, but would rather not. But isn't that a somewhat dreary form of dialectics? You don't love me, I don't have you tortured, I am not coercing you, therefore love me of your own accord. 'See, I could issue orders, I could treat you cruelly, constrain you' – and then, as though this were a possible alternative to unreciprocated love, 'But, no, Constanze, it is you, you yourself, whom I want to have to thank for your heart'. In plain terms, this means 'I want you, I want you to love me of your own free will, but not to be forced through cruelty. Love, though, there *must* be.' Constanze sees through the gambit. After the Pasha's more outspoken 'Tomorrow you must love me or else –', she repays his subtlety with bluntness: 'Must? What a ludicrous demand! As though love, like a thrashing, can be ordered!'

Perhaps the mild Pasha Selim derives pleasure from toying with his power. When Constanze lets slip that she will 'never' love him, he asks, 'And you do not fear the power that I have over you?' He hints not merely at death, but 'torments of all kinds' too. 'Her grief, her tears', he admits to himself, 'bewitch my heart ever more.' To all appearance this kindly, loving, mighty personage derives a certain morose enjoyment from talking about cruelty as the last resort and from savouring the anxiety, if not the submission, of a young woman whom he loves.

Since he cannot but recognize that the direct threats of his fury evidently make no impression on Constanze's courage, he changes tack: 'I achieve nothing by harshness nor by pleas either. What neither threats nor pleas can attain, cunning shall effect.'

This is a different strategy of courtship, in which cruelty is either entirely absent or is mentioned directly, not as a possible threat which a clever woman can evade. Finally all is plain sailing. Constanze has proved her intrepidity and Belmonte shows himself just as brave, unconcerned about his own life, but anxious simply on his beloved partner's behalf. They have, all of them, thoroughly transgressed against the Pasha. He would not be unjustified in taking vengeance, but he feels how far below the standard of his own sensitivity and his melancholy humanity it would be doggedly to carry out such justice. He has not behaved feebly, nor has his conduct been above reproach. Upset and angry, he has repeatedly succumbed to the temptation to talk about cruelty in order to force his objective. But now, lonely in the face of a pair who have incurred guilt through love, he feels revulsion at the system of coercion and revenge. He wants to leave the ranks of the killers – not that he declares his mercifulness in such high-flown terms; his words sound bitter, contemptuous, almost cynical. Let no one be deceived, however. He really deserves the closing choruses of jubilation in his honour.

SERVILIA

Soprano. Sister of Titus' close friend Sextus. Is briefly selected by
the Emperor to be his wife, but successfully declines to become
empress because she loves Annius.

in *La clemenza di Tito*

The subjects of mild rulers can and may obey their own feelings – if they
are courageous enough honestly to admit to them.

The Emperor's decision to marry Servilia (after his repudiation of
Berenice, whom he has loved, but who is a foreigner) can not have been
long considered, or else Sextus, her brother, would not be as much
surprised and upset as honoured at the Emperor's flattering noti-
fication that his family is to become so closely allied to the imperial
dynasty. Neither Sextus nor Annius, her betrothed, ventures to argue
with Titus, however.

Servilia, on the other hand, remains unswerving. The short, sincere
and serene A major duet (no. 7) lays down irrefutably in two-four time
that nothing can outweigh her and Annius' love for one another. In *Don
Giovanni* the A major duet 'Là ci darem la mano' ('there my hand shall
plight our troth') is also in two-four time, carries the instruction
andante, and was composed as no. 7. Anyone who wants to be
convinced that *La clemenza*, though different in character, is equal in
quality to Mozart's more popular operas should study these two pieces.
Moreover, students of genre may ponder how in the former the duet
breaks the bounds of *opera seria* and how that in *Don Giovanni* fits into
dramma giocoso; not that such findings have much aesthetic significance.
Still, one can recognize the form of accomplished simplicity, over and
above all dramatic interest, which Mozart devised in the year of his
death. The duet's blissful stillness, comparable in more than one
respect with *Così*, is not inferior to, merely different from, the wonderful
paralysis exercised by the *Don Giovanni* number over Zerlina's feeble
resistance. The difference consists in its more static composition,
despite its rich variation.

Servilia stands unconditionally by her feelings and by her intentions, and the Emperor holds her in high esteem for it. Indeed, she demands similar conduct from others, such as Vitellia. In her lyrical D major aria (no. 21) she persuades her brother's beloved not to leave Sextus in the lurch, but to confess that it was she, Vitellia, who incited him to seek his imperial friend's life. Tearful pity without action, sings Servilia (like an unconditional existentialist for whom action alone, not sentiment, counts), is to no avail and 'Oh, how very similar to cruelty'.

More than any other protagonist in *La clemenza*, Servilia is enviably clear about herself, her wishes, and her feelings of love.

SEXTUS

Soprano. Selflessly in love with Vitellia and on terms of warm friendship with the Emperor, Titus. This brings him into a severe conflict of 'obligations' from which he emerges safely but in a state of shock, for although in thrall to Vitellia he is no coward.

in *La clemenza di Tito*

His infatuation has undermined Sextus' character and renders it possible to seduce him from his loyalty to his Emperor and friend; none the less, he remains decent and courageous. If not exemplary, he is at least interesting, and the music allotted to him makes his weaknesses appear amiable.

He is touching in his belief that he can talk Vitellia round by sensible reasoning, although in fact she is less concerned with her poor lover than with Titus, by whom she feels affronted because he has previously preferred Berenice and whom she hates for family reasons. Sextus says: 'See matters in their right light, beloved, and consider. Oh, let us not kill Titus, this world's good fortune, Rome's father, our friend!'

Such homage to the monarch she hates understandably excites Vitellia beyond all measure. How much more anomalous her temperament is than that of Sextus is shown at the beginning of the opera in the duet where she repeats her words in an imploring tone and spans an enormous compass while Sextus, though lyrical enough, remains much more restrained. (The ratio of fifth to octave with Sextus corresponds to a ratio of ninth to almost double octave in Vitellia's case.)

What Vitellia is not prepared to grant her lover is bestowed on him by Annius – the contentment of an unproblematic harmony (duettino no. 3). There is no longer any need for the alternations between forte, piano and mezzo-forte which were used at the start of the andante duet (no. 1, Vitellia and Sextus) to convey a truly unstable character. The insistent demonstration by text and music of Sextus' pliability – even when he really knows best what he ought or ought not to do – alerts us to see, hear and find the evidence for his spinelessness. Our ears detect even in his noble adagio aria (no. 9) what Mozart probably did not mean to impute: his trait of complete dependence. It is as though his cantilena follows the lead of the solo clarinet and, when the horrifying thought of what he has to lose if he loses Vitellia enters his mind, he behaves as though under its remote control.

He does not perform what the plot and his lover demand of him, however. He is aware – just as is his friend Titus, whose enemy he has to become and whose punishment he must incur – of how difficult it is to be 'evil'. After his imagination had been fired by Vitellia, this seemed somehow within reach, but once the mischief has been done and Titus' rage has been aroused, he is horrified and stands 'deformed' before his powerful friend, whom he cherishes. In the finale of Act I his despair at the murderous intrigue is such as to increase his strength of dramatic expression. The high-minded minor intervals when the admission of his guilty conscience is wrung from him – 'Earth, open up to swallow me down, a traitor, into utmost depths' – intimate the transition from an interesting dependent character into a tragic one. It is not easy for him to accept his fate: 'Shall I flee or remain? In this perplexity I cannot take any decision.' These are the reflections of a man temporarily taxed beyond his capacity.

Later, though, he does not make anyone pay for inflicting disgrace on him. When taken prisoner, he does not betray that Vitellia was the plot's originator. He does not even renounce his love for her. With death staring him in the face, he suffers less from fear than shame at having involved himself in the uprising. His rondo (no. 19) reveals that he has at last acquired a self-assurance burdened by feelings of guilt. He has not betrayed his beloved (which would be his last chance of reprieve), nor does he wish to plead for anything. The pure, wide-ranging A major melodic phrases are not concerned with seeking pardon. But drama enters into the rondo when he implies what he cannot say outright – 'Could you see into my heart, your severity would be less great'. Vitellia's confession saves him, but he will never cease to reproach himself.

Mozart's music is far more interested in what is heartfelt and sincere in this role than in what makes it 'interesting'. Subtleties of character delineation are present, but they concentrate only on the touching sensitivity of this ill-starred hero, not the man as a whole.

SPEAKER

Bass. An old priest, full of wisdom and intensity, who takes words and aims so deeply seriously that an aura of solemnity surrounds him. Perplexes Tamino thoroughly.

in *The Magic Flute*

The Speaker, weighing words and refuting them, is an impressive figure as he stands there like a signpost showing Tamino a new world. Upon his appearance the opera's register changes. Whether or not he is identical with the First Priest is an insoluble problem because the facts contradict one another. (The *Neue Mozart-Gesamtausgabe*, contrary to normal performance practice, states in its preface: '. . . it is almost certain that in the Act I finale of the original performance the First Priest – now a spoken part – and not the Speaker, participated'. Irrespective of whether it is a Speaker, First Priest or old priest who comes on the scene, the earlier pace ceases and so do the spontaneous displays of temperament which have been responsible for such a rapid and varied wealth of events.

A few moments earlier the stage was populated only by youngsters like the Prince, threatened and in love with a portrait, and the imprisoned Pamina tormented by the inflamed Monostatos. The temperaments have been lively, like those of the Three Ladies, or even morbidly eccentric, like that of the affronted Queen of the Night. Even Papageno has been anything but a mystic seeker of truth.

The priest's entrance is steeped in suspense. 'Retreat!' rumbles from behind the doors to left and right. Here is the signal for sudden change. The allegro stops and upon the Speaker's appearance its place is taken by the E flat major adagio. The sanctuary is open. It is noteworthy that the music does not assume the archaic, old-fashioned, or chorale character which might well be expected when a venerable priest appears. Instead, with apparent effortlessness, Mozart anticipates Wagner's dramatic orchestral recitative. There ensues a freely flowing dialogue subject to occasional directions ('fast', 'slow'), sometimes symphonically elaborated, sometimes no more than thinly accompanied. Far removed from anything like a 'number', the term 'duet' would be mistaken, indeed a sacrilege. No wonder that Wagner, who knew Mozart's work thoroughly and greatly admired it, singled out the Speaker scene for special praise.

Priests and scribes, after all, are basically people who take words literally, and therefore insist on getting things right; so it is no wonder that the Speaker proves to be a sage. His personality and his cross-examination break down Tamino's confidence: 'Whither, bold youth, would you now go?', 'how will you love and virtue find?', 'declare yourself more closely; you have been deceived', 'but tell me then your reasons!', 'has all that you do say been proven?'.

The older man accepts the younger at his own value. He allows him 'boldness' and approves the 'loftiness' of his aim. The Speaker is, however, forceful as well as wise: 'Dich leitet Lieb' und Tugend nicht, weil Tod und Rache dich entzünden' ('virtue and love are not your guides, for death and vengeance do inflame you'), he thunders – forte, in G minor.

At first Tamino does not permit himself to be browbeaten and he continues to charge Sarastro with wickedness, until the older man's patience snaps. 'Wenn du dein Leben liebst, so rede, bleibe da!' ('if you value your life, so speak now, and remain!'), an exclamation that the audience and Tamino cannot interpret other than as a threat. Perhaps, though, this menacing utterance is intended in a more spiritual sense: 'for the sake of your life and its truthfulness, which you value, let yourself to truth be brought'. At this point a dangerous undercurrent mingles with the calmly reflective flow of the dialogue. The youth condemns a world he does not know, and he must be forced to become acquainted with it. The priest's zeal waxes to such a degree that he mocks the witness who has slandered his master: 'Ein Weib tut wenig, plaudert viel' ('a woman does little, chatters much'). It is the only moment where, because he has been offended, the Speaker's guard is really down. His weakness may also seem exposed when he admits that what Tamino says about Pamina's abduction is factually correct: 'Ja, Jüngling, was du sagst, ist wahr!' ('indeed, good youth, what you say is true'). But this renders him trustworthy, for Tamino senses that he is not a liar but ready to acknowledge the truth even if it undermines his own position. Tamino is at his wits' end – 'Wann endlich wird die Decke schwinden?' ('when will at last this dark be lifted?').

The priest has questioned him closely, uttered furious threats, confirmed Pamina's abduction, and has then paternally addressed his alarmed partner in this discussion as 'beloved son'. Now, in A minor, he answers the despairing question with an incomparably cogent idea: 'Sobald dich führt der Freundschaft Hand ins Heiligtum zum ew'gen Band' ('when you are led by friendship's hand through hallowed ground to lasting bond'). The A minor motif, reverberating through Tamino's utter despondency, is intensified by the gentle force of an invisible choir, a community which allows the prediction to appear not just as the assertion of an old priest, but as resting on mysterious and mystical authority. Although the whole dialogue lasts only a few minutes, anyone who has heard Dietrich Fischer-Dieskau in this role knows that the Speaker is compounded both of intensity (he is not merely effortlessly 'wise', but profoundly serene and committed, honest and convincing) and a mystic veracity. At this point in *The Magic Flute* a living spiritual principle defies the play of temperaments.

SUSANNA

⌣

Soprano. Figaro's bride, Countess Almaviva's lady's maid, Basilio's music pupil. Count Almaviva is after her. In his castle she links all the characters 'by being the one person who participates in all ensembles (six duets, two trios, one sextet, and three finales)'.[34] When her heart and her temperament are obscured by her nimbleness, it is perhaps possible to catch a glimpse of *commedia dell'arte*'s Columbine, from whom she derives. When in the Act III sextet she ecstatically realizes her good fortune and in Act IV transforms a planned scene of jealousy into a depiction of natural emotion, a confession of love, then Columbine appears to have entered the age of Sensibility and Early Romanticism.

in *The Marriage of Figaro*

The charming Susanna, whose name is a favourite for daughters in regions where *The Marriage of Figaro* is treasured, is not easy to analyse. It is as though she were less an individual than an embodiment of the genius inherent in a particular race – gay, supple, unsentimental, loving and lovable Southern womanhood. She displays no tiresome petulance, no inflated sentimentality. Love and passion appear in her neither sombre nor selfish, while her enjoyment of laughter and mockery is neither cynical nor forced. It is clear that if all her enormously positive qualities were lumped together as an item for the lonely-hearts or situations-wanted column, she would make just as ideal a wife as domestic help, holiday companion, or professional colleague. Recalling how Beaumarchais – in love with his own creation – described Susanna in *The Follies of a Day* (the play's alternative title), she seems to be a type rather than an individual, an ideal figure of comedy rather than an ordinary being. Beaumarchais characterized Susanna as follows: 'Clever young person, intelligent and gay, but without the almost impertinent merriment of our spoiled soubrettes'.

Her attraction is unobtrusive, and that is why it attracts. During her first aria in Act II, talking to and about Cherubino, Susanna says, 'If all the women love him so, then for certain they know why'. The graceful manner in which she expresses her enchantment, blithely fiddling about with the young man preparatory to dressing him as a woman, is so vivacious and so captivating that her charm is irresistible. And when she merrily demands of him (as though his handsomeness were a deliberate performance), 'Little viper, please now stop being so good-looking', her remarks constitute a delicious combination of charm and exuberance.

In Almaviva's castle a strict feudal hierarchy does not separate people from one another as distinctly as in *Don Giovanni* or in *The Magic Flute*. Sometimes, however, we are reminded of certain class differences. It is clear in principle who gives orders and who has to obey, and anyone who kicks against the pricks knows very well what he risks. 'Naturally' Susanna does not treat the Count, the Countess, and the very young gentleman Cherubino as equals. She is no less self-assured for being aware that the smelling-salts the Count offers are not for the likes of her: such socially superior indispositions do not happen in the world of *donne triviali*, simple women. And she confesses to the Countess that the Count had not wanted to seduce, only to buy, her: 'With women of my station he takes no such trouble' (a slight exaggeration: the Count does take a fair amount of trouble in pursuit of her).

The Countess, who sometimes treats Susanna like a sister, in a soliloquy shows herself abashed in her class-consciousness. 'To what a fatally humiliating condition a cruel husband has reduced me. After first . . . loving, then insulting, and finally betraying me, he now reduces me to seeking help from a maid!' It sounds arrogant, but it is not her last word. In the very next number, the 'letter' duet (no. 20), she will join forces with Susanna in sisterly thirds. It is she moreover who furnishes Susanna with the money to ransom Figaro from Marcellina. This link, it is worth noting, is not merely incredible to her husband (the Count: 'But if she [Susanna] paid the old plaintiff? She pay! How?'), but occurs only in Beaumarchais. Da Ponte and Mozart forget to mention it, but just take it for granted. In any case it hardly matters. At that joyous moment (the Act III sextet) the bridegroom Figaro is being showered with purses from all sides.

How does Susanna behave in a world where class differences are clear-cut, but on the other hand people can cross these barriers to come together, to associate and to confide trustingly in one another? Whether talking to Figaro, Marcellina, the Count, the Countess or Cherubino, Susanna has an instinctive gift for adaptability, though not for opportunism. She may echo the tone of whoever she is speaking to and she may join in someone's game, but she does not efface her real self. If it proves necessary or she knows best or her self-confidence renders her bold, she can spy and seize the chance to modify or change her partner's designs and observations.

In the duettino no. 2, for example, without producing a glaring contrast, she discreetly tones down into G minor Figaro's lively and unsuspecting B flat assertion about how pleasantly practical the situation of their new room is. Woe to the singers who fail to appreciate that! As though enhancing the urgency of the allegro parlando, Susanna explains to her beloved what further significance lies in the fact that the ringing of their employers' bells can be heard so easily. By the time he begins to understand the meaning of her discreetly sharper and darker tones, her music is back in B flat – and Figaro the wiser by a fateful piece of information which he slowly begins to digest.

Marcellina and Susanna – both of them out to marry Figaro – feel a genuine antipathy for one another, at least initially. The younger, more attractive Susanna derives childish fun from provoking the older woman into a fury. Her pretence of politeness in allowing Marcellina to take the conversational lead as well as to walk ahead of her is a pert way of pointing up the respectful restraint owed by young girls to elderly ladies. The musical counterpart is that Susanna at the beginning always reacts to Marcellina's utterances with an excess of modesty and politeness either by exactly repeating Marcellina's initial tones (first and fourth reactions) or by hitching on to her last ones (second and third reactions). There is venom in her method. Then she becomes impatient with her own mimicry. Suddenly, in her first forte in this duet (bar 24), she selects a tone which has nowhere occurred in Marcellina's preceding utterance. Her style is now distinctly saucier: 'La donna d'onore . . . di Spagna l'amore' ('the lady of honour . . . all Spain's great beloved'). Whereas Marcellina is obviously on the verge of losing her nerves and her poise, Susanna thoroughly enjoys deriding her rival. Her mockery of Cherubino's adolescent love will be kinder (though mockery still).

She savours ironically the Count's embarrassment when, instead of Cherubino, whom the Count and the Countess expect, she herself enters 'molto andante' the Countess's chamber from the neighbouring room. Complacently she notes the Count's drawn sword and she courteously invites his excited lordship to see for himself who is hiding next door.

Healthy common sense and quick-wittedness are the foundations of this adaptable, self-confident girl's serene, bantering sovereignty. She believes in her good luck although, being the more spontaneous of the two, she loses heart more quickly than Figaro. If a situation becomes critical, she will moan 'Nothing could be worse', almost faint, and superstitiously accuse the 'cruel stars'. 'I have no hope at all', she whispers to Figaro, who is already approaching with his prudently organized chorus of ironic homage for the Count. She brings off a brilliant feat when at the beginning of Act III she hoodwinks Almaviva. His initial moroseness, caused by her former rebuff, is reflected in phrases in a minor key which she first adopts, then transposes into a tender major mode. Now, at precisely the right moment to inspire confidence, she ventures to pretend that class barriers cannot separate two such loving hearts as theirs. She reacts with convincing sugariness to his justified question why, if she loves him, she had been so cool to the pimping Basilio: 'What need have we of a Basilio?'. The enamoured Count fully takes the point, but the adroit Susanna, who cannot but sense his vehement passion, does not find it altogether easy to keep up her reckless deception. Dietmar Holland has acutely observed that, having to give soothing answers to Almaviva's repeated questions ('You will come?' 'Yes.' 'You will not keep me waiting?' 'No.'), she once blunders.[35] In duet no. 17, bar 45, she gives herself away by saying 'No' where 'Yes' would be appropriate. Shaken, the Count repeats 'No', whereupon she at once emphatically corrects it to 'Yes'. Her fibbing evidently rather weighs on her conscience. Ludwig Finscher (to whose friendly helpfulness I owe several very valuable corrections and suggestions) thinks that in fact Susanna's (Freudian) slip has 'been familiar to everyone since 1786' but one must acknowledge the sensitive insight with which Holland has drawn attention to the fussiness of her correction, in other words her badly disguised shock.

Susanna is a past-mistress in the war of the sexes and the conflict of classes. Fortunately, where her heart is committed, she too can make the odd mistake. Believing that she has caught out Figaro, she is livid and mistrusts him completely. Where swift and violent jealousy is concerned, he and she are a well-matched pair.

Behind the clever Susanna who had to learn that she must always keep a cool head, and who thoroughly digested the lesson, another Susanna is hidden – one who neither defends herself aggressively, nor flirts, nor mimics, nor tells inspired lies, neither boxes anyone's ears nor takes fright in an emergency and runs to Figaro for help.

This other Susanna is met, rather late, in Act III's sextet. With what tempestuousness (not for an instant guessing the familial reason for Marcellina's and Figaro's embrace) had she broken into what seemed to her their infuriating harmony, singing the same dotted notes of desperate defiance as the Count had done, with more reason for his rage.

The others enlighten her, and now her smoothly flowing melismata – her range of expression at the end of the sextet (bar 103 onwards) spans almost two octaves – present a Susanna more happy, warm and dreamily approving than we have ever seen her. In the succeeding recitative it is she who, more sensitively than any of the others, manifests her blissful satisfaction at the turn taken by events, which indicates what tensions are now beginning to relax inside this courageous girl.

But there is still one intrigue which she wants to continue, though she is too much in love to see it through to the end. She pretends to be keeping her rendezvous with the Count, combining pleasure and expediency; he is to be duped and Figaro, who, like a voyeur, wants to overhear his own ignominy, is to be made ashamed of his jealousy. 'Well, one wants to overhear, the other to come to his assignation. The game can start.' We have here a straightforward dramatic action – the love scene which she enacts for the Count's benefit (although he is not as yet there) is purely meant to punish Figaro. Yet this attempt at vengeance unexpectedly evolves into a tender and heartfelt protest-ation of her love for him. That is how Walter Felsenstein interpreted the ardent allegro vivace assai recitative and the succeeding andante, the so-called 'roses' aria. The recitative certainly sets off at a brisk pace (or at any rate not so sentimentally as it is usually interpreted). But is it not a fairly unassuming and innocuous piece of music? Its rage seems pretty thin. A lot of emotion needs to be read into the few minor key moments in the twenty-four bars of this recitative, which changes course from C major to F major. The 'roses' aria follows. That, according to Dietmar Holland, is where the change happens, when 'the serenade's string accompaniment is superseded by suddenly rising first violin figures and thus the structure of the vocal melody with pizzicato accompaniment . . . is gradually abandoned in favour of an orchestral fabric. The beloved of whom the text at this point speaks becomes real and is Figaro.'[36] In other words, as long as the pizzicato accompani-ment is prescribed, the change from an empty parade of feelings to real protestation has not yet occurred: that takes place at the moment of the marvellously sincere 'I shall garland your brow with roses'.

There is one point which tells against this interesting interpretation. Right at the end, as a postlude, the pizzicatos, early 'abandoned', recur in the first and second violins as well as in the violas. The psychological development is not altogether clear. And the decision to regard those first thirty-six pizzicato-accompanied bars as less than straight-forward, a downright pretence of love in musical terms, is one of which many sopranos will fight shy – rightly so, because with great music it is better to risk treating too seriously something that may have been intended to be indirect or ironic than to repudiate something that was perhaps meant in good earnest. Aloys Greither explains the F major aria more simply: 'Susanna sings this love song – hence the dramatic power which is inherent in the scene, though expressed only in the music – to her truly beloved, whereas he imagines it to be for the benefit of Almaviva'.[37]

TAMINO

〰️

Tenor. A prince, aged twenty. Goes through no mere tale of
adventure, but a passage from adolescence to adulthood.

in *The Magic Flute*

The name of the Prince may derive from a misapprehension by Mozart,
at least according to the Egyptologist Siegfried Morenz: 'Pamino and
Tamina floated into the ken of *The Magic Flute*'s creators as Egyptian
names. Mozart remembered from his work on Gebler's drama that
Thamos was a male name, and was thus led to mix up the gender
elements which of course he was unaware of.'[38] In 1773 Mozart had
composed choruses and entr'acte pieces for a drama, *Thamos, König in
Ägypten* (*Thamos, King in Egypt*), by Baron Tobias Philipp Gebler,
incidental music which in 1779 he considerably expanded. It was much
performed and distinctly anticipated certain passages from *The Magic
Flute*. According to Morenz, 'the initial letters were transposed, and the
names should properly read Pamino and Tamina . . . Pa-min signifies
"the man appertaining to Min", i.e. Min's servant, Ta-min correspondingly "the woman appertaining to Min"'. What a lot scholarship
can discover, and how little difference it makes!

The score and many performances suggest that there are two
Taminos. The Prince in Act I informs us about the plot developments,
his doubts and his conflicts. As a candidate in Act II, he demonstrates
exemplary obedience, zeal and diligence, even at the expense of his
beloved. Since the 'test' so requires, he addresses not one consoling
word to poor Pamina, even though she is ready to kill herself on account
of his imagined coldness. Even right at the end he asks like a good boy,
'Am I permitted to speak to her?'. No wonder that in the farewell trio
Pamina complained, 'O liebtest du, wie ich dich liebe, du würdest nicht
so ruhig sein' ('Oh did you but love as I love you, you would not remain
so passive'). Although Tamino does not accept this reproach, he does
put up with a good deal, even when Pamina pays the price. In Act II he
behaves precisely as is required of him – a disciplined man who knows

176

his duty, chokes down his grief, and, with a sad look, helps cause the distress of his beloved (who suffers far more severely, because she is being 'tested' without knowing it and must regard Tamino's reserve as heartlessness instead of obligatory taciturnity). Tamino needs his nerves mainly to keep the utterly unheroic Papageno on the straight and narrow path.

At his first entrance the magnificently clad young Prince, whose good looks are at once extolled by the Three Ladies, does exactly the same as Pamina does at hers: both faint with terror. On regaining consciousness, Tamino tells Papageno who he is and where he comes from, explaining that he has not entered the Queen of the Night's realm in complete ignorance, for his father, a powerful ruler, has told him much about the nocturnal Queen. Tamino therefore seems not unprepared for the conflict he approaches. He is no unsuspecting prince on his travels, but one whose curiosity has somehow been aroused. This may be why he reacts so promptly to the portrait of Pamina which the Queen allows him to see.

Tamino's 'portrait' aria clearly and tenderly shows how love originates and develops. The trouble is that singers, who at the start of the opera are understandably nervous, do not always bring out distinctly the rising wave of emotion in which the audience is meant to participate. The first sixth, 'dies Bildnis' ('this portrait'), then resounds far too loudly, as if Tamino were already aflame, whereas he is gradually becoming accustomed to his passion.

The Prince has a strong visual sense. When the Third Lady hands him the portrait, he is immediately absorbed in contemplating it: the stage direction is 'His love increases inasmuch as he seems deaf to all the talk around him'.

The 'portrait' aria begins with a quietly flowing piano and two descending melodic phrases as sequence. It demands a detached rendering, one of scrutiny, as it were, and of objective comment. Then emotion takes over – 'ich fühl es' ('I feel it') – and the sixth expands, with the first sforzato marking, to a seventh: 'Götterbild!' ('divine image!'); and love, the 'neue Regung' ('passion new'), his longing, begins to grow. All this is described by way of the recurrently scaled tension of a seventh – 'O wenn ich sie nur finden könnte! O wenn sie doch schon vor mir stünde!' ('Oh were I but able to find her! Oh did she but stand before me now!') – to which are added constantly brisker movement, constantly richer harmonization, and a forte accentuating the 'mein' in 'Und ewig wäre sie dann mein' ('and forever would she be mine') with which Tamino ends the aria.

Tamino is a handsome young man of noble birth, about whom Sarastro transmits some personal details: 'Son of a king and twenty years of age'. At the outset he is not a hero, for his flight from the snake betrays little heroism, unless of course one is alert enough to interpret the snake, torn into three pieces by the Three Ladies' three javelins, as a sexual metaphor. If I may quote: 'The snake is a penis symbol that among freemasons stands for the band of brothers and for much else'.

Yet surely it was a real live snake from which the well-dressed young man was seen fleeing? Papageno, as well as the Three Ladies, certainly thought so. Tamino's visual sense, his habit of examining closely what he sees, is confirmed after the 'portrait' aria by the impression made on him not only by the wise, frank words of the Speaker, whom he at first opposes, but also by the architecture in Sarastro's temple grove. The fine portals and pillars show him 'that wisdom and labour and the arts here prevail'. Tamino is no dreamer, but an aristocrat who walks the world with his eyes open.

His eyes are not open to everything, though. Papageno's impediment – being deprived of speech by a padlock – leaves the Prince coolly amused: 'Can do nothing but commiserate because I am too weak to help'. He is all the more deeply moved by the apparition of the Queen of the Night who, amidst the glittering stars, prophesies that he will become her daughter's saviour, victor, and future spouse: 'Was it reality that I saw? Or did my senses quite deceive me?' The quick succession of events confuses him, but gradually he learns to adapt himself. He stakes no special claim in the ensemble. Indeed, there is one inconspicuous detail which shows all the more convincingly that he even regards Papageno as an equal. The Three Ladies have said farewell, so that the adventurous journey can begin. 'All prepare to leave', the stage direction tells us, when something occurs to the Prince: 'Doch schöne Damen saget an . . .' ('but lovely ladies do declare'). He has no need to continue because Papageno takes over in harmony as though the two of them were one: '. . . wo diese Burg man finden kann' ('where this stronghold may be found'). They then repeat their thoroughly reasonable question twice over in duet.

Tamino has seen the portrait of the imprisoned Pamina. He has let the architecture of Sarastro's temple have its effect on him. The Queen of the Night, in a vision, has honoured and bewildered him. Sarastro's Speaker has impressed him (sung by Dietrich Fischer-Dieskau, the Speaker's part can provide the greatest, most moving, and most modern moment of expression in the entire work). The Three Boys have appealed to his self-control.

At the start of the Speaker scene everything is clear to him. In a fine E flat major phrase free from complication he defines his quest as 'Der Liebe und Tugend Eigentum' ('love and virtue's right possession'), and, more turbulently of course, as 'Rache für den Bösewicht' ('vengeance on the villain'). Slowly the realization dawns that the temples of wisdom in Sarastro's realm command his respect. At first he is reluctant to trust appearances. His 'So ist denn alles Heuchelei' ('duplicity is but all this'), however, sounds less like arrogant defiance than desperate rearguard action. Forte. A diminished seventh chord. He has an uneasy feeling of being faced with a 'mystery'. The Speaker's calm, lofty, A minor promise 'Sobald dich führt der Freundschaft Hand ins Heiligtum zum ew'gen Band' ('when you are led by friendship's hand through hallowed ground to lasting bond') leaves him utterly perplexed: 'O ew'ge Nacht! Wann wirst du schwinden? Wann wird das Licht mein Auge finden?' ('Eternal night, when will you wane? When shall I see the light again?').

What a journey! First he was helpless before the snake, then the Queen of the Night made her stormy entrance, and now he has to thread his way through so many contradictions. Perplexed as he is, he is comforted only by his flute and his love.

As for the flute, its power works at once. The wild beasts dance delightedly to its C major solo. When Tamino starts to moan and groan about Pamina, one can hardly blame them for stopping in some annoyance.

At last, although in great peril – Tamino is the prisoner of Monostatos, who has already retrieved Pamina and Papageno – the lovers meet. Mozart shows how the *Singspiel* hero and heroine remain loyal to one another even amid deadly dangers. He also shows that Pamina is invariably the more spontaneous. It is she who begins their duet, just as it is she who supplies the motif material Tamino adopts: 'Er ist's' – 'Sie ist's' (''tis he!' – ''tis she!'). She is the first to sing 'Es schling mein Arm sich um ihn her, und wenn es auch mein Ende wär!' ('let my arm be laid around him, and even though my end it were!'). Tamino answers with the same phrase, but she is the more ardent of the two. Later, when this couple, whom Mozart denied a large-scale love duet, have passed all the tests, it will again be Pamina who leads off, on a lyrically chaste F major, with 'Tamino mein! O welch ein Glück!' ('Tamino's mine! Oh what rapture!'). Is this mere chance or over-interpretation? After all, one of two individuals is compelled to begin a dialogue, unless both start simultaneously.

Such questions show insufficient confidence in a Mozart score. If Prince Tamino, right in the middle of his appearance during the Act I finale, were the first to sing 'Es schling mein Arm . . .', a sceptical reader, if he thought about the matter at all, could say that it is only natural for the man (particularly in a fairy-tale) to speak first and for the loving woman to give a bashful response, and that this tells us next to nothing about the relationship between the pair. But if the loving woman repeatedly and resolutely takes command of the dialogue, that is neither natural nor trivial. In Act II Prince Tamino behaves forcefully and with more deliberation. Nevertheless there can be no doubt that Pamina reacts more spontaneously, faster, less reservedly and more amorously – whenever a distinction can be made at all between the lovers' reactions.

We know how Tamino arrives at his decision to submit to any and every test. His conclusion is, 'Wisdom's lesson be my victory, Pamina, the beloved maiden, my reward'. Nothing can now deter or disconcert him, even when the Three Ladies tell the lie, 'Tamino, dir ist Tod geschworen' ('Tamino, death is sworn to be your lot'), which is sufficient to make Papageno's knees quake a little. There is no one to console him as at the beginning of Act I the Third Lady had still done ('be not afraid') or, following her, the Queen of the Night: 'O zittre nicht, mein lieber Sohn' ('be not afraid, beloved son'). During Act II's tests, trembling seems to be delegated to Papageno and fear to Pamina, who has not been let into the secret of the tests. Thus the Prince, previously liable to confusion and error, becomes an imperturbable personality devoted to wisdom and love, a proper *Singspiel* hero. Still, we can understand why Goethe in his sequel lets the marriage of Tamino and Pamina begin with a number of complications.

TITUS

Tenor. Roman Emperor, anxious at all costs to be the enlightened and benevolent ruler of his loyal subjects.

in *La clemenza di Tito*

Titus: the mild monarch, a 'puppet representing magnanimity', as Alfred Einstein scoffed, and most critics agree with him.[39] 'Thus the *Clemenza* figures, latecomers in a genre, really do seem aimed at reducing *opera seria* to the ridiculous. The borderline between the lofty and the absurd is here practically effaced' (Wolfgang Hildesheimer).[40]

All this is correct only, though, if the figures in *La clemenza* are compared with the personages in *Don Giovanni*. Characterization in *Singspiele* and *opere buffe* may be direct, dramatic and overwhelming, but it should not make us forget how in *opera seria* character is delicately conveyed by arias, ensembles and recitatives whose compact and lovely form can capture quintessential qualities. A far greater appreciation of music is required to enjoy aesthetically the subtle distinctions among the figures in *La clemenza* than to love *Figaro*. To enthuse over Cherubino and Zerlina is easy; the veriest dunderhead of an opera-goer can do that. Even to suspect how much sublime and craftsmanlike purity and sincerity went into *La clemenza* requires great sensitivity. The miracles of this work tend to be discovered late, if at all. They are a surprise for maturing Mozart admirers who fancy that they know his masterpieces and now encounter mysteries. These noble, reticent mysteries may lack the sparkle of wind instruments, descending chromaticism, and direct dramatization, but they exist in their own right as sheer inspiration realized in melodic form.

Granted, Titus is especially difficult to come to terms with. Clemency – in real life something necessary, pleasurable, humane – is usually boring, undramatic and flabby on the stage. Coriolanus, Shakespeare's unruly aristocrat, after enraging the plebeians by telling them unpleasant truths to their faces, is asked by his patrician supporters to use a little flattery next time to win back the commoners whose votes he needs: 'The word is, mildly'. False accusations must of course be so answered as to preserve his honour; 'Ay, but mildly'. The scene closes on a grotesque note when the rugged warrior hoarsely repeats: 'Well, mildly be it then. Mildly!'. In the theatre the mild man is mildly ridiculous.

Is Titus really never anything more than a mild and magnanimous puppet? Is the Emperor's benignity simply that of a colourless, spiritless plaster saint?

After succeeding the overthrown Emperor Vitellius he received from his predecessor's daughter Vitellia first love and then jealous hatred because, instead of living with her, he cohabited with Berenice (not even a Roman, she comes from Judaea; her father's name is Herod and her stepsister is Salome).

This story was dramatized by Corneille and Racine, and has often been set to music. It begins with Titus' parting from Berenice. As his wife he selects Servilia, sister of his friend Sextus. She, most unpleasantly surprised and pained, has the courage to confide in Titus that her heart is already bestowed elsewhere. Titus does not mind. He relinquishes this plan, which was obviously no more than a political move, just as quickly as he has proposed it.

His next choice is Vitellia; but he is too late. Her rage at being spurned has made her incite the infatuated Sextus to rebel against the Emperor, a plot which incidentally involves setting the Capitol on fire. The coup fails, Sextus is caught. He admits his guilt. He is repentant, but he does not name the real culprit. Vitellia's fierce temperament abruptly turns against herself. She confesses to her prospective husband that she instigated the conspiracy. Titus was reluctant to punish his friend, whose remorse seemed genuine and whose behaviour seemed to conceal some secret. He now also forgives his Empress, who acted not from innate wickedness, but because she fancied that she had been scornfully rejected.

This plot could be narrated in such a way as to illustrate Titus' feebleness of will, but also to demonstrate his open-mindedness, his contempt for power, and his respect for his fellow-humans. How does the opera deal with Titus' clemency?

We meet Titus as a man who receives homage and who uses the tribute due to him to help the victims of the eruption of Vesuvius. In a recitative Sextus asks his Emperor – and surely this denotes a considerable degree of intimacy between them – whether he has given Berenice her marching orders. Titus replies, 'Ah, friend Sextus, what a dreadful moment! Never did I think . . . Enough!' ('che terribil momento! Io non credei . . . basta!'). With this curtly discontinued outbreak and his 'basta!' Titus thrusts the painful recollection aside. One of the mighty who does not care for might? A sufferer who conceals his pain? Does he fancy that he can occupy the imperial throne and yet live on equal terms with his subjects? Is he driven by a compulsive hankering for harmony? No, Titus is certainly sufficiently wide-awake to understand that his life was in danger and to see that 'mildness' for all transgressions would jeopardize the law and the state. He is perfectly clear about this.

In Act II he is greatly agitated on realizing that his life has been threatened by a friend whom he must now regard as a miserable hypocrite. That is audible in Scene 8 – 'Let it be – the vile traitor shall die!' – during the *recitativo accompagnato* (this, unlike the *secco* recitatives, was written by Mozart himself). Yet, even as Titus expresses himself so vengefully, the music intimates that he is estranged from his true self, and to this end it modulates into D flat major.

Titus dreams of a golden age of unrestrained friendship. He hopes that noble-minded trust between noble-hearted men will bring about what he has failed to find in love. We observe how difficult it is for him to act despotically, let alone malevolently. His first aria (andante) shows that it is not enlightened rationalism that makes him wish to behave benevolently; he simply cannot do otherwise. Its accompanying quavers are an inescapable reminder of the larghetto semiquavers accompanying the equally enlightened Sarastro in his 'In diesen heil'gen Hallen' aria. Titus feels that the exercise of power is onerous, degrading and odious. 'To reign would be no plague, but happiness and bliss', were all to speak so frankly and freely as Servilia has done by confessing how great is her love for another. There would then be no need to pry into people's inmost thoughts.

He is an emperor who needs complete trust as he needs air to breathe. The malignancy of enemies he rationalizes as a sign of their lamentable ignorance. Sometimes this hankering for harmony has something absolutely compulsive about it, as though he cannot bear to witness the execution of a sentence, any cruelty, any shedding of blood (and that, while the beasts in the Colosseum are waiting for the condemned to be thrown to them, to the accompaniment of the splendidly *chiaroscuro maestoso* brilliance of the G major (no. 24) chorus with its richly embellished harmony, comparable to the most exciting marches or choruses in *Idomeneo*).

Titus' state of mind seems to have less to do with the humane objectives of the French Revolution (the period when Mozart and his librettist Caterino Mazzolà were at work on this opera for the Prague coronation festivities) than with a vision of Paradise. Saved from assassination, hailed by friends and supporters, he feels neither hatred, vengefulness nor fear, but utters only serenely hovering tones of pure joy. He cannot be alone or unhappy when so many hearts still love him, he declares in the ethereal F major chorus that he sings together with patricians, Praetorians, and his people.

In Titus' second aria Mozart has a strikingly stark transition (bars 43–4) from F sharp to D major. Perhaps it indicates how compulsive, direct and dominant is the Emperor's optimistic desire for happiness. How joyous, indeed exuberant, appears the allegro jubilation of his third aria (no. 20) when he has managed to arrange and to construe matters in such a manner that he no longer need suffer any conflicts. He fears the fear of others. He loathes loyalty whose roots are in fear. The idea of having to exercise coercion causes him revulsion, gloom, descent into a minor key; not to have to do so represents his happy ending, an invitation to a tenor's coloratura, the essence of his being.

We have already mentioned his wrath with Sextus: it was justified, but in a state of D flat major alienation. On learning that his chosen spouse has been plotting nothing less than his assassination, he is at first highly incensed: one guilty party follows another, he exclaims. Mozart shows, however, how little stomach he has for violent resentment. The vigour of his minor key at the beginning of his *recitativo accompagnato* (no. 25, bars 1–8) virtually collapses, forte is transformed into piano, A minor into F major. Once or twice still his fury flares up, but the maxim 'to understand all is to forgive all' inexorably takes its course in him, and it invests the Emperor with such radiant self-assurance that in the final sextet with chorus his is the voice which emerges from among the soloists as by far the most dominant.

It may be worth providing some historical background to the formula used above, that Titus' state of mind seems to have to do with 'a vision of Paradise'. *Opera seria* was not just entertainment, but also a mirror for princes, exhorting them to rule well. In Mozart's lifetime this was still discussed, as, for instance, in Johann Georg Sulzer's *Theorie der schönen Künste* (*Theory of the Fine Arts*, in two volumes, published in 1771 and 1774 respectively). This applies especially to an opera composed for a coronation. Ivan Nagel goes so far as to claim that, in principle, *opera seria*'s function related not merely to coronations, but even to the establishment of political states. On this occasion, with Leopold II being crowned King of Bohemia in Prague as successor to the enlightened Joseph II, the opera written for the event hinted pretty broadly how much clemency was expected from the new monarch's rule. Pressure to rule with clemency was disguised by the excitement of *opera seria* and the figure of Titus.

VITELLIA

Soprano. Eccentric daughter of a dethroned emperor. Passionately and submissively loved by Sexus, she is intensely hurt at fancying herself scorned by Titus.

in *La clemenza di Tito*

Act I of the opera belongs to the active and resolute Vitellia, while its titular hero, who has to cope with the consequences of her sanguinary intrigues, only really comes to the fore in Act II. Mozart used the opportunity afforded by the opening duet (its text was added by Caterino Mazzolà to Metastasio's libretto) to give a clear picture of Vitellia and her more restrained, more scrupulous friend Sextus, who is helplessly infatuated with her.

Clear? In this *opera seria*, dating from the year of its composer's death, that does not mean direct, obvious, or entirely realistic. It does not matter that the commission was urgent, for Mozart was never slow in putting notes down on paper; of course we can hardly tell how long he had already been carrying an inspiration around in his head. Nevertheless we must accept that urgency and maturity of style in this instance moved him to put his trust more in triads and passages within the scales. Titus' role exemplifies aesthetic reduction, an *opera seria* ideal of severe, restrained diatonic clarity. The worst 'sufferers' are the conventional *secco* recitatives, not written by Mozart himself, and also the fairly conventional orchestrally accompanied recitatives which bear no comparison with those in *Don Giovanni* or even *Idomeneo*. The overture, based partly on pure triads and scales, already displays this ideal of refined simplicity. Anyone susceptible only to chromatic charms or mass effects will underestimate most of *La clemenza*'s beauties – or regard them as trite. Yet anyone who can accept and sympathize with the work's compositional premises will soon fail to understand what it was that he initially misunderstood.

Is it really so difficult to follow the contrast Mozart presents in the very first duet between the lovingly overzealous Sextus and the venomously goading Vitellia? 'Command, demand, as you please, if you will but guide my steps', he begins. 'My destiny lies in your hands, all you bid I shall do.' And then, somewhat more effusively repetitive, 'all you bid I swear to do'. The cadential movement grows correspondingly more ambitious and more comprehensive in range. The melodic movement encompassing a fifth (bar 10) expands to the compass of an octave (bars 11–13).

Vitellia replies at once. The orchestral accompaniment's demisemiquaver appoggiaturas are not alone in heralding greater, more incisive excitement amidst the innocuous F major and C major landscape, and Vitellia at once reiterates over the same harmonic structure her cantilena rhythm. 'An empire he robbed him of [Titus deposed her father] that destined was for me', a phrase that in her agitation she repeats with great passion. Whereas with Sextus a fifth was transformed into a restrained octave scale, Vitellia's performance assumes far more vigorous scope. The range of a ninth (octave plus a second, bars 18–21) grows to almost a double octave. Her outburst stretches from the G down to the deep A of the small octave (bars 22–5).

This shows us what a strange temperament she has, and what violent extremes her hot blood drives her to. One could always provide a psychological explanation for the fact that in the allegro portion she and Sextus come precisely together: she has just succeeded in bringing him to the same frame of mind as herself. It is only that the strange hanging back at the close of this duet, where we might expect a spectacularly tempestuous ending, as well as a few dissonant sevenths and minor sixths in the instrumental epilogue, markedly missing in the vocal duet itself, do suggest that the impetus has been cut short in some strange way. This last may of course be due to the conspiracy in progress rather than Vitellia's temperament.

Her personality fills the stage and dominates it. Bernhard Paumgartner called her 'perhaps the wildest, most demoniac woman who ever entered Mozart's musical sphere'.[41] (Let the 'perhaps' be underlined, for the Queen of the Night, Donna Anna and Donna Elvira have something to offer in this respect too.)

And yet, as Hermann Abert complains, doesn't her immediately following larghetto aria put all these conclusions in question? No: there is no inconsistency in her being able to conduct herself with lofty and calm authority when she claims from her lover unreserved, unquestioning trust and in turn to promise lasting devotion (she protracts for three bars a single D symbolic of dependable loyalty). It simply proves her intelligence and her fascination, to which Sextus cannot be blamed for surrendering so abjectly. Her behaviour here is that of an unbending Fiordiligi. She achieves what she wants – Sextus acts.

True, she has at once reason to regret her resoluteness. In the trio with Annius and Publius she is again in a fury, for she is caught in the meshes of her own intrigues, and seems to be raging against herself. Her mangled phrases, at the start before the others join in, seem to stand in a strangely close relationship to one another, like articulate cries embedded in the excitement of the orchestra. 'I come . . . Wait . . . Sextus! . . . He is gone.' An incandescent temperament fans the flames of a crisis. Naturally, Annius and Publius do not understand these confused utterances. They have not the slightest idea that, now she has been told of the Emperor's proposal, she no longer has any reason to seek his death with Sextus' help but that Sextus has already set off to perform the murder. Her unintelligible behaviour therefore strikes them as slightly unhinged. Their explanation is nicely conventional: 'all too great a pleasure does distort her senses'. Mozart's *opera seria* devices here may be simple, but there is nothing naive in what he does with them, and they fully suffice in this trio to describe a mixture of excitement, uncertainty, fear, and apparent joy. In the third bar from its close Vitellia's dramatic soprano is tested by a treble D.

Just as she had earlier demanded that Titus be sacrificed, so 'Non, più di fiori' (no. 23), that extended *concertante rondo* probably written before *La clemenza* was ordered, announces another strange choice – self-sacrifice (at the end the decision fortunately proves superfluous). But this decision seems more rhetorical than diabolical, placed in the mouth of someone from whose dramatic coloratura Mozart requires that she shall not merely three times in succession drop to small A but here even to the G one step below it.

How married life proceeded between Titus, compulsively shy of conflict, and the tirelessly quarrelsome Vitellia, history does not record.

ZERLINA

Coloratura soprano. A peasant girl. Delightfully natural and pretty shrewd. Anyone who thinks Zerlina merely 'innocent' probably is so himself.

in *Don Giovanni*

Miss Zerlina stands out straightaway, to both sight and hearing, from the group of young peasant girls. Decked out as a bride, she is about to get married – on the very day when Don Giovanni espies her. Zerlina always acts with such liveliness, lovability, intelligence and simplicity that all male opera visitors enthuse over this deliciously spontaneous creature exactly as the ladies do over the aristocratic seducer. Her two arias, sung to reconcile or to console her bridegroom, are oases of lyrical sincerity in *Don Giovanni*. Theodor W. Adorno, in his beautiful *Huldigung an Zerlina*, emphasizes that melodically her arias suggest a *Lied* quality and that she is no longer a rococo shepherdess, although not yet a *citoyenne* of revolutionary France.[42]

For the Vienna production of *Don Giovanni* Mozart added a big scene (recitative and duet) between Zerlina and Leporello, including it in the catalogue of his works. It is a lengthy piece, well over a hundred bars, which has however in recent decades been tactfully suppressed in performances of any note and in recordings. This may be because the composition (not an excessively inspired one, but still lively, coherent, and with direct reference to Leporello's G major aria no. 20) was not thought worthy of the master, or, more probably, because the goings-on in it have not been regarded as worthy of Zerlina.

In this libretto addendum she shows that she has not forgotten the predicament in which Leporello landed her nor how ruthlessly he got rid of Masetto at Don Giovanni's behest. The sweet little country girl drags the badly shaken Leporello right across the stage by his hair. Not for an instant does it occur to her to fall for his desperate blandishments. She repulses him as scum of the earth and with the help of a passing peasant shackles him to a chair. His pleas for pity are ignored, she ties him down 'with great vigour'. Leporello whimpers miserably about the tightness of his bonds and the blows that he receives. But Zerlina, whom he calls a 'fury', rejoices, 'What pleasure and what delight now quiver in my breast. This, this is the way to set about all these men.' She goes to fetch Masetto and Donna Elvira, but before her return the mortally terrified Leporello escapes with the chair still tied to him.

How curious. These strict moral standards suggest that Zerlina's graceful proposal to Masetto could be viewed in a slightly different light. What she says and sings to her betrayed fiancé is not, as it used to be translated with charming prudery, 'Chide me, chide me, dearest lover, like a lamb I must endure it'. Instead she makes Masetto, who refuses to give her his hand or to touch her at all, an unambiguous proposition: 'Batti, batti, o bel Masetto' ('beat me, beat me, my dear Masetto'). In other words, slap me, thrash me to your heart's content. Do with me what you will. Then, though, we shall be at peace again.

Curious indeed: not precisely a feminist proposition, but a subtly feminine one. Who can doubt that Zerlina deserves a thrashing much more than the unfortunate Masetto, who subsequently receives one from Don Giovanni? In Act II furthermore, after Don Giovanni has badly mauled Masetto, her consolation is not confined to fine words: she lays the hand of her unfortunate fiancé against her bosom. Such a remedy is sure to help: 'You feel it beating here?'

What is common to Zerlina's behaviour in these three scenes? It hardly deserves fanciful names like sado-masochism, but it is still an unusual mixture of shrewdness and corporeality. For each of the situations in which she culpably or innocently finds herself she supplies an appropriate physical dimension. She consciously brings her body into play.

You don't want to touch me any more? Very well, punish me with a good hiding (whereby contact, even if painfully at first, would be re-established as a preparation for peace). You have aches and pains because Don Giovanni beat you up? Very well, here is my heart, my bosom – a balsam that will heal you. You, Leporello, as the constant companion and accessory of your master, have played the devil. Very well, I'll tie you up painfully and avenge myself on you in the name of all affronted girls. That is how the libretto defines Zerlina if one ignores the playful exaggeration in her words and attends only to *what*, not *how*, she sings.

At her very first entrance she enjoys continuing to warble, that is, at the end of the phrase simply to go on melismatically carolling on a single syllable for the sheer joy of life. (Masetto, incidentally, should he join her, confines himself to the second register. There is no question about which of these two wears the trousers.) She has a certain something, and she probably knows it too. Don Giovanni hits the nail on the head shrewdly when he does not just tell her that she is beautiful, but gives her clearly to understand that she is of a mettle above her station: what a shame that it is wasted on a country bumpkin.

Zerlina makes no excessive efforts to ward off Don Giovanni's gentlemanly importunity. She politely praises her good-hearted Masetto, but for the rest she unceremoniously forgets him and never thinks of remaining loyal to him. Neither da Ponte nor Mozart leaves the door open for the unfaithful creature later to declare that she was horridly deceived. She looks on as Masetto is dismissed with menaces – Don Giovanni puts his hand to his sword. Leporello, moreover, mockingly repeats for his own part to the peasant girls 'with whom he is joking' Don Giovanni's transparent euphemism about offering Zerlina 'my protection'. (Against whom?) So at the very first opportunity she betrays and dupes her bridegroom on their wedding day.

Obviously, Don Giovanni has put a spell on her. The A major duet 'Là ci darem la mano' ('there my hand shall plight our troth') conveys the most loving womanly dependence. Bewitched, Zerlina can no more than repeat over again what the hypnotic nobleman has already hinted, spoken, or sung to her. She does indeed construe the substance in her own way, embellishes it, and goes on merrily trilling. She is therefore entirely identical with the girl first seen among her friends, gaily following Don Giovanni's irresistible lead. The urgency of her sensual desire even renders her prone to anticipation (bar 24 in the duettino no. 7), to blissful coloratura flourishes or ecstatic expansiveness. At the end of this duet, 'Andiam, andiam mio bene' ('let us go, let us go, my well-beloved'), complete harmony and solidarity are the order of the day. Arms around each other's waist, the ill-matched pair proceed towards Don Giovanni's pavilion.

Heartfelt exuberance and high-spirited flights of fancy are part of Zerlina's cheerful singing. Just as in her first exchange with Don Giovanni she docilely attunes herself to his recitative melodic lines, so later she adapts herself to him and his wooing. (It is undeserved good fortune that at the close of the opera she can, more or less intact, fold Masetto in her arms. Or is it? Possibly warmth of feeling and irresistible frankness do ultimately furnish a kind of protection.)

Zerlina's earlier reconciliation aria seems unobtrusively shaped not by pure song-like melody, but again by her bent for elaboration and embellishment (variegated strophic form). Music can have no greater delight to offer than the transitional passage to the repetition of 'Batti, batti', the melody's dissolution into sixteenths, and the untroubled merriment of her coloratura warbling in the rapidly flowing final section.

After the first interruption we may hope that Zerlina no longer 'loves' her aristocratic admirer with quite so blind a confidence; indeed, he now inspires her with fear on her own and on Masetto's account. Both of them, Masetto and Zerlina, have fairly underhand motives for attending Don Giovanni's party in spite of all that has befallen. He is still not completely satisfied, and wants to be sure whether she has been and will continue to be faithful to him. She, believing him to be in danger from Don Giovanni's fury, pretends not to want to imperil Masetto by refractory behaviour which might involve him in wrangles which he could not cope with. At certain moments she appears in a trance rather than acting decisively to any purpose. Perhaps it may be possible – how splendid that would be – to combine the pleasant (being with Don Giovanni) with the legally respectable (being with Masetto): hence the agreement to go dancing as a threesome. All Zerlina's self-control slips through her fingers.

At any rate she no longer acquiesces helplessly in Don Giovanni's openly forcible insistence. When he pulls her into the closet, her loud screams from there are anything but sham. Fear, not lechery, lies behind them. In that instant she really gives the impression of being a victim. She provides palpable human proof of Don Giovanni's villainy. The finale of Act I is the crucial touchstone. Now even she knows, and no two ways about it, where and to whom she belongs.

When Zerlina offers poor Masetto her bosom as consolation, when she gives Leporello's limbs (especially since she cannot lay her hands on Don Giovanni's) a thorough drubbing to avenge the honour of betraying women, and at the end, when Don Giovanni has gone to hell and the survivors are picturing their future in vivid and concrete terms, she decides, 'We'll go home and eat in company' – she reveals herself as she is, a fanciful, blithely chatty, affectionate country girl who is not without her frailties.

Guide to the Operas

by Karin Heindl-Lau

Idomeneo, King of Crete

Act I. Ilia's apartment in the palace; at the back, a gallery: The Trojans deported to Crete after the city's defeat included Ilia, daughter of King Priam. Her secret love for Idamante, son of Idomeneo, the victorious Cretan ruler, causes her more anguish than her captivity. Idamante's avowal of his own love for her and his desire for goodwill and peace between their peoples, in token of which he frees the prisoners, cannot induce Ilia to show other than still greater reserve towards him. Idamante believes his suit to be rejected. Their encounter has been observed with smouldering jealousy and foreboding by Electra, daughter of Agamemnon, who, after the murder of her mother Clytemnestra by her brother, fled to Crete. Arbace enters and announces that the Cretan fleet, with Idomeneo aboard, is in danger of shipwreck. Idamante hurries to the scene of the disaster. — *A precipitous coastline pounded by breakers and with wreckage strewn along the beach*: While the survivors of the storm are still struggling to save themselves, Idomeneo vows in return for the lives of himself and his followers to sacrifice to Neptune, god of the sea, the first human being whom he meets on land. The winds and the waves drop, but joy at salvation yields to despair when the victim promised by Idomeneo proves to be his own son. Idamante cannot understood his father's attitude and feels himself to be inexplicably spurned by him. — *Intermezzo. The sea is now perfectly calm. Idomeneo's soldiers sing a paean to Neptune. Their womenfolk rush in, embrace them, and all join in a dance of homage to the god.*

Act II. The royal apartments: Arbace advises Idomeneo, in order to evade the sacrifice of his son, to send Idamante with Electra to Argos. — *The harbour of Sidon and a fortified coastline*: Electra sings a song of farewell to Crete in glad anticipation that in her own country, far removed from her rival, she will succeed in regaining Idamante's love. Barely have the ships been boarded before a storm arises, the waves are lashed into fury, and the Cretans flee ashore to escape Neptune's wrath.

Act III. The palace garden: While Ilia sadly confides to the breezes and the flowers her love for Idamante, he comes to say goodbye to her. He intends to liberate Crete from the monster which, having risen from the sea at Neptune's command because of Idomeneo's unfulfilled vow, is devastating the island. Fear for her secret beloved leads Ilia to reveal her true feelings. Their discovery by Idomeneo and Electra cuts short their happiness. Without affording further explanation the King orders his son to find another home elsewhere. Electra, blind with jealousy, swears revenge. — *A large square with statues in front of the palace:* Neptune's high priest demands from Idomeneo the victim whom he has sworn to sacrifice to the god of the sea. The Cretans realize with horror that Idamante is to be the victim. — *Outside the temple of Neptune. The sea can be seen in the distance:* Idamante has killed the monster and now offers himself in fulfilment of his father's vow. Everything is ready for the sacrifice, when Ilia throws herself between father and son, demanding that instead of her beloved, the hope of his countrymen, she, a Phrygian and therefore hereditary foe of the Greeks, shall become the victim and thus appease the gods. Neptune at last relents. Amidst the rumblings of an earthquake a voice proclaims what shall be done: 'Idomeneo shall abdicate; Idamante shall ascend the throne and take Ilia to wife!'. Electra alone cannot rejoice in the turn of events. Rather than see Idamante united to her rival she will descend to the vales of perpetual suffering and tears. Amidst the Cretans' acclaim, Idomeneo surrenders his power to Idamante as the oracle has demanded, and pronounces his blessing on the couple.

The Abduction from the Seraglio

Act I. The square in front of Pasha Selim's palace overlooking the sea: Belmonte tries to obtain entrance to the palace. Through his servant Pedrillo, himself a prisoner, he has learnt that this is where Constanze, his betrothed who had been captured by pirates, has been brought. His efforts are foiled by Osmin, Pasha Selim's steward, a fanatical Mussulman with a rabid distrust of foreigners. He does however meet

Pedrillo and is assured by him that not only is Constanze alive, but that so far she has successfully withstood Pasha Selim's passionate wooing. Pedrillo's idea is to enable Belmonte to enter the seraglio by introducing him to Pasha Selim as an architect. This works in spite of Osmin's protests. Having returned from an excursion, Pasha Selim renews his pleas to Constanze. Despairingly she tells him that she regards herself as entirely pledged to another. The strength of her feelings impresses him, but it also inflames his love for her even more strongly. He allows her to postpone her decision for one more night.

Act II. The palace garden. At one side Osmin's house: Unable to prevent Belmonte's entry, Osmin would at least like to show Blondie, Constanze's maid, who is master in the house. A mistake, for as an 'Englishwoman born to freedom' she simply laughs at the Oriental view of women as men's property. Meanwhile Constanze, wracked by inner doubts, reflects on her sad lot. Harried again by Pasha Selim, and finally threatened with 'torments the most varied', she nevertheless avows her loyalty to her distant beloved and is prepared to suffer the worst. Pedrillo is now able to give his sweetheart Blondie the news of Belmonte's arrival and his abduction plan. She hurries to Constanze. All that remains to be done is to outwit Osmin. The process is not all that difficult. A flask of Cyprian wine makes him drowsy enough for the lovers to meet undisturbed. After their initial joyful greetings, though, doubts are suddenly expressed as to the girls' sustained fidelity. Blondie reacts characteristically; Constanze leaves Belmonte to draw his own conclusions. Reconciled, the time for escape is set for midnight.

Act III. The square in front of the palace. The palace at one side, Osmin's house opposite. At the rear a view of the sea. Midnight: Pedrillo has impatiently reached the second verse of the song which is to act as a signal when the girls appear and are helped over the seraglio's wall. At the very last moment Osmin awakes, instinctively senses something to be wrong, and prevents the escape. Revenge is in sight for him because now Pasha Selim's eyes will be opened to Christian treachery. He reports the frustrated abduction with gleeful anticipation of the reward for his vigilance. Pasha Selim, on hearing that Belmonte is not merely Constanze's betrothed but likewise the son of his greatest enemy, retires with Osmin to deliberate the prisoners' manner of death. Belmonte and Constanze prepare for their ordeal. Pasha Selim has however concluded that far greater satisfaction than returning evil for evil is to be obtained from redeeming by generosity an injury inflicted.

He releases Pedrillo and Blondie as well as Belmonte and Constanze.

The Marriage of Figaro

Act I. A half-furnished room: Susanna, upset by the light-heartedness with which he sets about furnishing the room allocated to them by Count Almaviva, explains to Figaro the truth of the matter. Here, between the bedrooms of his lordship and her ladyship, there will probably soon be opportunity for Almaviva to bring his pursuit of her to a successful conclusion. Figaro decides to be on the watch. But Dr Bartolo, who has not forgiven him for helping the Count to wed his ward, and Marcellina, who for her part would gladly have become Figaro's wife, are likewise out to do everything to prevent his marriage to Susanna. True, after a back-biting exchange with her substantially younger rival, Marcellina must initially beat a retreat. The page Cherubino rushes in and begs Susanna to use her influence with the Countess to have his dismissal by her husband rescinded. Just in time to hide behind an armchair as the Count enters, he becomes witness to Almaviva's wooing of Susanna. With Basilio's arrival the game of hide-and-seek reaches its climax. Cherubino leaps into the chair, hiding under a dressing-gown, while the Count conceals himself behind it and has to listen to Basilio revelling in insinuations about an affair between Cherubino and the Countess. Almaviva emerges from his lair and within a few moments Cherubino is discovered. An officer's commission imposed on him, he has now irrevocably to leave the castle. Figaro has meanwhile called together all the servants to join him in thanking the Count for his repeal of the 'droit de seigneur' and to ask for an early date to be set for the wedding between himself and Susanna. The Count intimates his agreement, but rules a postponement which will allow for the festivities to be duly celebrated. Figaro finds an outlet for his rage by scaring Cherubino with a description of the 'pleasures' awaiting him in his military career.

Act II. A splendidly furnished room with a closet: The Countess is aware of her husband's infidelities, but she hopes with Figaro's and Susanna's aid to recover his love and loyal devotion. A plan has been concocted whereby Basilio is to bring the Count a letter telling him of a secret rendezvous by the Countess. At the same time Susanna is to pretend readiness to meet him in the garden at night, Cherubino being dressed as a girl and sent in her stead. A rehearsal, with Cherubino pulling the Countess's crinoline over his uniform, is interrupted by the Count's unexpected return. He has received the *billet doux* through Basilio and he finds his wife's door locked. Cherubino is quickly thrust into the Countess's dressing-room. Almaviva is admitted. On the Countess's refusal to surrender the key to the closet (where allegedly Susanna has retreated), he forces her to accompany him in a search for tools to break down the door. Having fortunately, just before the Count's arrival, come back with a set of clothes for the disguise operation and then concealed herself, Susanna is able to release Cherubino. His only way of escape is to jump out of the window. Susanna takes his place in the closet. There the madly jealous Count discovers her and, through the women's pretended confession to having played a practical joke, matters would seem to take a turn for the better, were it not that the gardener Antonio throws fresh suspicion on Cherubino. He saw someone, not unlike the page, jumping out of the Countess's window into the middle of the flowers and losing a paper, Cherubino's commission, in the process. Figaro manages to dispel suspicion, but he looks helpless against the accusations made by Dr Bartolo and Marcellina of having promised the latter marriage, a bond that he must now redeem unless he can buy himself free.

Act III. A richly decorated chamber prepared for wedding festivities and embellished by two thrones: Susanna and the Countess revert to their plan for decoying the Count into the garden in the dark, but this time the Countess, disguised as her maid, is to await him. A new twist occurs in the dispute between Figaro and Marcellina. The few details he knows about his birth are sufficient for Marcellina to recognize him as her own and Dr Bartolo's illegitimate son. To the Count's annoyance two weddings are to be celebrated now because the turn of events has also persuaded Dr Bartolo and Marcellina in favour of marriage. When Almaviva again unmasks Cherubino (he has not only remained in the castle, but mingles among the girls paying homage to the Countess), it seems that even a third wedding, between Cherubino and Barbarina, the gardener's daughter, is in sight. The beginning of the festivities sees Susanna secretly slipping the Count the invitation, fastened with a pin, to the nocturnal rendezvous.

Act IV. A narrow corridor, then a densely wooded garden with two parallel pavilions: Figaro learns through Barbarina, looking for the pin of Susanna's *billet doux*, of the latter's contents and swears revenge in the name of all betrayed men. He calls on Basilio, Dr Bartolo and Marcellina to be his witnesses. Soon the Countess, dressed as Susanna, enters and is at once subjected to Cherubino's importunities. Almaviva arrives, zealously courts the supposed Susanna and is watched with increasing fury by Figaro. He has seen through the respective disguises and throws himself at the feet of the 'Countess'. Susanna lacks in such matters a sense of humour and rewards his 'unfaithfulness' with a vigorous box on the ears. Almaviva, in search of Susanna, lights on the pair and imagines that he has caught out the Countess. Only her appearance is able to appease his rage and, thoroughly ashamed, he pleads for forgiveness. Amid general jubilation the 'crazy day' ends with the gaiety of wedding music, songs and dances.

Don Giovanni

Act I. Garden in front of the Commendatore's house. Night-time: With Leporello keeping watch outside, Don Giovanni, his master, is inside the house trying to seduce the Commendatore's daughter. Donna Anna, however, can hold her own, but while pursuing her would-be ravisher to the street she is unable to tear the mask from his face. The Commendatore, hurrying forward on account of his daughter's cries, challenges the assailant to a duel in which he is killed. Donna Anna has gone to fetch her betrothed, Don Ottavio. They come too late. Beside the dead father's body Don Ottavio swears to avenge him. — *A street:* Barely has the day dawned, but Don Giovanni is already proceeding to a fresh amorous adventure. The new love turns out to be an abandoned old flame. Leporello has to jump in again and cover his master's retreat with the wordy explanation that Donna Elvira shares her lot with no less than 2,063 ladies from every class in Italy, Germany, France, Turkey and of course Spain. A new victim appears in the shape of Zerlina, a peasant girl, on the way with her bridegroom Masetto and their friends to her wedding. Don Giovanni at once avails himself of his opportunity. Leporello is told to invite the entire company to spend the festive day at his castle. Meanwhile he tries to conquer the bride with the most flattering compliments. Zerlina is in danger of succumbing to his blandishments when Donna Elvira intervenes. As she leads Zerlina off, Donna Anna and Don Ottavio enter. Don Giovanni offers them his services, but Donna Elvira returns and warns them of his hypocrisy. He fancies himself able once more to get the better of the situation by telling them that Donna Elvira is not right in the head. He escorts her away. By some word or gesture he has, however, betrayed himself, for Donna Anna now tells Don Ottavio the whole truth about the fateful nocturnal events. Once more he swears vengeance. — *A garden with two gates, two pavilions, and later a brilliantly lit apartment prepared for ball festivities:* Regardless of previous setbacks, Don Giovanni joyously anticipates his victory over Zerlina, but he is foiled in his attempt to lure her into one of the pavilions. A favourable chance seems to occur during the dancing when Leporello distracts Masetto's attention so as to enable Don Giovanni to pull Zerlina into an adjacent closet. Her resistance is nevertheless such that he has to release her. His trick of trying to present Leporello as the guilty party helps him little when confronted by his accusers. Suddenly too he sees himself faced by the vengeful trio, Donna Elvira, Donna Anna, and Don Ottavio. They have obtained entry as masked guests and now, as the miscreant again gives earthly justice the slip, call down divine judgement upon him.

Act II. A street: Leporello has, not for the first time, had enough of his master. The latter, though, knows how to use his purse to retain him. To achieve his purpose more quickly with his latest beloved, Donna Elvira's maid, he exchanges cloaks with Leporello and even permits him to take his place below the balcony on which Donna Elvira appears. Leporello serenades her, the deception succeeds, Donna Elvira hurries into the arms, as she imagines, of her former flame, and together they flee into the protective darkness from the false street alarm created by Don Giovanni. Hardly has he finished singing his canzonetta to the lady's maid before Masetto comes on the scene with a party of peasants. Mistaking him for Leporello, he lets his supporters go in further search and, held back by Don Giovanni, becomes the recipient of a sound thrashing before being left quite alone. Found in that condition by Zerlina, she tenderly nurses his bruises. — *Dark antechamber, with three doors, in the house of Donna Anna.* Leporello is not very happy in Don Giovanni's cloak. He is about to try and slip away unnoticed from Donna Elvira when Zerlina and Masetto, then Donna Anna and Don Ottavio cross his path. Donna Elvira, in the belief still that Don Giovanni has repentantly returned to her, valiantly defends her nocturnal escort. The deception uncovered, she joins the rest in their imprecations on master and servant. — *Walled cemetery with a statue of the Commendatore. Moonlight:* Don Giovanni and Leporello meet. As they compare notes, the statue suddenly speaks and warns Don

Giovanni against further misdeeds. Boisterously Don Giovanni tells Leporello to invite the statue to dinner and notes just as nonchalantly its acceptance. — *Room in Donna Anna's house:* Donna Anna answers Don Ottavio's urgings at last to fulfil her promise of marriage to him with the plea to wait until her father's death has been avenged. — *Chamber in Don Giovanni's castle. The table is laid:* Dinner is served. Donna Elvira makes a last attempt to redeem her beloved. Derided by him, she turns to the door, but retreats in horror. Outside stands the Commendatore's statute, and he too demands repentance of Don Giovanni. The latter remains true to himself. A defiant 'No!' on his lips, he is swallowed by hell-fire. Donna Anna, Don Ottavio, Donna Elvira, Zerlina and Masetto find only the terrified Leporello with whom, before they go their several ways, they join in a final condemnation of Don Giovanni.

Così fan tutte

Act I. Naples. A coffee-house: Guglielmo and Ferrando, in hot dispute with the old cynic Don Alfonso about women's fidelity in general and that of their fiancées in particular, lay a wager that is to prove Fiordiligi's and Dorabella's integrity. — *Garden by the sea:* The two unsuspecting ladies sing their lovers' praises while the lovers prepare their plot – a pretended call to the 'field of honour' is to give them an opportunity to steal in disguise into their respective beauties' house and hearts. — *Elegant room in the sisters' house:* The sisters, sunk in the pangs of parting, tell their maid Despina of their sad fate. Despina takes a far more realistic view: why not repay the gentlemen's inconstancy, by their departure for the wars, in the same coin? Asked by Don Alfonso for help in arranging a rendezvous on behalf of two young friends madly in love with her mistresses, she is at once available. Not so the two ladies. Fiordiligi, fierily eloquent, turns the strangers out of the house. Don Alfonso and Despina, left cold by such steadfastness, plan the next assault on the girls' virtue. — *Garden:* Fiordiligi and Dorabella are exchanging melancholy thoughts about their distant dearly loved ones when the two men – unrecognizable, of course, in their exotic disguise – rush in, declaiming their determination to end their rejected wooing by taking poison. Despina and Don Alfonso hurry to fetch a doctor, leaving the ladies alone with their apparently dead suitors. The ladies' pity is strongly stirred and their joy at the resuscitative effects of the magnetism practised by the doctor (alias Despina) correspondingly great. When however the patients demand a kiss for their complete recovery, the sympathy just won is immediately transformed back into furious repudiation.

Act II. Room in the house: Despina does not give up so easily. After some argumentation back and forth she manages to convince the sisters that an evening garden rendezvous need not amount to a breach of fidelity. — *Garden by the sea:* After initial embarrassment, with Don Alfonso and Despina respectively taking the initiative on behalf of the apparently still hesitant men and the genuinely still hesitant women, Guglielmo gains a first victory. Without too great resistance Dorabella allows him to substitute a bejewelled heart for the locket with a portrait of Ferrando hanging from her neck. Fiordiligi too is secretly smitten, but, the more serious of the two sisters, is ready to struggle for her fidelity to Guglielmo and against her dawning love for the stranger. The men tell each other what has so far happened. Proud alike of his effect on women and the reliability of his 'Penelope', Guglielmo leaves Ferrando, madly jealous, alone with his conflicting emotions. — *Room in the house:* Dorabella is by now so enchanted with her new suitor that she talks of marriage. Fiordiligi is more attracted to her stranger than she cares to admit to herself. She is not, though, as yet ready to surrender. In her despair her decision is that she and her sister, in military dress, shall follow their loved ones to the field of battle. In this state of mental stress she encounters Ferrando and eventually capitulates before his passionate wooing. Now it is Guglielmo's turn for jealous raving. 'Così fan tutte', they all do it, is the sole comment of that old cynic, Don Alfonso, on his friends' defeat which, according to Despina, is to end in a double wedding. — *Festively lit hall. A decorated table laid for four:* The wedding feast has been prepared and the notary reads the marriage contract. A roll of drums announces the unexpected return from the field of the soldiers who in the morning went on campaign. Quickly the two strangers/suitors/sweethearts, pushed into a neighbouring room, change back into Guglielmo and Ferrando and embrace their brides, trembling for fear of discovery. The situation cannot be long maintained. The notary is revealed to be Despina, but the marriage contracts admit of no doubt. When, moreover, Guglielmo and Ferrando divulge their identities as the day's seducers, the confusion is as great as is the ultimate joy of reconciliation.

The Magic Flute

Act I. A mountainous region sparsely covered with trees. Hills to left and right. A temple: Tamino, a 'Javonian' prince fleeing from a poisonous snake, has strayed into the territory of the 'star-blazing' Queen of the Night and is saved in the nick of time by her Three Ladies. Could not this handsome youth free Pamina from the clutches of Sarastro? They hurry at once to their sovereign lady. Tamino is still recovering from his shock when Papageno enters, on his way to the Queen to present her with his latest catch of birds in exchange for sugar-bread and wine. All he receives this time, though, is stones, water, and a golden padlock to his mouth for having misled Tamino into thinking that he had killed the snake. When the Prince, presented with the picture of Pamina, swears to do everything to save her, the hills part and the Queen of the Night appears to assure him of her help. He and Papageno are to gain access to Sarastro's stronghold and liberate her daughter. For their protection Tamino is given a magic flute and Papageno a set of chimes, instruments with the miraculous power of improving the tempers of men and beasts alike. In addition they are to be provided with an escort of Three Boys who, in the capacity of tutelary spirits, will guide them and act as their advisors. — *A room furnished in magnificent Egyptian style:* In Sarastro's realm the Moor Monostatos has just foiled an attempted escape by Pamina. His secret approach to her is interrupted by Papageno who, the sooner of the two, recovers from his shock at encountering the Devil in person and tells Pamina of her impending liberation. They sing a paean in praise of love. — *The scene is transformed into a grove. A beautiful temple at the rear carries the inscription 'Temple of Wisdom'. Two lanes, flanked by pillars, lead forward to the right to a temple inscribed 'Temple of Reason' and to the left to one inscribed 'Temple of Nature':* The Three Boys have brought Tamino into Sarastro's sacred precinct and have admonished him to remain steadfast, patient and discreet. A priest, the Speaker, comes out of the Temple of Wisdom and asks him what he is doing here. Tamino gives free rein to his fears on Pamina's behalf and the hatred for Sarastro inspired in him by the Queen of the Night. The Speaker replies that Sarastro did indeed abduct Pamina, but for just reasons, and that she awaits Tamino inside the sanctuary. Tamino, to find her the quicker, plays on his magic flute. Its sound entices in the first place only wild beasts; they prance peaceably around him. Pamina and Papageno, however, have also heard the flute and hasten in search of him. Monostatos surprises them and tries to stop them, but against magic he is helpless and must give way before the sound of Papageno's chimes. Loud cries of acclaim herald Sarastro's arrival. Papageno goes tremblingly into hiding. Pamina courageously faces Sarastro and admits to her attempted escape, motivated by Monostatos' pursuit of her. The Moor has meanwhile ferreted out Tamino and exhibits him triumphantly to the assemblage. In this manner Tamino and Pamina are for the first time able to sink into each other's arms, only to be at once parted by the 'initiates' because Tamino must first undergo the purification tests.

Act II. A forest of silvery palm-trees with leaves of gold. Eighteen leafy seats: Sarastro has summoned the entire priesthood to proclaim the will of the divinities Isis and Osiris – Tamino must, to be accepted as the spouse of Pamina into the circle of the 'initiates', pass the order's severe tests. Pamina despairingly tries to warn her beloved of the impending dangers, but he is determined to follow this path. — *Night. Distant thunder. A small temple forecourt with remainders of pillars and pyramids:* Two priests prepare Tamino and Papageno for the tests. Papageno feels queasy about the whole business and he is only ready to accompany the Prince if a Papagena is held in store for him as reward. The Three Ladies ascend from the depths of the temple and urgently warn the two adventurers against placing any faith in Sarastro. Before they can do any harm, they fall into an abyss. — *A pleasant garden with trees planted in a horseshoe shape. At the centre is an arbour of flowers and roses wherein Pamina lies asleep, her face lit by moonlight. In the foreground a grassy bank:* In Sarastro's garden Monostatos again makes an approach to Pamina. He is disturbed by the Queen of the Night, who calls on her daughter to inflict vengeance. Although Pamina dearly loves her mother, she cannot bring herself to kill Sarastro and thus to recover for her mother the 'Shield of the Sun' which Pamina's father voluntarily presented to the 'initiates' before his death. Monostatos, eavesdropping, thinks his hour has struck. Her love for him or her death are the alternatives with which he confronts Pamina. Unexpectedly Sarastro intervenes, chases the Moor away, and calms Pamina: 'within these sacred precincts', understanding and forgiveness, not revenge, prevail. — *A hall with space for the Three Boys' aerostructure. In the foreground two grassy banks:* For Tamino and Papageno the second part of the tests has begun. The earlier precept to maintain silence continues without unduly impressing Papageno. He chatters cheerfully to Tamino and launches straightaway into lively conversation with the old dame who has fulfilled his request for water. Thunder and lightning put an abrupt end to her effort to establish herself as Papagena. Tamino plays his flute to indicate to Pamina where he is. Papageno tucks into the rich dishes on a table laid by the Three Boys. Since Tamino staunchly refuses to answer any of her questions, Pamina believes herself betrayed by him too and sadly turns away. — *A vault of pyramids:* Pamina tries once more to warn Tamino about the 'Portals of Horror', entrance to the final tests. He is however determined to see everything through – unlike Papageno, who is roaming lonely through the vault and prepared to relinquish all 'higher things' for the sake of a beaker of wine and a girl. Again the old dame appears and again she is torn away from him when she tries to identify herself as Papagena. — *A small garden:* Almost crazed with despair, Pamina thinks of ending her life with the dagger given her by her mother to kill Sarastro. The Three Boys stop her and bring her to Tamino so that she can accompany him during the final, most difficult tests. — *Two high mountains. The noise of a raging, rushing waterfall from the one can be distinctly heard while the other spits fire. Each has a trellised entry behind which fire and water are to be seen:* Protected by the magic flute which Pamina's father once carved from a thousand-year-old oak, Tamino and Pamina pass the tests by fire and by water and so jointly overcome desperation and the perils of death. — *The garden previously seen:* Life is of no interest to, and impossible for, Papageno without his Papagena. The Three Boys have again to intervene and bring the pair together. Under Monostatos' guidance the Queen of the Night and her Three Ladies try once more to storm the temple and to abduct Pamina. Thwarted by Sarastro, they are now ultimately consigned to destruction. — *The loudest of all chords, thunder, lightning, tempest. The scene is transformed into a sun. Sarastro stands on high. Tamino and Pamina, in sacerdotal robes, are flanked on both sides by Egyptian priests:* 'The rays of the sun drive out the night and destroy the hypocrites' usurped power.' Tamino and Pamina are accepted into the circle of the initiates; people and priests, nature and civilization are again in harmony.

La clemenza di Tito

Act I. Vitellia's apartments: Vitellia, daughter of the murdered Emperor Vitellius, is obsessed by two ideas: she will regain power either by marriage to Titus, the reigning Emperor, or, should he reject her, by having him murdered in turn. Sextus, friend of the Emperor and passionately in love with Vitellia, is now to undertake the second of these courses, since Titus has evidently selected Berenice, his former mistress and daughter of King Herod Agrippa I of Judaea, to become his Empress. Hearing from Annius, friend of Sextus and in love with his sister, Servilia, that Titus has persuaded Berenice to leave Rome for good, Vitellia's hopes are again aroused and Sextus is instructed to postpone the assassination. — *A section of the Forum Romanum, splendidly embellished with arches, obelisks, and trophies. A magnificent avenue leads to the Capitol, in the foreground:* Senators, emissaries from the conquered provinces, and a large crowd pay tribute to Titus as the father of his country and Rome's tutelary divinity. On their departure Titus informs his confidant Sextus of his decision to wed Servilia instead of Berenice. Annius, seeing his friend's hesitation, fulsomely praises the Emperor's choice and is therefore chosen by Titus to make the proposal to his own beloved on his behalf. Servilia realizes with dismay that Annius' loyalty to the Emperor extends to readiness to sacrifice their mutual love for one another. — *Room in the imperial apartments below the Palatine Hill:* Publius, prefect of the Praetorian Guard, has news of a projected attempt on the Emperor's life and warns him. Servilia enters and tells Titus of her love for Annius. The Emperor, impressed by her courageous frankness, relinquishes his claim on her. Vitellia, mad with jealousy, wrests from Sextus an oath to murder Titus; hardly has he left her before Publius and Annius bring the news that the Emperor has selected Vitellia to become his Empress. — *Capitol:* More than ever in conflict with his feelings, Sextus rushes into the building to execute his horrible deed.

Act II. As before: Sextus seeks refuge with his friend and future brother-in-law. Annius can offer consolation – Titus is not only alive, but he has hardly been hurt. Were Sextus to throw himself on his mercy, he could assuredly count on pardon. Sextus fears, though, that this will incriminate Vitellia; he prefers to try and escape from Rome. — *Hall of Audience, furnished with throne, table and chairs:* When Titus learns that Sextus was the leader of the conspiracy for his overthrow and the person who tried to strike him down, his distress is immeasurable. The two men come face to face. Sextus is filled with loathing of himself and solely concerned with how he can make atonement; Titus is tormented with the problem of whether justice and the law will permit mercy for his former confidant. Vitellia too can find no peace of mind – should she, for the sake of power and the imperial crown, allow Sextus to be sentenced to death on her behalf? A severe inner conflict precedes her decision to confess everything to the Emperor. — *A sumptuous apartment leads into an enormous amphitheatre whose interior is glimpsed through archways. The condemned stand in the arena, ready to be thrown to the wild beasts:* Once more Annius and Servilia appeal to the Emperor's great-heartedness, but a turning-point in the crisis occurs only when Vitellia confesses that it was she who, on account of wounded vanity and jealousy, incited Sextus to attempt the murder. Titus forgives them all and so helps *la clemenza* to victory over political considerations.

REFERENCES

1 Cosima Wagner, *Die Tagebücher*, ed. and annot. Martin Gregor-Dellin and Dietrich Mack (Munich/Zurich, 1976), vol. 1, p. 198.

2 Hermann Abert, *W. A. Mozart* (revised and enlarged edition of the standard work by Otto Jahn, 1856–9), 8th edn. (Leipzig, 1973), part 1, p. 779.

3 Anna Amalie Abert, *Die Opern Mozarts* (Wolfenbüttel/Zurich, 1970).

4 Wolfgang Osthoff, 'Die Opera buffa', in *Gattungen der Musik in Einzeldarstellungen* (Berne/Munich, 1973), p. 684.

5 Emily Anderson, *The Letters of Mozart and his Family* (London, 1938), vol. 3, p. 1264.

6 Ibid., vol. 3, p. 1145.

7 Hermann Abert, *W. A. Mozart*, part 1, p. 699.

8 Anna Amalie Abert, *Die Opern Mozarts*, pp. 54, 56.

9 Wolfgang Amadeus Mozart, *Don Giovanni – Texte, Materialien, Kommentare*, ed. Attila Csampai and Dietmar Holland (Reinbek, 1981), pp. 19–21.

10 Constantin Floros, *Mozart-Studien* (Wiesbaden, 1979), p. 97 ff.

11 Walter Felsenstein, 'Donna Anna und Don Giovanni' (1966), in W. F. and Joachim Herz, *Musiktheater* (Leipzig, 1976), quoted from *Don Giovanni*, ed. Csampai and Holland, p. 262.

12 Alfred Einstein, *Mozart*, reissue (Frankfurt a. M., 1968), p. 459.

13 Wolfgang Hildesheimer, *Mozart* (Frankfurt a. M., 1977), p. 302.

14 Anderson, *The Letters of Mozart and his Family*, vol. 2, pp. 1036–7.

15 Ibid., vol. 3, p. 1140.

16 Hermann Abert, *W. A. Mozart*, part 1, p. 703.

17 Anderson, *The Letters of Mozart and his Family*, vol. 2, p. 978.

18 *Don Giovanni*, ed. Csampai and Holland, p. 34.

19 Ibid., p. 36.

20 Hermann Abert, *W. A. Mozart*, part 2, p. 664.

21 Rainer Riehn, ' "Die Zauberflöte" oder Mozart, der dialektische Komponist', in Wolfgang Amadeus Mozart, *Die Zauberflöte – Texte, Materialien, Kommentare*, ed. Attila Csampai and Dietmar Holland (Reinbek, 1982), p. 245.

22 Götz Friedrich, 'Die Ausgangssituation im Musiktheater', in *Jahrbuch der Komischen Oper* (Berlin, 1960–61), p. 23 ff.

23 Anderson, *The Letters of Mozart and his Family*, vol. 3, p. 1144.

24 Ibid., vol. 3, p. 1150.

25 Arnold Schönberg, *Briefe*, ed. Erwin Stein (Mainz, 1958), p. 44.

26 Oswald Jonas, 'Improvisation in Mozarts Klavierwerken', in *Mozart-Jahrbuch 1967* (Salzburg, 1968), p. 181.

27 Egon Komorzinsky, *Emanuel Schikaneder*, reissue (Vienna, 1951), p. 192.

28 Walter Felsenstein, 'Warum flieht Pamina?', in *Jahrbuch der Komischen Oper* (Berlin, 1960–61), p. 53.

29 Wolf Rosenberg, 'Mozarts Rache an Schikaneder', in 'Mozart. Ist die Zauberflöte ein Machwerk?', *Musik-Konzepte* 3 (Munich, 1978), p. 10.

30 Hildesheimer, *Mozart*, p. 336.

31 Rainer Riehn, ' "Die Zauberflöte" . . .', in *Die Zauberflöte*, ed. Csampai and Holland, p. 248.

32 Aloys Greither, *Die sieben grossen Opern Mozarts* (Heidelberg, 1970), p. 205 ff.

33 Gustav Radbruch, 'Das Strafrecht der Zauberflöte', in *Geistige Welt* (April, 1946), pp. 23–30.

34 Anna Amalie Abert, *Die Opern Mozarts*, p. 80.

35 Dietmar Holland, 'Was in unseren Zeiten nicht erlaubt ist, gesagt zu werden, wird gesungen', in Wolfgang Amadeus Mozart, *Die Hochzeit des Figaro – Texte, Materialien, Kommentare*, ed. Attila Csampai and Dietmar Holland (Reinbek, 1982), p. 26 ff.

36 Ibid. p. 27.

37 Greither, *Die sieben grossen Opern Mozarts*, p. 100.

38 Siegfried Morenz, *Die Zauberflöte* (Münster/Cologne, 1952), p. 43 ff.

39 Einstein, *Mozart*, p. 424.

40 Hildesheimer, *Mozart*, p. 317.

41 Bernhard Paumgartner, *Mozart* (Zurich/Freiburg, 1945), p. 438.

42 Theodor W. Adorno, 'Huldigung an Zerlina', in *Moments musicaux* (Frankfurt a. M., 1964), p. 37.

INDEX

～

Chapters on the characters are referred to in **bold** type. The Preface has been indexed; the Guide to the Operas has not.

Index